A Psychology for People of God

E. Rae Harcum

Hamilton Books
A member of
The Rowman & Littlefield Publishing Group
Lanham · Boulder · New York · Toronto · Plymouth, UK

Hamilton Books
4501 Forbes Boulevard
Suite 200
Lanham, Maryland 20706
Hamilton Books Acquisitions Department (301) 459-3366

10 Thornbury Road
Plymouth PL6 7PP
United Kingdom

Printed in the United States of America
British Library Cataloging in Publication Information Available

Library of Congress Control Number: 2012932384
ISBN: 978-0-7618-5870-6 (paperback : alk. paper)
eISBN: 978-0-7618-5871-3

Cover photograph courtesy of Dr. James D. Maxwell

™ The paper used in this publication meets the minimum requirements of American National Standard for Information Sciences—Permanence of Paper for Printed Library Materials, ANSI Z39.48-1992

Dedication

To my grandchildren, James Davis Maxwell, Jesse Christian Maxwell and William Rae Harcum. Thank you, Jamie, Chris and Will for joy today and hope for the future.

Table of Contents

List of Figures and Tables

Keynote Message

One ship drives East, another drives West,
While the self-same breezes blow;
It's the set of the sail and not the gale
Which bids them where to go.

Like the winds of the sea are the waves of the fates
As we voyage along through life;
It's the set of the soul that decides the goal
And not the winds or the strife.

Ella Wheeler Wilcox

Preface

This book was written because I became concerned that I was teaching psychology as a rigorous empirical science during my working day, hoping thus to help solve the problems of daily living, but praying to God in gratitude for my evening meal. I came to feel that I must reconcile the two devotions in order to feel comfortable with my mission in life. I felt that Christians deserve psychological answers to questions about life and living together that are compatible with their religious convictions. Therefore, the present book accommodates psychological and spiritual perspectives in a way that does not deny the validity of either.

Indeed, whenever my Christian friends asked me what they could read to learn a little more about psychology, I had no ready answer. I could not recommend any of the current college textbooks in introductory psychology, because such books are written primarily as foundations for later scientific study in the field, not as useful guides for a casual reader, and, for the most part, not for the Christian reader. Indeed, they are full of details of empirical studies, many of which are of little immediate interest. In contrast, the present book attempts to include only useful information. So, if you are reading in order to gain a little practical information for use in your daily life, the present book is for you.

Indeed, this book is written for the men, women and youth who are sitting in the pews of our churches, possessing minimal formal training in psychology, but clinging to their faith despite repeated frontal attacks by reductionistic scientists. The book is also aimed at those citizens who would be in the pews except for the pseudo-scientific attacks by the non-believers. This book firmly assures the reluctant believers that their faith has nothing to fear from the most rigorous application of science.

Although I do not claim expertise in theology, I do claim an enduring Christian faith, supported and bolstered by over 70 years of membership in the United Methodist Church. I am a qualified professional psychologist, scientist and teacher with the Ph.D. credential from a superb university, fellowships in two national associations of psychologists and the American Association for the Advancement of Science. I have over 35 years of experience in college teaching. Although I have taught most courses in the psychology curriculum, most semesters I taught courses in Introductory Psychology and in Research Methods.

This book explains what, in my opinion, the readers should know about the field of psychology in order to render Christian service in the best possible manner. The book aims to be fully practical and useful, and thus attempts to avoid facts and details that are not helpful to the Christian mission to serve. The book emphasizes that we must first understand, as best we can, the nature of human beings before we can solve the serious problems that face our society today. Because I believe that the human being is something more than a collection of physical mechanisms, the whole person must be understood and directed by also recognizing the spiritual qualities of the individual.

The trade books also have restrictive treatments of psychology, but of a different sort. The popular books narrowly encompass abnormal, sensational and even supernatural topics, but ignore much of the important basic information of psychology and the spirit of religion.

To be sure, psychology is partly a physical science. But, I emphatically assert that psychology cannot be reduced to a physical science, because the hard-science approach sadly de-emphasizes the humanistic and spiritual aspects of human beings. In fact, the narrow scientific study of human beings expressly blocks the use of more humanistic views; a conception of"mechanical man" thwarts a superior conception of "holistic man." Unfortunately, religion has been unwisely excluded by most authors of psychological textbooks. The exclusion also of humanistic ideas, such as freedom of will and the dignity of the individual, from the study of behavior is unnecessary and surely detrimental to the welfare of our society.

Unfortunately, the word humanism often has unwelcome connotations for people of faith. But that is only appropriate if humanism is taken as an alternative to religion, and not as an approach to psychology. In particular, the psychological approach of humanism accepts that human beings possess freedom of will, which is a necessary assumption of religion.

Therefore, this book is not a scholarly treatise on the intersection of psychology and religion. Already the literature on that topic is increasingly large. Rather, this book accepts without question the truths of the Christian religion and embraces psychological theories that are compatible with that religion. This means that the book rejects certain allegedly scientific restrictions on available thought. Unfortunately, much of psychological thought today is anti-religious. I think that such attitudes are not only unnecessary, but wrong.

To my best knowledge and belief, there is nothing in this book that conflicts with accepted scientific fact in psychology. But, also, there is much more in this book than can be proved by scientific inquiry, no matter how broadly the methods are conceived. Thus, this book proposes a broader conception of psychology and its subject matter. It adds a religious perspective without dismissing or detracting from its valid scientific evidence.

Thus, this book consistently and frankly advocates a particular metaphysical and theoretical orientation to psychology that is compatible with religion. The distinction between theory and fact is consistently acknowledged. Frequently, traditional textbooks in introductory psychology do not admit their narrow theoretical bias. For example, there tends to be a strong preference for a particular approach, called Behaviorism, which unfortunately is incompatible with religion. Although Behaviorism denies voluntary choice of behaviors, most people, and surely all Christians, believe in freedom of a human will. In fact, my personal research, to be described in this book, indicates that virtually no layperson believes that he or she does not possess som capacity for voluntary personal choice.

This crucial question of free will is central to the way that all of us run our personal lives. I submit that young people are even more concerned about this issue because we older persons have settled our minds on the question. I truly believe that the salvation of our world depends upon our commitment to a belief in human freedom to make choices. As my empirical research has shown, the perceived dignity or worth of a person in our society is based in part on the very assumption that the person makes worthy personal choices of his or her social responses. Without the concept of the worth of human life, there would be no caring about our neighbors, and therefore no helping behaviors. Our society would sink into a hopeless, unendurable, selfish morass.

The strong effort to support the concept of freedom of will in this book is made necessary by two factors. First, the Behavioristic scientists who deny freedom of will continuously assert—falsely, to be sure—that their view represents the only metaphysical position that is compatible with scientific thinking. Second, the belief in a freedom to choose is essential for coping with most personal problems in life and in supporting most interpersonal relationships.

Another important presumption of this book is that the entering attitudes and needs of the students about important knowledge in psychology are basically the same practical issues whether they are enrolled in a formal course or studying independently to pursue personal interests and goals. Indeed, almost all people, young or old, and especially Christians, want to be of use to their fellows on this earth. The Christian needs and wants a compatible psychology to help him or her in this important endeavor.

Another emphasis in the book is on a modern approach to science. Although conventional introductory psychology textbooks are compulsively current in reporting empirical research, their approach to science is outdated in three respects: 1) they present behavioral science as merely an objective compilation of rigorous research results and testable theories; 2) they avoid the issue of free will; and 3) they do not meet the strong needs of modern students for specific applications to common daily problems. The present book resolutely embraces a liberal view of what is admissible evidence for scientific study. This approach means that there is a full recognition of the inherent role of subjectivity in science, despite its problems. Psychology is finally recognizing the important role of spirituality, especially in clinical applications.

The book also confronts the difficult mind-body question that concerns the relationship between the physical body and mental awareness. Typically, such questions are not fully covered in the psychology textbooks because the authors consider such issues to be metaphysical, not psychological. Such cavalier pronouncements do not induce the new students to dismiss so easily their basic questions about life and behavior.

Finally, and probably most important, this book accommodates a religion that believes in the freedom of a human will to assume responsibility to love and care for the environment and for one's fellow creatures on this earth. Accordingly, this book asserts a most basic principle: for us as human beings to survive, we must focus our lives on serving others. The person who is fittest for survival is undoubtedly the one who serves.

Plan for the Book

The book begins in Chapter 1 with a general orientation to the study of psychology and the educational philosophy of the author. Following in Chapter 2 are discussions of the problems in defining the field and describing its characteristics. The causation of human behavior is discussed in Chapter 3, particularly the issue of freedom of will. General research methods are covered in Chapter 4. Proposed descriptive models to help us understand the psychology of human beings are presented in Chapter 5. General theories of behavior and specific theories of the mind are discussed in Chapter 6.

Acknowledgements

Gratitude for help with this book is due, as always, to my colleagues and students at the College of William and Mary, and also to a lifetime of Christian friends and pastors who have shaped my personal integration of psychology and religious faith. I owe an immense debt of gratitude to Becky Rose for her faithful, reliable and superb typing and comments on this book. Also the excellent work of formatting the final text earns my greatest respect and gratitude to Nan Maxwell.

Though many have helped with the ideas and thoughtful feedback, nevertheless I am solely responsible for the final result.

Chapter 1

Orientation

Without a doubt, all readers of this book already understand a great deal about psychology. In fact, only a newborn infant is a true beginning student of human behavior. And we know that such a beginner's status does not last for very long because the neonate soon learns how to make an impact on the surrounding world. Indeed, some infants achieve tremendous early success in controlling the doting adults around them.

Moreover, each of us has added each day to our practical knowledge and skills in real-world psychology. Truly, this universal developmental process never stops throughout the total span of each life because, as responsible people, we develop additional useful knowledge of psychology through individual successes and failures in coping with the common problems of our lives. The present book adds professional psychological knowledge and insights, and a religious orientation to this corpus of lay knowledge. This religious orientation is important because many psychologists portray psychology as a strict science with no room for subjective experience, personal feelings and values.

Miller and Delaney report that psychologists as a group are far below the general population in personal religious belief.[1] They report:

> Something else occurred in psychology over the course of the 20th century. It became, by far, one of the least religious disciplines in the United States. More than most other professions or scientific disciplines, more than academics in general, far more than the general population, psychologists disavowed religious affiliation, belief, and practice. In matters of spirituality and religion, psychologists drew progressively further away from the people we study and serve. Within clinical psychology in particular, substantial antipathy toward religion was often evident. Influential historical figures, (e.g., Sigmund Freud and Albert Ellis) expressed vituperative disdain for religion. Others such as Gordon Allport and Carl Jung gave prominent attention to spirituality and religion in their theories of personality. The modal response of psychologists to religion in research, practice, and training, however, became one of silence and neglect.[2]

Nevertheless, they conclude that:

> A psychology that ignores spirituality, however, necessarily promotes an incomplete understanding of the human person. Whatever the spiritual and reli-

> gious inclinations of psychologists, our conception of people should not exclude this crucial domain of human experience, identity, and culture.[3]

Fortunately, the situation with psychologists is changing. As Miller and Delaney conclude:

> Yet something is changing. During the last decade of the 20th century, psychology began to show signs of greater openness to, and even reconciliation with, its spiritual roots. The American Psychological Association began publishing a series of volumes (including this one) on the interface of psychology with spirituality and religion. Positive psychology arose, affirming secular values and areas of study that overlap substantially with traditional interests and values of major world religions.[4]

A number of new books reveal an interesting academic interest in psychology and religion, seeking to discover the psychological origins, commonalities and uses of the two disciplines.[5] For example, the book by Nelson attempts to establish a basis for dialogue between students of psychology and religion.[6] The book recognizes the need to know about both psychology and religion in order to connect the two. The resulting dialogue requires equal respect for the two fields. This task is not easy, given the volume of literature on that intersection of psychology and religion. Indeed, Nelson reports that the corpus of the literature is "enormous."[7] In fact, the impressive scholarship on this subject is revealed by some 3,000 items on Nelson's reference list.

The thrust of the present book is different from the books that attempt to integrate psychology and religion. The present book concentrates on presenting and developing a psychology that is compatible with a particular religious view, and confidently asserts the validity of both the views of that psychology and of that religion.

Thus, this book begins with an acceptance of certain tenets of the Christian faith, and accepts the theoretical aspects of psychology that are consistent or compatible with those tenets. Whereas Nelson favors an empirical science approach to psychology, the present book goes beyond the facts of empirical science, as is necessary for the people of God.[8] For example, Nelson avoids the issue of voluntary human choice. In fact, I did not find the word "voluntary" in his book. He defines human freedom as "Our ability to make choices, pursue goals, and be creative that exceeds what might be expected."[9] Presumably, this principle is involved in what Nelson calls "strong transcendence" as follows: "Sometimes, however, we encounter more radical forms of *strong transcendence* that defy comprehension, understanding, and control."[10] Thus, he appears to be rejecting the concept of human freedom of will in favor of unexplained variance in behavior, which presumably is caused by physical factors.

As Nelson points out, the dialogue concerning an integration of psychology and religion is substantially influenced by the context of the dialogue. For example, the dialogue of a committed Christian is very likely to be different from that of a disinterested academic scholar. Therefore, as a person of God, and thus a believer in the Holy Bible, I believe that human beings have the power of voluntary choice, even to transcending the press of heredity and past and present environments.

Perhaps the best evidence from the Bible for voluntary choice was given in Jesus' recruitment of His first disciples, as follows:

> As Jesus was walking beside the Sea of Galilee, he saw two brothers, Simon called Peter, and his brother Andrew. They were casting a net into the lake, for they were fishermen. 'Come, follow me and I will make you fishers of men.' At once, they left their nets and followed him.[11]

Jesus was obviously calling for a voluntary choice to follow Him, and got it.

Therefore, the present book is based on psychological theory (i.e., Humanism) that accepts the principles of freedom of will, and rejects theories (i.e., Behaviorism and Psychoanalysis) that are based on deterministic science. Indeed, the issue of freedom of will actually constitutes a major schism in psychology, and thus humanism is the only theory that is compatible with the Christian religion. Therefore, the only dialogue between psychology and religion that makes sense happens when both sides accept the principle of freedom of will. A Humanistic psychology is the only orientation that provides a compatible basis for the Christian religion.

To be sure, the formal definition of psychology does not include a particular theory of behavior. Indeed, a proper definition would be broad enough to include all approaches. Usually, psychology is formally defined as the study of animal behavior for the purpose of understanding its causation in order to predict and to control that behavior. Some say, in a more restrictive sense, that it is the science and art of dealing with people. In any case, a rigorous definition that would clearly distinguish between theories and psychological operations and non-psychological ones—for example, in biology, sociology or philosophy—is truly not possible. Indeed, confusion is necessarily entailed by the diverse character of psychology and its multiple overlappings with many other related fields. Nature does not recognize the discrete categories that we use in trying to simplify the educational process. But, to be sure, only a Humanistic approach to psychology is compatible with religion.

Despite its importance, a comprehensive, practical definition of the field of psychology will be delayed until the next chapter, so that I can turn first to my goals and assumptions in writing this book. Accordingly, I begin with statements of what I believe, what I want to accomplish and especially what I hope the readers will bring to their reading.

My first assertion is most important: the goals of the book will not be met if the reader merely tries to memorize its contents. The principles of psychology cannot be of greatest use to us if they are not truly understood. Principles are statements of uniformities in nature that we can use to guide our behavior. Meaningless memorized contents will not provide this useful guidance.

Another major contention of this book is that the same basic content is appropriate for the reader who is taking a formal course as it is for the casual reader who is reading for general edification. In either case, the reader tends to ask the same questions about people and life. Psychologists hope to help people understand the causation of behavior so that each person can make beneficial changes in selected target behaviors for either himself, herself or others. Which of your own personal behaviors should be improved? Are you doing enough to help others? The answer to these questions must be your personal call. I can never achieve the important goals that I have set for my readers without the active cooperation and individual effort of the readers themselves.

Knowledge of basic psychology will help you whatever your goals in life, but particularly if you decide to mentor others. Indeed, Annett pointed out long ago the importance of basic psychological knowledge for anyone who would teach or counsel young people, as follows:

> The writer has had in view the large number of religious educators, Sunday-school teachers, and others who, for one reason or other, are unable to pursue a full course in psychology, yet would like to know enough of the human mind, and especially of the child mind, to be quite sure that the methods they are using are sound and effective. Every such person who is charged with the responsibilities of a religious educator in however humble a capacity needs to become familiar with the laws of the mind which affect religious education. This does not imply a recognition as psychological experts nor the power to use the technical language expressed so freely nowadays, but it does mean an ability to use the simple, direct methods which a knowledge of the workings of the growing mind suggests. Only thus is any teacher worthy of his or her place in God's family. . . .
>
> The wise teacher will realize that nothing short of the best methods will do in dealing with the unfolding life. Let the facts be clearly and squarely faced. In an unfolding soul, peril and possibility are both at their highest; therein lies the charm of the work as well as its peculiar importance. No sensible person would care to place costly and fragile china in the hands of one who was unaware of its value; nor would a fine mechanician allow untrained hands to manipulate his delicate machinery.[12]

Murray supported the need for religious educators to become knowledgeable about psychology, as follows:

> Psychology is a science of life, especially as it relates to human conduct and to its explanation. It strives to give insight into the life of the individual. It is the science that will enable the religious leader to understand the human subject with which he must work, and to read meaning in his conduct, actions and behaviors.
>
> The Christian teacher cannot be proficient in his task of ministering to humanity without a knowledge of this science of man. . . .
>
> Individual psychologists may be materialistic, mechanistic or even atheistic, but in these they merely reflect their own personal views or inclinations. One does not ask whether Thomas Edison was a religious devotee, or a member of a church, or even what his religious convictions were, before making use of elec-

> tric lamps or the electric current in the home. If we are willing to use the work of others who have made available the benefits of electrical research and other scientific investigations and developments, why should we hesitate to use the thought-findings and the valuable facts of psychological research?[13]

Thus, the Christian worker is called, not to be an expert, but to be at least knowledgeable about psychology so that he or she can be of most effective service and guidance to others.

Carrington advised that all Christians are called to do pastoral work. Therefore, he asserted that we must do this work as best we are able, as follows:

> As with every kind of skilled operation we need the specialist for the more difficult and complex parts of the work, but there is a great deal of less highly skilled service for which the 'rank and file' can be trained. All Christian laymen can be trained to fulfil their total evangelistic calling, the proclamation of the Gospel by word of mouth, backed up fully by its exemplification in their lives, in the attractive quality of their fellowships, and in their pastoral service to their communities.[14]

This emphasis on Christian education is part of a plan to restore the critical place of religion in our society. Therefore, if the church is to regain its important place in our society, the people of God must become the best persons that they can be. Part of that improvement is to increase their knowledge and appreciation of psychology, as well a their devotion to religion. As Carrington said:

> The general worship, the preaching, the sacraments, and the various social and cultural activities of the Christian Church seem to have lost much of their appeal to millions of people, however valuable they may still be to the faithful. Because of this the leadership of the Church in many social, national, and international affairs has greatly declined, even allowing for the unassessable influence of the Church through broadcasting and the public Press.
>
> But more and more people everywhere are feeling the need for personal encouragement, help, and guidance in the complex problems and difficult dilemmas of modern life, in the everyday problems of personal relationships (especially in the intimate relationships of marriage and parenthood), and in the various problems of mental and physical illness and abnormal behaviour. They are also feeling the need for help in their inner emotional tensions and conflicts, their intellectual bewilderment and confusion, and their volitional frustration and indecisiveness.[15]

Carrington proposed that the problems of the church could be solved by the combined efforts of ministers and laymen in pastoral counseling. Although Carrington, a physician, authored a book on pastoral counseling, he argued that laity must become involved in solving the problems of the church, as follows:

> It may have some symbolic significance that a 'layman' should make bold to write a book on Pastoral Ministry. If this work is to be done in such a way as to

> cope with even a fraction of the need, the Christian layman must have a vital part in it. The author has no desire to tell the members of a 'sister profession' what they should be doing, but rather to use his own experience and opportunities to the fullest extent in the service of God.[16]

So should we all, particularly those of us who are mentors and teachers in church school. Indeed, all of us must be ministers if we are to achieve our goals as Christians.

Nevertheless, as Harcum has emphasized, we must be aware of our limitations as counselors.[17] We must be Christian friends, displaying love and caring, but not attempt to enter those realms of psychotherapy for which we are not qualified.

Giving Psychology Away

This book does not attempt to give the readers a gift-wrapped package of a tidy thing called psychology. Such a feat is not even possible. Just as soldiers cannot be given the outcome of a battle before it is fought, students cannot be given the riches of psychology without their own active search. Knowledge of psychology is not a finished product to be beautifully packaged and tied neatly with a colorful ribbon, passed from one person to another like a Christmas present. Also, it cannot be copied like a computer program. So, do not expect to be handed answers to all of your questions, by me in this book, or actually by anyone.

Psychology is a process and a frame of mind. It must be sought, wrought—and even fought for—by the student. Like religion, to be maximally useful it must be incorporated into the very self as part of an individual's personal life, a part of the person's views and habitual modes of responding. An author, such as I, merely opens the door to psychological knowledge for the readers by making them essentially junior colleagues in the field.

A major problem in using psychology is that one principle may guide a person toward one approach to a problem, but a second, equally worthy, principle suggests exactly the opposite advice.[18] For example, a child who is continually frustrated in solving problems may develop an attitude of learned helplessness. This attitude causes the child to avoid challenges because he or she has come to expect personal failure. An inexperienced mentor may therefore decide that it is important that the child is never defeated, and thus may give him or her only tasks that the child can easily conquer. But, under these circumstances, the child would never develop frustration tolerance, which is also necessary for the child to cope with the failures in life that are surely to come to all of us.

Because the child develops a tolerance for frustration by enduring a limited measure of frustration, he or she should occasionally be allowed to fail, or at least to take on a task in which failure is possible. Consequently, a child should be permitted to fail, but not too often. Careful judgment of the mentor is needed to steer the child between the two potential hazards of never trying and never failing. Sheer rote memorization alone of the two opposing principles cannot work. Because confidence comes from experience in successfully solving problems, give the child tasks at which he or she is likely to succeed, but at which failure is possible. The result of ultimate success is what Seligman called "learned optimism."[19]

Thus, the present approach to teaching psychology is what George Miller called giving psychology away.[20] Miller contended that it is the very understanding of psychological truths and approaches that must be given to the public. We should not attempt to give particular canned answers to difficult questions about specific problems.

Hebb, in his textbook on introductory psychology, agreed with Miller on the need for understanding, as follows:

> I have advised the student not to expect that the book will be fully intelligible on first reading; to understand Chapter 1 fully requires some understanding of later chapters, so the student is advised to go through the book rapidly once, then work through the whole thing twice more. . . . The teaching problem demands an oversimplification that does not prevent, but invites, the subsequent elaboration of the student's understanding.[21]

Some topics and terms will appear in several different chapters of this book. Such redundancy is unavoidable, even helpful. It is not even desirable to organize a book on psychology so neatly as to prevent such duplications or delays.

Developing Interest

Not all of the students of psychology intend to become professional psychologists. Therefore, as McCollom argued, a better goal is to develop an interest in the field, as follows:

> Psychology as a topic of general interest is possibly more popular with the general public than is psychology as an academic subject-field with college students. Furthermore, the content of the general-interest psychology is probably quite different from the content of a college course. What is there about the "good" psychology of the classroom that is less enticing than the "inferior" popular brand?[22]

Indeed, much of the content of the conventional textbooks in introductory psychology is of little interest or value to college students, any more than it is to the general public. I have objective evidence for this assertion.[23] On the first day of a second-semester class in introductory psychology, I presented some items from a final examination on introductory psychology from the first semester. The class was a mixed group of continuing and beginning students in a year course. The average score of only 55 percent correct on four-alternative multiple-choice items for those students who had taken the first semester of the course does not suggest a very imposing retention rate. I fear that this lamentable rate of retention is attributable to the often arid content of those books. Nevertheless, the beginning students, who had never studied psychology, achieved an average score of 43 percent, which is substantially higher than the 25 percent to be expected by chance. This high score indicates that there also was a corpus of useful information in those books that could be learned through the usual coping with life. So the introductory books contain much that is not seen as useful by the college students taking the introductory course, but there is also some important information about life in those books.

Relevancy

Relevant issues for the students involve crucial questions for daily living. Perhaps the most relevant issue concerns the possibility of freedom of a human will. Although this is a metaphysical issue, to be more fully discussed in the next chapter, it deserves mention here because of the practical issues. Unfortunately, this relevance is *not* one that is emphasized in the conventional books on introductory psychology. For example, in a survey of introductory psychology books, I found that fewer than three in 10 of these books even included the term *free will* in the subject index or glossary.[24] The term free will refers to the alleged capacity of a person to choose a response voluntarily, which means that it is not entirely caused by the joint influence of heredity and learning from personal experiences.

Actually, the term "free will" is misleading because it has a stronger meaning than the term "freedom of will." Taken literally, free will means that a person is not influenced by inherited physical factors, or by events in his or her past, or present physical environment. Although no one believes in that sense of free will, unfortunately such a misguided use of the concept is too often expressed in conventional books. Therefore, to be sure, no psychologist believes in a completely free will, because of the environmental constraints. Similarly, no Christian believes in a completely free will because of our reliance on the grace of God. For example, the clearest statement of belief in freedom of will by the United Methodist Church is given in its *Book of Discipline*, as follows:

> In his own strength, without divine grace, man cannot do good works pleasing and acceptable to God. We believe, however, man influenced and empowered by the Holy Spirit is responsible in freedom to exercise his will for good.[25]

In my study of introductory psychology books, I found that the philosophically opposite term, determinism, was also frequently omitted from the introductory books. The presumption of determinism is that, for everything that happens, given those particular prevailing conditions, nothing else *could* have happened. Such a view considers it impossible for there to be any voluntary component in the causation of human actions. Some behavioral scientists actually accept this very view, but others do not. As I said, Christians surely do not accept such a view.

The issue between the opposite views on voluntary behavior is the major one confronting psychologists today. Indeed, as is apparent from a little reflection, the issue of freedom of will pervades every practical facet of our society, including everything from law enforcement to social welfare programs. Most of our social judgments concerning praise and blame—the selection of heroes or villains—are based on our assumption that the individual made a voluntary choice to perform the particular behaviors. Specifically, the issues of premeditation and choice are vitally important in prosecution and sentencing for crimes. Similarly, welfare programs presume the recipients' willingness to work. Again, the Christian religion emphasizes the crucial importance of personal choice.

Because the question of voluntary control of behavior is a metaphysical issue, the question involves a presumably unprovable assumption about the nature of human beings. Many authors of introductory books in psychology thus mistakenly consider it outside the subject area of psychological science. In fact, only two of the 58 introductory books in my survey, mentioned above, even attempted to discuss and resolve the crucial issue of free will versus determinism. In contrast, virtually every person that I have known and studied passionately defends the belief that he or she personally possesses some freedom of will.

To my best knowledge and belief, there is no data on the proportion of psychologists who believe in a literal determinism. Because most psychologists are clinicians, who base their very livelihood on a belief in personal choice, it very probably is a minority view. But, research data on college students shows that only a very rare college student reported an acceptance of the principle of literal determinism.[26]

Some psychologists say, as a consequence of their belief in determinism, that such a belief is necessary for the search for causes of behaviors. This view says—falsely, to be sure—that only the strictest belief in a literal determinism is compatible with a science of behavior. I denounce such a view. Despite such pronouncements by psychologists who absolutely should know better, *no* psychologist embraces the assumption of a literally free will. Such a strict voluntaristic view is indeed incompatible with the study of behavior, and indeed with any definition of psychology. If behavior were controlled by a literally free will, all psychologists would be absolutely out of business, because the only possible explanation for a behavior would be that it was a particular unfettered choice of the person, which is actually no explanation at all. Indeed, the action of a literally free will could not be understood or predicted, and it certainly could not be controlled. There would be nothing for a psychologist to study, because the causation of such freely selected behavior could, by its very nature, never be understood, predicted or controlled. So, there could be no field of psychology.

Most psychologists, and most non-professionals as well, accept a middle metaphysical position, typically called soft determinism. According to this view, behavior can be jointly caused by both genetic and environmental forces, and also by some internal agent that can sometimes operate independently of such external factors. This view permits a science of behavior, but includes also absolutely necessary concerns for idiosyncratic personal choices. It says that sometimes behavior cannot be predicted at all accurately, and sometimes it can be predicted with great precision.

The foregoing discussion shows why the present book is necessary: the conventional definitions of psychology in introductory textbooks present an image of psychology that is not compatible with religion. The present definition includes support for subjective methods and a belief in freedom of will, both necessary for the faith and practice of religion.

This book further assumes that psychology is part of a liberal arts curriculum. Liberal arts courses emphasize personally relevant material, rather than technical content. These courses are characterized by openness to different ideas that can supplement rigorous thought. They emphasize the humanity—the distinctly human characteristics—of the person. Specifically, a scientific analysis of behavior is only one aspect of a holistic approach to understanding human beings. Therefore, psychology must study the whole individual, including physical, emotional, cognitive, social, moral and spiritual aspects. And, it should use all pertinent and useful methods for the study.

Indeed, the study of liberal arts considers the whole person striving to create independence, responsibility and responsivity in our citizens. Therefore, the study of psychology is a way of dealing with life. Indeed, these are desired characteristics of Christians.

Independence

Independence is the ability to form opinions on one's own, based on a personal analysis of all available information, plus a willingness to act in accordance with those personal convictions. The decisions of the independent individual can be reached without substantial outside help or influence. The independent person is willing to exercise his or her freedom of will.

To be sure, independence is a relative term. Everyone is touched by his or her neighbors. Independence must be tempered by responsibility and responsivity. Indeed, an independent person does accept guidance from knowledgeable people.

Responsibility

Responsibility means to honor one's commitments and obligations to others. Thus, there is a personal integrity and stability of good characteristics that other persons rely upon with confidence. A responsible person is a good citizen. A responsible person accepts the limitations on his or her freedom of will.

Responsivity

To be responsive is to be aware of the various differences in situations and human conditions in one's environment. It also implies a general willingness to take appropriate actions to improve those situations and conditions. A presumed attitude of caring is rather shallow and hollow without the responsible actions which back up and thus give it substance.

The responsive person is sensitive to the needs of others because he or she truly cares about the welfare of others. Indeed, there is not much point in learning how to deal with others if one does not truly care enough about them to help when help is needed.

Good Teaching

According to McCollom, good teaching means to help the students teach themselves.[27] Therefore, the teacher and author should concentrate on being a resource person and a motivator. If he or she is successful, the students will be interested enough in the subject to continue to study long after the formal course is completed. The successful student will be led to make choices that will improve his or her life, and also improve the society around him or her. An instructor, or author, who can achieve such goals has surely done his or her teaching job extremely well.

The students should be taught to use both scientific and humanistic methods to study behavior. Such training will enable the students to discover new facts and principles of psychology for themselves. This kind of training will continue to serve the student long after the book has been read. Knowledge of the methods of psychology will, in particular, show the students how to discover the specific causation of the behaviors of family, friends, colleagues and even strangers. Such discoveries should improve personal adjustments, bring about better interpersonal relations and thus increase the students' control over social situations.

The general methods also tell a student how to evaluate alleged facts and principles already put forth by professional psychologists, and also by practitioners in related professions, such as education and social work. The students will learn to decide for themselves what should be believed. In my view, the leaders in our society today have a general reluctance truly to evaluate anything. Therefore, innovative programs are retained merely because the innovators feel good about them.

The knowledge of methods to learn about people literally gives each person power in life. Learning about what makes people tick gives one the power to control others, and also to control oneself, in the best interests of everyone. It also gives one the wisdom to understand that some people cannot be controlled. For example, persons with disordered thought processes—i.e., in the vernacular, "crazy" or "insane" people—are not likely to be controllable by normal psychological means. Perhaps you could control them by reward and punishments, if you had the power under special circumstances. But, you are not likely to control them, anymore than they can control themselves without help through psychotherapy.

Methods of Study

The present book strongly advocates the use of liberal, humanistic approaches to psychology. This book demonstrates that alternative points of view about methods are in fact held by reasonable people in the field. The present holistic view accommodates all aspects of other views, except those that prohibit its main premises. For example, it does not in any way question the scientific validity of collecting, collating and summarizing empirical data. At the same time, it asserts the superiority of a scientific approach that includes the crafting and testing of hypotheses and theories. Hypotheses are tentative explanations for a given behavior. Theories are tentative explanations for a whole class or category of behaviors. Research puts the tentative explanations to empirical test by the collection of relevant data. If predictions from the theory are accurate, then the hypothesis or theory is supported. Thus, hypothesizing and theorizing guide research.

This book also approves so-called casual observations as sources of legitimate data for discovering the causes of human behavior. This book assumes and asserts that the profession of psychology needs practitioners who are broad in vision, and thus open to less rigorous and more subjective views. To be sure, one must constantly keep in mind the relative reliability and validity of the various sources of data. Although some data are to be trusted more than other data, none should be summarily discounted.

Teach Discovery

Students should develop the discovery approach in applying psychology to life. This approach means to learn about people from personal observations. Undoubtedly, we learn best by doing. Therefore, the student is encouraged to get as much "hands-on" experience as possible, always within the limits of his or her knowledge and research skills.

Solving problems of human relations is like seeking the answer to a puzzle. For the most part, the answer to the human puzzle must be discovered through active personal effort. The student will learn which principles of behavior apply to all people in general, and which particular ones apply only to specific people. Principles discovered for oneself in a particular situation will necessarily be relevant to the puzzle posed by that situation.

Such an independent, focused study will help the student to cope with some people, to enjoy others and to help those who need it. This discovery approach to living will help to put the students in control of their own lives, and in better control of the situations about them.

The principle of active discovery by no means rules out the use of the library and written reports. It is entirely appropriate to make use of the research and experience of others, especially professionals in the field. Reading a book or research manuscript is indeed an active process.

The most efficient method of study for achieving the goals of this book, called the PQ4R technique, emphasizes highly active learning—literally, a search for answers. The letters stand for Previewing, Questioning, Reading, Reflecting, Reciting and Reviewing.

Previewing

The student first scans the material quickly in order to get a general idea of what it will be describing and discussing. Thus, he or she will know how to direct the later, active search in reading.

Questioning

Next comes the self-questioning about what specific information the students should be actively seeking when they later read the material. This questioning directs attention to the important parts for subsequent reading.

Reading

Reading entails an active search for the answers to the questions that have already been raised. Ideally, it produces answers to the students' questions, thereby guaranteeing relevance.

Reflecting

The student thoughtfully evaluates these answers to his or her questions, in order to decide whether or not the reading has produced satisfactory answers. Can he or she think of relevant examples that have been experienced personally? Will the answers be useful in daily life?

Reciting

Then, the student puts down the book and notes, and recites what has been stored in his or her organized, meaningful memory. The student tells himself or herself, in his or her own words, what has been learned. Only by the success of this active recall will the student be sure that the material has truly been learned. In effect, the recitation, or active recall, is a practice test.

Reviewing

Finally, the student should at later times review what he or she has learned. The reviews are further recitation tests. They refresh the memory, and help to strengthen that which was previously learned. They also point out those places where additional learning is needed. Because one obviously cannot review material that has not already been learned, the original learning must be accomplished before any recitation or review is possible.

Emphasize Applications

The liberal arts approach considers that the life span incorporates a growth process. Formal study is just one upward step in learning how to cope with uncertain future events. A useful book encourages the students to continue the development of the skills that are necessary to be successful at each stage in life.

Thus, another goal of the liberal arts approach to understanding psychology is to develop a particular mental set in the students, which is a predisposition to respond in a certain way, to develop a consistent tendency in the student to look for practical applications of psychological principles. Unfortunately, college students frequently do not believe in the practical value of their academic courses. In contrast, older students in continuing education classes tend quickly to accept a principle when it is taught. They make the class come alive with their stories of personal experiences about how that very principle had appeared in their workplace, often on that very day. The acquisition of such an applied mind set is perhaps the most important achievement of the successful student.

This book explains that there are no sure cookbooks of psychological recipes for practical applications. The students must craft their own recipes for a particular behavioral pudding for a personally developed knowledge of the basic psychological ingredients. They must develop the ability to analyze a situation in order to recognize the controlling principles for themselves. The successful students will ask themselves what is happening psychologically. Simple pat answers about the causation of a behavior will probably be off the mark. Particularly, a proposed answer will probably not work if it is given by a person who is not aware of the particulars of the problem situation. People and situations are different, and these omnipresent differences are usually important.

The successful book in psychology must also help the students contribute in a practical way to the successful living of other. For this, the motivated students must increase their responsivity to people and to situations. They care whether or not life is good for all. Their new knowledge can work toward universal improvement in social climates through the general use of behavioral technologies. Everyone surely benefits from a general improvement in social behaviors.

Problems in Achieving Goals

The simplicity of listing the goals of a psychology book belies the great difficulty of achieving each goal. First, the subject matter is not easily circumscribed, because it is continuously evolving. Hebb uses an analogy to describe the state of research in psychology that also nicely describes the total discipline.[28] He said that the study of psychology is like a battle of a war in which the action occurs on many fronts by relatively isolated groups. The commander of the troops has little knowledge of just what is happening. Nevertheless, there are vigorous independent activities of isolated units directed toward specific goals. The successful leader does not detract from the vigorous efforts of the individual units by expending resources to control and to organize their efforts. Winning the war will best be achieved by allowing individual units to fight for the turf that they call their own, delaying attempts at consolidation and coordination.

Similarly, the practitioners of psychology should concentrate simply on learning to understand behaviors, without worry over distracting concerns about discrimination among disciplines, or sub-disciplines, within psychology or with other fields of study. Attempts at precise definitions may evoke premature rigid boundaries and constraints that will limit the discovery of new facts and principles.

As Hebb also said, progress in psychology can be made by building bridges with other related disciplines which also study the human animal, especially physiology.[29] Physiology, for example, can suggest different hypotheses from the ones crafted by psychologists. Biological knowledge, by establishing facts with which the psychological theories must be consistent, can impose constraints on excessive speculation.

Summary

The preferred goals and strategies of this book have been described as written with the interested voluntary reader in mind. The primary conclusion was that the goal of giving psychology away should be conceptualized in a liberal arts sense. Truly, useful knowledge of psychology cannot be given away as a completed package. The students must earn it by active striving, helped by a book that is oriented more to the needs and wishes of the students than it is to the needs of professionals who present themselves as rigorous scientists.

This book advocates an integrated behavioral science, which is suitable for a liberal arts curriculum, as well as for general interest. Thus, there is an emphasis on principles, rather than factual details, and on discovery, rather than memorization.

The proposed method of study is called PQ4R (Previewing, Questioning, Reading, Reflecting, Reciting and Reviewing). This technique emphasizes the proposed active role of the students in their own education.

Notes

1. William R. Miller and Harold D. Delaney (Eds.) *Judeo-Christian Perspectives on Psychology: Human Nature, Motivation and Change.* (Washington, DC: American Psychological Association, 2005).
2. Ibid: 3-4.
3. Ibid: 304.
4. Ibid: 4.
5. Raymond F. Paloutzian and Crystal L. Park (Eds.) *Handbook of the Psychology of Religion and Spirituality* (New York: The Guilford Press, 2005); Don S. Browning and Terry D. Cooper, *Religious Thought and the Modern Psychologies* (Minneapolis: Fortress Press, 2004); William R. Miller and Harold D. Delaney (Eds.) *Judeo-Christian Perspectives on Psychology: Human Nature, Motivation and Change* (Washington, DC: American Psychological Association, 2005); James M. Nelson, *Psychology, Religion and Spirituality* (New York: Springer 2009).
6. Nelson, *Psychology, Religion and Spirituality*, 2009.
7. Ibid: vi.
8. Nelson, *Psychology, Religion and Spirituality*, 2009.
9. Ibid: 528.
10. Ibid: 4.
11. Holy Bible, New International Version. (Grand Rapids, MI: Zondervan Publishing House, 1973). Matthew 4: 18-20
12. Edward A. Annett, *Psychology for Bible Teachers.* (New York: Charles Scribner & Sons, 1925). 2-3.
13. Alfred L. Murray, *Psychology for Christian Teachers.* (Grand Rapids, MI: Zondervan Publishing House, 1943). 6-7.
14. W. L. Carrington, *Psychology, Religion and Human Need: A Guide to Ministers, Doctors, Teachers, and Social Workers.* (Great Neck, NY: Channel Press, 1957). 295.
15. Carrington, *Psychology, Religion and Human Need.* ix.
16. Carrington, *Psychology, Religion and Human Need.* x.
17. E. Rae Harcum, *Incidental Psychotherapy Within Christian Relationships* (Lanham, MD: Hamilton Books, 2011).
18. Martin E. P. Seligman. In J. E. Levitt, B. Rubin and J. Brooks (Eds.) *Depression: Concepts, Controversies and Some New Facts* (Hillsdale, NJ: Erlbaum, 1983).
19. Martin E. P. Seligman, *Learned Optimism* (New York: Pocket Books, 1990).
20. George A. Miller, Psychology as a means of promoting human welfare. *American Psychologist, 24*: 1063-1075, 1969.
21. Donald O. Hebb, *A Textbook of Psychology* (2nd ed.). (Philadelphia: Saunders, 1966). x.

22. Ivan N. McCollom, Psychological Thrillers: Psychology books students read when given freedom of choice. *American Psychologist, 26*: 921-927, 291, 1971.
23. E. Rae Harcum, The classroom test as a dependent variable in transfer of learning. *New Directions for Education Reform, 1*: 69-74, 1992.
24. E. Rae Harcum, The fractionary psychology we try to give away. *American Psychologist, 4*: 483-484, 1998.
25. United Methodist Church, *Book of Discipline of the United Methodist Church.* (Nashville TN: Methodist Publishing House, 2004). 68
26. E. Rae Harcum, Ellen F. Rosen and Barry N. Burijon, Popular vs. Skinnerian views of the relation between human freedom and dignity. *Journal of Psychology, 123*: 257-267, 1989.
27. McCollom, Psychological thrillers, 1971.
28. Donald O. Hebb, Alice in Wonderland, or psychology among the biological sciences. In Harry F. Harlow and C. N. Woolsey (Eds.) *Biological and Biochemical Bases of Behavior.* (Madison WI: University of Wisconsin Press, 1958). 451-467.
29. Ibid.

Chapter 2

A Compatible Psychology

The brief practical definition of psychology in Chapter 1 is adequate for casual conversations, but it does not provide a sufficiently comprehensive definition of the profession for such important issues as professional memberships, licensing requirements and identification of academic disciplines. To be sure, psychologists are not the only professionals who study animal behavior, who describe relationships among individuals and groups of individuals and develop ways to improve behaviors of people in society. But, on the other hand, some psychologists would actually like to restrict the definition of psychology to include only the strictest scientific methods for studying behavior and statements of empirical facts. Thus, psychologists must unfortunately admit our very inability to define our field in a way that would satisfy everyone.

Indeed, many psychologists are concerned that attempts at formal definition could produce constraints on our vitality and productivity as a separate discipline. For example, Sheridan contended that, although psychology represents a unique and common core of knowledge, we should not even try to delineate this core explicitly, as follows:

> Various attempts were made at previous national conferences to identify a list of core subject areas. Although this is an understandable undertaking to help students meet extra university requirements associated, for example, with licensing and credentialing, such explicitness is inimical to the educational purposes of a university-based discipline. Instead, for such a cognate discipline, a core need not be thought of in terms of specific areas of courses, but rather in terms that are common to (a) broad subject matter content, (b) outcomes that follow attempts to develop scientific and professional attitudes and ethics, and (c) a family of methodologies and skills that culminate in a unity of identification with the discipline of psychology.
>
> The intellectual-educational enterprise just described is common to the education of doctoral students in most disciplines, and it is common to the education of all psychologists, whether they are preparing for a career as an academician, practitioner, or scientist.[1]

When I was chairman of a state licensing board for psychologists, I was frequently frustrated by my inability to explain to some non-psychologists—occasionally including circuit court judges—why certain professionals in related disciplines were indeed not psychologists. Often, the central issue was whether or not the practitioner could receive third-party payments for his or her services.

Ultimately, psychology is operationally defined by the daily actions or practices of psychologists. But, even so, the practitioners of psychology are too diverse to satisfy such a tidy definition of the field. For example, clinical social workers have much the same training as psychologists and perform many of the same services. Thus, the field of psychology is admittedly so varied and broad that many non-psychologists can possess talents, skills and knowledge that substantially overlap parts of the field.

I venture to say that the distinctive quality of a psychologist is his or her emphasis on understanding the basic mechanisms of individual human behavior. The desire to be useful comes second, and naturally requires the need to understand.

Historical Antecedents

The polymorphous qualities of psychology are rooted in its multiple antecedents. Psychology began its short official history in 1879, when the first laboratory for performing psychological experiments was established. But, the complex root system extends much farther into the past, within three major antecedents: philosophy, biology and mathematics.

Philosophy

From philosophy, psychology inherited a concern for such areas of study as metaphysics, which is concerned with unprovable assumptions about nature. For example, it asks whether or not human beings have some freedom of personal will. Psychology is also connected with ontology, which investigates the nature of existence. Psychology also involves epistemology, which is concerned with the bases of knowledge, i.e., how we truly prove a proposition about nature.

Thus, psychology shares with philosophy a general concern about the nature of reality. In particular, psychology studies the nature of the mind, the nature of the body and the possible relations between them. For example, an important question concerns whether or not the human mind incorporates some sort of non-material essence (spirit) in addition to a material component.

Biology

From biology, psychology inherited an interest in how the physical body works. The physical structure and states of the body, as in the Greek word *soma*, undeniably affect the responses of a person. Such effects include the content of conscious experience, as in the Greek word, *psyche*. Therefore, the words psychosomatic and somatophysic imply that there are two stuffs that make up a human being: a material body and a non-material spirit. Psychosomatic refers to the causal effects of mental events (thoughts or cognitions) on the physical body. Somatopsychic refers to the effects of bodily conditions on conscious experience (mind). To be sure, many psychologists doubt that there is a non-material component of the mind, thus reducing it to unspecified material components.

There is general agreement among psychologists that human existence does entail physiological mechanisms that affect both conscious experiences and overt physical behaviors. The relationship between the body and the so-called mind—however it is conceived—shows that such physical factors as bodily health, or chemical changes due to the administration of certain drugs, can influence the thinking and the emotional state of a person.

Also, certain physical changes in a body, characteristic of a particular emotional state, can be produced just by thinking about some past event that provoked such emotion. Therefore, the presence of particular thoughts that continuously arouse can produce particular behaviors. Similarly, you may be able to shut off, say, the juices of anger by thinking tranquil thoughts. That is an important way of protecting your body from the psychosomatic ravages of anger. Again, the question is whether or not the thinking involves something other than physical parts.

Mathematics

From the field of mathematics, psychology inherited valuable quantitative tools to deal with its data. For example, psychology borrowed and developed quantitative methods to describe functional relationships between particular environmental events and subsequent behaviors. Thus, mathematics has helped to develop various statistical techniques that are tools in psychological research.

Also, psychology has adopted mathematics for its own specialty in assessing differences among individual persons. Psychologists are the experts in assessing human differences in aptitudes, capabilities, skills, etc.

Finally, mathematics has provided the tools for mathematical models of behavior. A model is an analogy used to represent relationships among the parts of some psychological entity. In such models, symbols can represent psychological entities and their relationships, from which quantitative predictions of behaviors can be made.

Relations to Other Domains

Because psychology is the study of the appropriate basic unit of analysis in our society—the individual person— it is arguably the best starting point for understanding our society. Questions such as how human beings understand our world, and how we conceptualize this reality are fundamental to our understanding. Thus, psychology is at the center of a liberal arts curriculum, and thus the starting point of knowledge.

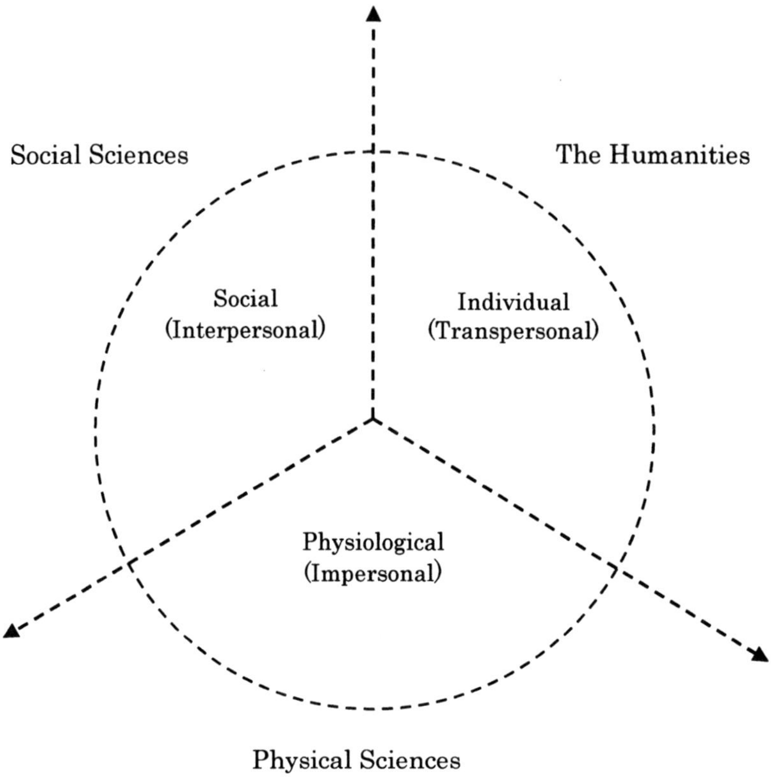

Figure 2-1. Relationships between psychology and other academic disciplines

To be sure, nature does not recognize even the indistinct lines that we use to delineate academic disciplines. The relationships between psychology and other academic disciplines are illustrated in Figure 2-1. This figure partitions studies of the universe into three familiar components: social sciences, the humanities and physical sciences. These divisions are by no means absolute as indicated by the dashed lines. The domain of psychology is indicated by the dashed circle at the center. The subject matter of psychology that falls within the three general areas of study are: social psychology (in social science); individual, or personality, psychology (in the humanities); and physiological psychology (in physical science). Each of the three general areas in psychology is associated with the sources of data (behavior) that they prefer to use and emphasize, shown in parenthesis.

Social Psychology

Relatively speaking, social psychology emphasizes interpersonal behaviors, using a global level for describing behaviors. Social psychologists examine how people react to one another in groups. Mostly, they describe naturally occurring behavior, and they look for consistent relationships among these behaviors. Such description involves factual or objective sensory data, called empirical data, which means that anyone who is present can observe and report the overt event.

Physiological Psychology

The physiological psychologists are likely to employ an impersonal or reductionistic approach, which assumes that the human being can be reduced to just physical structures. Such rigorous scientists also concentrate on objective facts, and abhor subjective experiences. Thus, these psychologists also tend to depend on empirical (objective) data.

Individual Psychology

The individual, or personality, psychologists emphasize transpersonal methodologies, which naturally include subjective data. This branch of psychology studies the properties of individual persons that distinguish them from other persons. These usable data include private experience, subjective meaning and personal intuition, and thus represent less rigorous approaches to psychology. Nevertheless, the students of personality also permit the use of the more objective data.

Inconsistencies

It should be emphasized at this point that the simple diagram in Figure 2-1 overlooks many obvious inconsistencies and anomalies. For example, the field of biosocial psychology attempts to account for certain social behaviors—such as aggression and altruism—in terms of inherited (i.e., biological) dispositions. Moreover, the personality psychologists attempt to account for certain social behaviors, such as the tendency of a person to loaf when working in a group, in terms of a personal (individual) appraisal of the level of effort that is appropriate when individual output is not identified.

Overlaps

The dashed circle in Figure 2-1 also indicates that the professional psychologists are not discretely different from practitioners in other professions. Thus, the psychologist and the non-psychologist at times perform the same services and operations.

Summary

In summary, there is no universal agreement about the similarities and differences between psychology and any of nominally different activities, in terms of either the subject matters or in the methodologies within an area of study. All areas of interest are so broad and multifaceted that the substantive content and methods of the different areas of study are often commingled. But, nevertheless, often there are substantial and discrete differences in the component parts of the disciplines.

Relation to General Society

I will now mention a few specific examples of the relevance of psychological studies to other professions. This list is surely not exhaustive.

Social Science

In relation to Business, psychology considers leadership styles, decision-making, job satisfaction and buyer confidence. With respect to Law, psychology is involved with such things as insanity defenses and jury behaviors. In Military Science, psychology deals with national intentions and diplomacy, and is involved in the design of man-machine systems of warfare. In Education, psychology is concerned with educational philosophy and the design of learning programs. In relation to Sociology, psychology helps to design environments and social welfare programs, and also studies communications networks and organizational structures. With respect to Anthropology, psychology studies cross-cultural differences in peoples and behaviors. Man is a social animal. Therefore, psychology studies all of the interactions of men in groups.

The Humanities

Specific examples of relevant issues for psychology and the humanities include, first, the psycholinguistics and communication in English language and literature. As mentioned before, the topics in Philosophy of epistemology, ontology and metaphysics are relevant. Psychology shares with Religion a concern for how beliefs affect particular behaviors, such as the practice of abortion, interpersonal behaviors, maintenance of public health and the practice of psychotherapy. The concern for aesthetics is held in common with Fine Arts. An interest in perception is shared with Music.

Physical Science

The many specific examples of overlapping issues for psychology and the physical sciences include a shared interest with mathematics and computer sciences in the use of mathematical models and simulation. With biology, there is a mutual interest in anatomy and the functioning of the body, especially the brain. Psychology and medicine share a concern for the nature and treatment of thinking disorders. Psychology and marine science are both interested in the reproductive behavior of aquatic animals. Finally, psychology shares with geology a concern for conservation practices.

Organization of Psychology

To be sure, any system for organizing the field of psychology involves unclear dividing lines, and thus will quickly break down if it is closely examined. I identify seven possible systems for organization, as follows: 1) Science versus Humanism, 2) Schools of Theory, 3) Primary Goals, 4) Levels of Analysis, 5) Kinds of Variables, 6) Mediating Processes, and 7) Fields of Application.

Science versus Humanism

As has already been discussed, psychology contains within itself the same schism between the scientific and the humanistic attitudes in the general culture. Therefore, psychology can be divided into parts that favor only objective data, formal logic and rigorous description of relationships, in contrast to parts that favor the subjective categories of data. On the other hand, some extremists even object to the scientific analysis of human behavior, as inherently dehumanizing.

Schools of Theory

A school of psychology is a group of psychologists who accept the same theoretical ideas, and who follow a prominent leader whose work exemplifies the beliefs of that theory. Typically, a school represents a subdivision of a theoretical approach. The main theoretical approaches are Psychoanalysis (which attributes adult behavior to problems at some psychosexual stage of development), Behaviorism (which attributes behavior to learning experiences as they interact with inherited dispositions), and Humanism (which attributes behaviors to the joint influences of experience, heredity and the free choice of the human agent).

The followers of a given scholar share the same theories and beliefs and use the same methodologies. For example, we often refer to particular psychologists as Freudians (after Sigmund Freud within Psychoanalysis), Rogerians (after Carl Rogers within Humanism), and Skinnerians (after B. F. Skinner within Behaviorism).

Primary Goals

The primary goals of psychology may be generally divided into two categories: research versus application. Relatively speaking, the research goal is to discover the basic facts and principles of behavior, and the applied goal is to use those facts and principles to solve some existing behavioral problem.

Often, we professionals casually refer to the research goal as "experimental," and to the applied goal as "clinical." Because not all research uses the experimental method and not all applied psychology is performed in the clinic, these are not good terms.

Sometimes, we consider the research objective as representing so-called pure science (also called basic science), in contrast to applied science. The idea behind this difference is that pure research is, in theory, not contaminated with concerns for its practical application. Similarly, the applied efforts are not aimed at giving us insights about how people behave. But, to be sure, good research leads to some understanding of the mechanisms of behavior, which must be ultimately practical. It is also possible to learn about the mechanisms of behavior by observing the behavior of people in practical settings. Moreover, we can validate our understanding by observing whether we have in fact succeeded in predicting correctly, or in controlling the behavior in applied situations.

Perhaps, the only real difference in these two approaches is in terms of our expectations about when a use will be found for the results. Some evidence may be gathered in order to solve a currently existing problem, thus with an obvious (identified) application. For example, we may perform research in a supermarket, using older citizens as subjects, in order to find out what cognitive and motor skills are necessary for them to locate and secure certain items in the store. The information thus obtained can suggest an organization of the shelves to make the practical task of shopping easier for our senior citizens. But, to be sure, from this same data we also learn something about the cognitive functioning of the subjects themselves.

Other evidence could be gathered because a given problem is only anticipated. That effort would imply a mixture of both applied and basic connotations. For example, at one time behavioral scientists studied the effects of weightlessness on humans before we had placed a human being in space because we anticipated that future space travel was possible.

Other evidence could be collected without a particular anticipated use in mind, although there was a general belief that the evidence will be useful some day. Such basic research may superficially seem wasteful from a practical standpoint, but it is truly most practical and efficient in the long run because it is aimed at virtually an infinite number of practical problems that just have not been identified. Obviously, if we knew everything about the causation of behaviors, we would know all that we needed to know for every applied situation. This important point should be kept in mind when critics of basic research contend, as they often do, that they can see no practical value to society for a certain piece of so-called basic research.

Arguably, basic research is cost effective because nominally applied research often becomes obsolete as soon as a new device comes off the assembly line. For example, I once conducted applied research on the visibility against a simulated night sky of a scale model of a new American bomber. The military needed the results immediately. But the empirical results for that particular configuration (physical model) of a bomber were obsolete once a revised configuration of the bomber had been put into service.

Levels of Analysis

Psychologists can also be distinguished by the level of analysis of behavior that they find interesting and useful. For example, as I write, my behavior could be described on a very molar, or global, level of analysis, such as creative writing. Or, the exact same behavior could be described as hitting the keyboard with my fingers (a finer level of analysis). It could also be described, at a very molecular level, as intermittently flexing and relaxing of certain muscles in my fingers (a yet finer-grained analysis), and even as the activity of certain particles in my brain and muscles (a very fine-grained analysis indeed). I recall a lecture at a professional meeting about certain structural changes at the fifth plexiform layer in the retina (location of the sensory receptors) of the eye as a consequence of visual stimulation. Although such a topic may seem at first more physiological than psychological, the process of change fits the psychological definition of learning: a change of behavior as a result of experience.

The preference for different levels of analysis affects the kinds of variables that different researchers choose to investigate, and the type of theory that they find most appealing. For example, a social psychologist might describe a person as "hostile," which is a molar description, whereas a physiological psychologist might describe that person as physiologically "activated" or "aroused" because of tension in certain muscles and electrical patterns within the brain. The levels should not be confused. For example, it would not be fruitful for the researcher on the fifth plexiform layer of the retina of the eye to propose that a molecule voluntarily decided to transform itself in a hostile way. Indeed, it would be silly.

It would be patently presumptuous for any psychologist to say that the preferred approach of another is wrong or useless. In fact, an ultimately satisfactory general theory of behavior would account for all behaviors at each level of description.

Kinds of Variables

A variable is something that can change, with the changes consequently influencing behavior. Three major categories of variables in psychology are: a) Stimulus, b) Organism, and c) Response.

Stimulus Variables

The stimulus variables are those physical forces in the environment that evoke or influence a response. This input includes such things as the physical character of the environment, the intensity of the stimulation, its duration, the configuration of various arrays of stimulations and so forth. For example, electromagnetic energy of certain waves lengths constitute visible light because they stimulate the visual receptors in the eye.

Organismic Variables

Organismic variables lie within the subject-person. They include such things as personal characteristics, habits, skills, motivations, emotions, levels of arousal, attention and attitudes. A special category of organismic variables are antecedent variables, sometimes called historical variables, which reflect the lingering effects (memories and habits) of earlier experiences. They may persist in the form of actual continuing activity in the nervous system as a result of the prior stimulation.

The effects of earlier stimulations have various degrees of stability. For example, some effects are very temporary because they are simply lingering traces of the stimulation. Somewhat more persisting traces would be considered to reflect a mental set producing a tendency to respond in a certain way. If the effects are even more stable over time, we refer to them as a mood, or mental state. This is a condition of uniformity or consistency among the various attributes that define the consciousness of the individual. So, for example, a person may show persistence over time of such characteristics as depression, disinterest, etc., that we would say represent a state of sadness. It presumably will change, and therefore it is not an enduring personal characteristic of the person.

If such lingering characteristics of the person are very stable over time, we are likely to refer to them as traits, or personality characteristics that are consistent long-term dispositional factors within the person. Therefore, we would say that a person who was always sad would have a personal trait of depression.

If a personal characteristic is so enduring, so strong, that it dominates other characteristics in controlling the behaviors of a person, we refer to a personality type. That means we would classify the person into a discrete category that is exemplified by that particular characteristic. For example, we might say that a person with dispositional factors to display depressed behaviors as a depressed person, or has a depressed personality.

Psychologists are wary of such labeling of persons, however, because the labeling necessarily ignores individual differences within the category. For example, if we identify someone as a firefighter, we know something about him or her—say, he or she is brave and willing to serve—but we are not considering many other distinguishing characteristics of that person which might make him or her different from other firefighters.

Some intervening variables are called moderating variables because they do not themselves directly produce behavior, but they interact with other variables to change their effects. Therefore, they are important because of their interactions. An interaction occurs when the level, or strength, of one variable influences the effect of another variable. I call it an "it-all-depends" effect, because the effect of the variable of interest depends upon the state of another variable. For example, the effect of a procedure designed to increase the level of motivation depends upon the moderating variable of the prior existing level of motivation in that person. Specifically, if he or she were already working as hard as he or she could, an additional increase in motivation might not be possible. And, if the expected increase actually occurred, the effect on performance could actually be detrimental in a person who had already been working near his or her peak level of performance. In this case, we would say that the person became stressed. Indeed, a stressed person usually performs less effectively than when he or she is not stressed.

Obviously, moderating variables are difficult to identify, and their mechanisms difficult to understand. Consider the trait of insecurity in a person, which could cause the person to act aggressively when threatened, or cause the person to turn down a free trip to Hong Kong. Interactions mean that psychologists often cannot predict behavior accurately, because we do not have sufficient information about the moderating variables.

Response Variables

The third category of variables, response variables, includes those characteristics of the person that influence the frequency, reaction time, probability, duration and quality of responding. For example, an aged person cannot be expected to respond as rapidly to a particular question as a younger person, even though he or she may know the answer just as well. Similarly, a very young child should not be expected to manipulate a pencil as well as an adult. Or, a skilled typist could turn out much more copy with a typewriter or computer than with a pencil.

Response variables are important because, for example, a poor typist might be incorrectly considered uncreative, if creativity is measure by the number of works typed per minute in an imaginative story. Or, a child with poor motor skills might erroneously be judged to be slow in thinking ability, if the test requires motor dexterity.

Mediating Processes

Processes are the mechanisms by which things change from one state or one condition into another. The following list of processes in humans is surely not exhaustive or mutually exclusive: Learning (changing behavior as a result of experience); Memory (retaining learned material for a later test); Sensation (taking in, or becoming aware of, raw stimulus input); Perception (interpreting the meaning of a sensation); Cognition (reaching conclusions about the nature of the environment); Thinking (making decisions about how to respond to the environment); Motivation (arousing or energizing the organism to achieve a particular goal); Emotion (physical arousal that is characterized by certain feeling tones or affective states); and Attention (directing consciousness, or awareness, toward one particular stimulus or cognitive event).

Fields of Application

Psychology contains within itself a number of sub-fields of application, or job specializations. The following list is surely by no means exhaustive or mutually exclusive.

Experimental psychology includes research on basic mechanisms of behavior, as in the processes of perception, learning and reasoning. Clinical psychology includes testing, counseling and treatment of persons with problems in realistic or rational thinking. The field of Personality involves studying the stable characteristics of people, which determine how they function in various situations, and the study of individual differences in such human characteristics. Social psychology studies the functioning of people in groups, in contrast to performance when they are alone. Physiological psychology studies nerve action and biological and chemical mechanisms, particularly in the brain, to determine the effects of various physical factors and functionings on behaviors. Developmental psychology studies the acquisition of certain human attributes, such as intelligence, social skills, language and normal and abnormal methods of responding. Quantitative psychology studies the theory of measurement, mathematical models of behavior and methods for analyzing research data. Environmental/community psychology studies the total stimulus conditions that surround persons in order to understand how these factors contribute to such human responses as mental health, happiness, aggression, cooperation and design of social programs. Industrial/organizational psychology considers all variables that influence work performance, including incentives, working conditions, management styles, job placement, job satisfaction and the design of machines and work places. Educational psychology studies how children and adults acquire such attributes as habits, skills and attitudes, and it evaluates which educational systems and programs work best for such purposes.

There are many yet smaller sub-specializations. For example, the subspecialty of forensic psychology studies all aspects of the legal system, including jury behavior, sentencing guidelines and insanity defenses. Therefore, it clearly involves specialists in social, clinical and experimental psychology. Similarly, a psychologist studying aesthetics would share interests with many subfields, such as art therapy, environmental therapy, design of workplace and educational settings and the study of perceptual processes. A psychologist studying gender issues would be interested in all of the processing and structural differences that would either differentiate, or fail to differentiate, between males and females of a species.

Science vs. Humanities

A schism between science and the humanities has unfortunately developed in our general society, and also in the field of psychology. In general, the humanities are the branches of knowledge that are concerned with the nature of human beings and their culture, whose methods are based on human values and human expression. Thus, the boundaries of the humanities do not coincide with artificial divisions represented by various academic disciplines, university departments or rigorous conceptions of science.

To be sure, certain elements of study are more pertinent to some fields than others. Relatively speaking, the sciences are more oriented toward general laws that are independent of individual differences, whereas the humanities are more oriented toward understanding the individual. Therefore, we can say that the humanities emphasize the detailed study of the individual human being after the sciences have established general laws for the species.

The sciences require rational and objective thinking, whereas the humanities emphasize imagination and subjectivity. Thus, the humanities are concerned with understanding the world according to a more simple-minded logic of everyday experience, accessible to everyone, as opposed to the more formal logic of science, which requires special technical skills. Therefore, the humanities are based on personal experience of the type of events that are available to such experience, such as the creative works from human endeavor.

Snow claimed that the members of each culture were very similar in intellectual life and background, but so different in psychological climate that they "had almost ceased to communicate at all."[2] In Odegaard's words, "I regard this two culture, mind-body, human and nature split among intellectuals in our time as incredibly unfortunate and far-reaching in its damaging consequences."[3] Sadly, sometimes the two groups are firmly oppositional.

Bird concluded that the tendency has been for science to provide the generally accepted model for understanding the world, with the humanities on the defensive.[4] Nevertheless, he also perceived an encouraging tendency of society to support the humanities.

As Bird pointed out, the language of the sciences is more descriptive and cognitive, whereas the language of the humanities is subjective and noncognitive. Therefore, the differences do not entail subject matter so much, but modes of approaching the subject. This means that a discipline in a so-called natural science can be studied in a humanistic manner and a so-called humanistic discipline can be studied scientifically. For this reason, apparent conflicts between them are often the result of semantic and other linguistic confusions. Indeed, there is a commonality of elements within the methods, content and goals of each, which are relevant to all of the various subject fields.

Thus, the differences between these approaches are relative, rather than absolute. Nevertheless, Harré contended that, although the truth of the two extreme positions are not differentially supported by any weight of empirical evidence, they do have differential practical consequences:

> Although these profoundly different ways of interpreting and explaining human thought and action have their origins in preferred linguistic forms rather than any compelling facts of the matter, they do have profoundly different practical consequences. They carry with them very distinctive stances as to the moral, political and clinical problems with which modern people are beset.[5]

And that is the very point of this book. There is a matter of the practical value of the methodological approach. Thus, the relevant basis for choosing between the two competing orientations is not which of them is true and correct, but which provides more practical consequences under specified conditions. In fact, the present book contends that a combination of the two views is more harmonious with real-life situations of ordinary people trying to cope with common problems of living.

Actually, the question of which approach is more useful cannot be answered in the abstract, in some absolute way. I propose that the answer is relative to the particular problem and the context in which that problem appears. This proposed solution is the natural consequence of a particular comprehensive perception of the field of psychology. An adequate comprehensive definition of the field naturally crosses both content and methodological distinctions which are used to distinguish between the two cultures of society.

Position of Psychology

Harré described the science versus humanities schism in psychology as follows:

> Two images of human psychology compete for our attention. Academic psychologists, particularly those who work in the 'experimental' tradition, make the implicit assumption that men, women, and children are high-grade automata, the patterns of whose behavior are thought to obey something very like natural laws. . . . Lay folks, clinical psychologists, lawyers, historians, and all of those who have to deal in a practical way with human beings tend to think of people as agents struggling to maintain some sort of reasoned order in their lives against a background flux of emotions, inadequate information and the ever-present tides of social pressures.[6]

Korn argued that we should consider psychology to be a humanity as well as a science, because it meets the five criteria for a discipline in the humanities: 1) uses expressive language symbols to communicate a feeling, 2) uses qualitative art to guide interpretation, 3) asks about the meaning and purpose of life, 4) focuses on values of what is best in thinking and living, and 5) employs imagination to understand what cannot be directly deduced from data.[7] Moreover, humanistic psychology argues that facts are not immutable and eternal. Korn asserted that the most enduring generalization about behaviors is that generalizations change over situations and time. Therefore, in developing our personal plans for most effective living, we must learn to live without certainty. The psychology of some psychologists does not meet Korn's criteria because it tries to be rigidly objective.

Other authors agree with Korn. For example, Koch concluded that "psychologists must finally accept the circumstances that extensive and important sectors of psychological study require modes of inquiry rather more like those of the humanities than the sciences."[8] Greenway argued similarly that the humanistic approach "emphasized the individual's personal experience,"[9] and therefore is more like an art than a science.

Deese also argued that psychology is in fact an art as well as a science:

> Some psychological knowledge is scientific—it comes from general principles that in turn are based on reliable experience. Some psychological knowledge, however, comes from unmodified, intuitive experience, and that part is art. In all science there is more art than the layman or the casual student would be led to expect from accounts of the philosophy of science, and psychology is no exception.[10]

The main impediment to a harmonious interface between the sciences and the humanities is the lack of a mutually satisfactory metaphysical foundation, although resolutions have been proposed by both philosophers and psychologists.[11] According to Baars, the best hope for a theoretical integration of the field is the so-called cognitive revolution in psychology.[12] The cognitive revolution encourages the inference of unobservable constructs based on observable phenomena. Because these internal constructs represent concepts such as purpose, thought, consciousness and meaning, they are quite consistent with common sense, as well as religion.

We should replace outdated positivisitic views of science, that science deals only with observable events or facts, with modern post-positivistic orientation, which holds that truth is contextual. The modernity view entails the holistic study of persons in real environments, studied by all methodologies and employing humanistic concepts to supplement reductionistic conceptions of human beings.

Many have in fact proposed to supplement a fractionary reductionistic behavioral science with an integrated or holistic approach. Harman described the holistic approach as follows:

> Holistic science departs from the reductionistic faith that the whole can be explained from knowledge of the component parts. Living organisms have emergent properties that are not predictable from their physics and chemistry (for example, tropisms of plants or instincts of animals) . . .similarly, science dealing with human consciousness involves concepts beyond those needed to describe non-sentient organisms. Thus, there is a natural hierarchical relationship among the sciences, higher levels of organization involving more holistic concepts.[13]

This hierarchical arrangement would put the reductionistic and deterministic physical sciences at the bottom, the more teleological life sciences on the next levels, and the human (social) sciences at the top. Because each level involves emergent concepts, and thus cannot be reduced to the lower levels, the insights relevant to the different levels are complementary. One must not, however, confuse the level of discourse, such that one level is imported or injected to solve a problem posed at another level.

According to LeShan, the prevalence of the rigorous approach to thinking in physical science has caused the shift of physical science from thinking in terms of final causes (Why has an event occurred?) to thinking in terms of efficient causes (How did an event come about?). Le Shan asserted that this emphasis on efficient causes was devastating when applied to behavioral science, as follows:

> The problem that arose for us is that people—the subject matter of psychology—operate in important matters different from Final Causes (why). I go down the street to buy a newspaper. That is my Final Cause. It is *why* I go down the street. To study my going down the street without including my goal is arrant nonsense. A car goes down the street because in the interaction of its parts and the road. This is *how* (Efficient Cause). The car has no *goal*, no Final Cause. To study *why* it goes down the street, its *purpose*, is nonsense.[14]

Therefore, the approach of physical science, to ask how an event was caused, is not entirely appropriate for behavioral science, which should also ask why a person behaves in a particular way.

The field of psychology is in fact moving toward a more humanistic approach, but the slow pace of the change is surprising. Ironically, as O'Hara asserted, the only challenges to positivism have come from fundamentalist clergy and particle physicists.[15] Despite the numerous criticisms of the old conception of science, and many advocates for change, such a major change in approaches does not seem near. As Staats complained, "But the criticism has had little effect. Psychology continues on its way, doing the same things it has always done, under the guidance given it by its mission of becoming a science."[16] As Rychlak observed: "What is so dangerous about this state of affairs is that it is seemingly uncorrectable."[17]

I have argued that the adherence by psychologists to "hard" science is caused by a fear of being considered unscientific.[18] I attributed the resistance to the adoption of flexible methodologies to basic inferiority feelings of psychologists with respect to the natural sciences, thus producing the basic intolerance of ambiguity[19], which is so characteristic of the positivistic tradition. Maslow also interprets this avoidance of the humanistic attitudes to a fear of ambiguity, as follows: "It can be a flight from a world seen as messy, unpredictable, and uncontrollable, a sort of high IQ return to the womb."[20]

Harman argued that truly meaningful reality is contacted through deep intuition, fostered by a more holistic conception of science. Therefore, humanists, religionists and transpersonal psychologists should aggressively confront the issues concerning the appropriate approaches to truth. As Harman said, "Perhaps the time has come to tiptoe no longer, but to quietly, firmly, self-confidently insist on the need for a restructuring of science to accommodate all, rather than just part, of human experience."[21]

Consistent with religious thought, I have accepted the proposition that there are two qualitatively different components of the human being: a material body and a non-material spirit.[22] To be sure, this idea can only be a metaphysical assumption. It is unresolvable, except on a utilitarian basis. Does the assumption help us deal with the problems of life?

Historically, despite rejection by the outdated views of science, many people have believed in the spiritual level. The spiritual level is necessary to control the individual exploitation by the lower levels of analysis and explanation. Therefore, a re-structured science that makes room for spiritual matters should have popular appeal as an alternative to rigorous science.

Discussion

Because mainstream psychology has not been responsive to the mood and attitudes of the general culture, it has not been as effective as it could be in contributing to the welfare of the general culture. The potential strength of the profession is the concept of the whole person in contact with the overwhelming universe of which he or she is a part, attempting resolutely to cope with it. While glorifying a diversity of views, theories and methods, psychology should nevertheless strengthen its identity by focusing on the cognitions of the individual person as the ultimate basis of causality of human behavior.

The relation to other disciplines is strongly related to our conception of science and human nature. But, as O'Hara charged, psychologists have not incorporated the latest epistemological advances in their thinking, and have not provided the proper philosophical underpinnings for the profession.[23] This is important for the credibility of psychology because, as Van Kaam asserted, the viable application of psychology to social problems is critically dependent upon its conception of human nature.[24] A more humanistic base is needed. As Grusky has warned: "the fact that the practice of psychotherapy is badly splintered into competing professional groups also bespeaks a large confusion about the nature of its foundations."[25]

As LeShan contended, we are not prepared for the problems of the twenty-first century.[26] Psychologists must promote human welfare and save psychology by studying human beings in context, both in terms of levels of discourse and in coordination and integration among disciplines at each level. Psychology, in choosing to model itself after the physical sciences, lost sight of what it means to be human. Unfortunately, we divorced ourselves from the humanities and the spiritual aspects of human beings, and borrowed our basic concepts from nineteenth-century physics.

LeShan concluded that therefore we psychologists could understand, predict and control the behaviors of rats and pigeons, but not any of the important behaviors of human beings.[27] Thus, psychologists could be of no real help in solving the serious problems of human behavior, such as killing each other, poisoning the earth and overpopulating it. LeShan said further that to conceptualize people as steam engines cannot make them better, only worse, because the healthier person is more free and unpredictable, whereas the damaged or defective person is more rigid and controllable. Thus, the machine orientation treats people as predictable, mob-like and controllable.

We should study purpose—that is, final causes—and not efficient causes. Our questions should concern why, and not how, a behavior was produced. We do not look to behavioral laws to explain why Columbus crossed the ocean: it is the result of the action of what Harcum called a Responsive Will—a choice made for a reasonable purpose, not necessarily a determined response tied to a set of environmental conditions.[28]

But, the mind is coming back to psychology. As Jeeves reported, the tendency of psychologists to emphasize the study of behavior and eschew concern for mental events is waning. He said,

> One feature of the past two decades in psychology has been the continuing cognitive revolution. After gathering momentum in the early 1970s, it has become a major influence in psychology and neuroscience. 'Mind talk' is respectable again after more than a half century when psychologists, primarily in the United States, were able to foist upon generations of students the belief that the only thing worth studying was behavior, and that any reference to mental life was, in some unspecified way, unscientific.[29]

The early distinction between psychological principles of the laboratory and those of real life has been exaggerated. Scientists can try to capture real-life variables in the laboratory and humanistic psychologists can instill rigor in their research without destroying the validity of either approach. When the two approaches provide converging evidence, the interpretation will become both easier and closer to the truth, and hopefully more acceptable to the people of God.

The components of psychology that is compatible with religion have already been proposed. Miller listed the eight basic tenets for what he called a theistic understanding of human nature, as follows:

1. There is a spiritual aspect of life.
2. There is a God that represents the ultimate standard of good and evil.
3. Sin occurs when humans fail to achieve the high standards of God.
4. Because humans make voluntary choices, they must take responsibility, within limits, for their actions.
5. Spiritual health is maintained through the practice of religion.
6. People of faith show responsivity to the conditions of others.
7. People of faith look to God for hope for the future through divine intervention.
8. Religious faith provides the belief in abrupt personal transformation for improvement.[30]

A psychology will adhere to all eight of these tenets by following two assumptions which are already accepted by some psychologists: 1. That human beings possess a measure of freedom of will; 2. That all methods of research can provide useful information for psychologists. In fact the present proposal for a compatible psychology makes these two assumptions.

Summary

Chapter 2 attempts to define and describe the polymorphous field of psychology. Admittedly, any attempt to capture the totality of psychology in a single chapter will surely fail because psychology is simply too diverse and too complex. In any case, the true definition of the field is established by the daily practice of psychologists.

A major cause of the diversity in psychology comes from its antecedents in philosophy, biology and mathematics. From philosophy, psychology inherited a concern for the nature of human beings. From biology, it inherited an interest in the effects of physical structure on behavior. From mathematics, it inherited quantitative tools, as manifested in individual testing and statistical methods.

Some psychologists prefer the model of the physical sciences, favoring objective evidence and deterministic metaphysics. Others prefer the more liberal view that subjective evidence is also useful, and that human beings can at times transcend environmental influences by personal acts through a freedom of will.

Aspects of psychological science overlap the three traditional areas of academic study: the humanities, the social sciences, and the physical sciences. The psychology that concerns itself with the whole intact and autonomous individual is related to the humanities. The psychology that is concerned with the relations among persons and groups of persons is related to the social sciences. The psychology that involves the physiological mechanisms of behavior is closely related to the physical sciences.

Various individual plans for organizing the field of study for psychology, including theoretical and practical bases, are not sufficiently comprehensive individually. In fact, there is no single accepted way for organizing the field. Various organizational bases include: 1.) Science vs. Humanisn; 2.) Schools of Theory; 3.) Primary Goals; 4.) Levels of Analysis; 5.) Kinds of Variables; 6.) Mediating Processes; and 7.) Fields of Application.

Notes

1. E. P. Sheridan, Science versus practice or science and practice. In L. Rickman and H. Ellis (Eds.) *Preparing Psychologists for the 21st Century*: Proceedings of the National Conference on Graduate Education in Psychology. (Hillsdale, NJ: Erlbaum, 1990). 223-230, 226.
2. C. P. Snow, *The Two Cultures and the Scientific Revolution.* (New York: Cambridge University Press, 1959). 2.
3. C. E. Odegaard, A historical perspective on psychology dilemmas. In L. Rickman and H. Ellis (Eds.) *Preparing psychologists for the 21st century*: Proceedings of the National Conference on Graduate Education in Psychology. (Hillsdale, NJ: Erlbaum, 1990). 17-24.
4. O. A. Bird, The Humanities *Encyclopedia Britannica.* (Macropaedia) Vol. 20. (Chicago: Encyclopedia Britannica, Inc. 1985). 731-735
5. R. Harré, *Personal Being.* (Cambridge, MA: Harvard University Press, 1984). 4.
6. Ibid.
7. J. H. Korn, Psychology as a humanity, *Teaching of Psychology, 12*: 188-193, 1985.
8. Sigmund Koch, The nature and limits of psychological knowledge: Lessons of a century qua "science." *American Psychologist, 36*: 257-275, 1981, 269.
9. P. Greenway, The methodological implications of phenomenological assumptions in humanistic psychology. *Australian Journal of Psychology, 34*: 231-237, 1982, 231.
10. James Deese, Psychology as Science and Art. (New York: Harcourt Brace & Jovanovich, 1972). v.
11. D. C. Dennett, *Brainstorms.* (Montgomery, VT: Bradford Books, 1981); Howard R. Pollio, *Behavior and Existence* (Monterey, CA: Brooks/Cole, 1981).
12. Bernard J. Baars, *The Cognitive Revolution in Psychology*. (New York: The Guilford Press, 1986).
13. W. W. Harman, The transpersonal challenge to the scientific paradigm; The need for a restructuring of science. *ReVision, 11*: 13-21, 1988, 16.
14. Lawrence LeShan, *The Dilemma of Psychology.* (New York: Dutton, 1990). 91.
15. M. O'Hara, Comment on Carl Rogers, "Toward a more human science of the person," *Journal of Humanistic Psychology, 25*: 25-30. 1986.
16. A. W. Staats, Paradigmatic behaviorism: Unified theory for social personality psychology. *Advances in Experimental Social Psychology, 16.* 125-179, 128.
17. Joseph F. Rychlak, Newtonianism and the professional responsibility of psychologists: Who speaks for humanity? *Professional Psychology: Research and Practice, 15*: 82-95, 1984, 91.

18. E. Rae Harcum, Defensive reactance of psychologists to a metaphysical foundation for interpreting different psychologies. *The Journal of Psychology, 122*: 217-235, 1988.
19. Else Frenkel-Brunswik, Intolerance of ambiguity as an emotional and personality variable. *Journal of Personality, 18*: 108-143, 1949.
20. Abraham H. Maslow, Humanistic science and transcendental experiences. *Journal of Humanistic Psychology, 5*: 219-227, 1965, 222.
21. Harman, The transpersonal challenge to the scientific paradigm. 1988. 21.
22. E. Rae Harcum, *A Psychology of Freedom and Dignity*. (Westport, CT: Praeger, 1994.)
23. O'Hara, Comment on Carl Rogers, "Toward a more human science of the person." 1986.
24. Adrian Van Kaam, Humanistic psychology and culture. *Journal of Humanistic Psychology, 1*: 94-100. 1961.
25. Z. Grusky, The practice of psychotherapy: A search for principles in an ambiguous art. *Psychotherapy, 24*: 1-6, 1984, 5.
26. Lawrence LeShan, The Dilemma of Psychology. (New York: Dutton, 1990).
27. Ibid.
28. Harcum, *A Psychology of Freedom and Dignity*, 1994.
29. Malcolm A. Jeeves, *Human Nature at the Milennium: Reflections on the Integration of Psychology and Christianity*. (Grand Rapids, MI: Baker Books, 1997). 8.
30. William K. Miller, What is human nature? Reflections from Judeo-Christian Perspectives. In W. K. Miller and H. D. Delaney (Eds.) *Judeo-Christian Perspectives on Psychology*. (Washington, DC: American Psychological Association, 2005). 11-29.

Chapter 3

Science and Metaphysics

Metaphysical issues involve questions about nature that cannot be answered directly and conclusively by the empirical methods of science. Empirical methods provide information about the world through our sensory systems. Indeed, much of our research about the nature of the world is based on what we can experience objectively and collectively through our senses—i.e., facts. Metaphysical issues, by contrast, cannot be resolved by this procedure. We cannot see, hear, feel, etc., positive proof of the correct answers.

But, in truth, even the empirical methods involve metaphysical issues, because one such issue concerns the true nature of reality, which questions the very validity of proof itself. For example, how do I prove to myself that my desk is real? Because I can see it and touch it, indeed, it passes those personal empirical tests. But I know that under some unusual situations, I can perceive a desk when none is present. For example, a person under hypnosis can perceive a nonexistent disk. Or a person may hallucinate a desk when under the influence of a high fever. Even under normal circumstances, we can always make perceptual mistakes. Each of us, at one time or another, has experienced something that turned out not to be real. Only if such distortions are unusually frequent for an individual is there concern about his or her mental normalcy.

We resolve the question of what to believe on the basis of converging evidence. That occurs when the weight of the evidence points to, or converges upon, one conclusion. Thus, most of our convictions about reality are conclusions from sensory data. But, even empirical evidence does not provide a secure answer to all of our questions. I will discuss later the possibility that we also can reach conclusions on the basis of intuition when there is no, or inadequate, sensory evidence. That very conviction is an example of an intuitive conclusion. Not all psychologists agree that such convictions exist.

Given the uncertainty about the true answers, then why do we bother with metaphysical issues? The answer is that they do have real answers. You just cannot prove that your personal answer is correct by the methods of empirical science.

In contrast to so-called scientific proof, in which a community of experts must be convinced, the individual person must decide for himself or herself what he or she will accept as true about a metaphysical question. Presumably, the answers of each person work for him or her in the course of a personal adjustment to life. Indeed, I could not lead an ordered life if I often doubted the reality of my desk. The same things apply to certain of my religious convictions.

The main purpose of this chapter is to induce the reader to hold fast to his or her right to decide these metaphysical issues. To be sure, the most respected scientists also can make mistakes. For example, the eminent psychologist B. F. Skinner asserted that good science requires the abandonment of the concept of a human will that can choose behaviors for the individual.[1] Indeed, this chapter asserts the contrary proposition, and provides compelling practical arguments for acceptance of the concept of freedom of a human will. Surely, a human will could not be seen, touched, etc., as is possible for the desk. The question thus goes beyond the validity of empirical evidence. In any case, the issue of freedom of will is a most important one for all of us.

Nature of Proof

Acceptable proof of a proposition requires a sufficient empirical, logical or intuitive basis to convince a reasonable person. Both empirical and logical evidence are accepted by all scientists, but not all scientists accept intuition as a basis for belief. Intuition is an experiential process by which the person, through minimal cues and similarities among perceived events and mysterious processes beyond our understanding, becomes aware of information about the environment. Conclusions based on intuition are called faith. Just as I must believe in the existence of my desk in order to live an ordered life, I must also believe in the existence of certain spiritual things in order to live an ordered life.

Because empirical evidence is based on actual experience with events observable by all observers through their sensing systems, it represents so-called facts. An observer senses something that is in agreement with what other competent observers also report sensing, or could have sensed if they had been present.

Logical evidence is based on deductions from presumed facts by certain accepted rules and criteria. For example, we can draw a reasonable conclusion that is necessarily valid if the presumed facts themselves are correct.

Intuitive evidence is specifically important in dealing with questions about values, reason and purpose. According to English and English, intuition is responsible for most of our practical judgments about persons and complex issues.[2] In fact, intuitive proof is most important in the absence of compelling empirical and rational evidence. It is holistic, relevant and personal. Intuitive decisions do not depend upon objectively weighted factors in precise formulas to determine which one is supported by the strongest evidence. Intuitive perception is obviously most appropriate for answering the metaphysical questions. The present conclusion is that scientific inference should be based on all available information, with proper consideration for the fact that some sources produce more reliable bases for conviction than others. These issues will be discussed later in this chapter, from the standpoint of the practical value of a belief in freedom of will, and also in Chapter 6, in a speculative description of the personal agent of action.

Physical vs. Social Science

The world of physical science is qualitatively different from other disciplines in ways of discovering the truth. In physical science, empirical proof is most heavily weighted. How much of what kind of observable evidence does it take to convince the doubter? If one reasonable person is able to doubt the truth of a proposition, how can it therefore be considered proved to another? Even in the case of empirical evidence, actually we are ultimately discussing faith or belief, rather than proof in an absolute, incontrovertible sense. Intelligent people can disagree.

Often we must be satisfied with something less than full knowledge of an alleged absolute truth. Deese has explained nicely the situation of science with respect to its search for truth, as follows:

> Most psychological theories fail to approach the ideals set for them by the philosophy of science in respect to correctness, or truth value. Many concerned laymen and not a few scientists take the view that the whole purpose of science is to search for truth. These same people often think that the truth consists of a set of propositions that remain unchallenged forever, once properly established. The truth is the truth. But, at the same time, everyone knows that scientific theories change. In fact, the history of any particular science shows that there is almost nothing that remains an eternal verity. . . . One can only decide that, given the circumstances at the moment, one theory is in some way better than another.[3]

Indeed, the nature of science means that new data can falsify a previously alleged truth. Deese pointed out further that the importance of certain facts and theories is actually derived more from the fads and fashions of scientists than from some orderly progression of rational study. Therefore, we must be chary about claims to absolute scientific truth about the universe. Indeed, I learned in high school that the atom was the irreducible particle of matter, and I learned in graduate school that color television was impossible. So, how much of what you think you know about the world is not true?

Royce also proposed that rigidly empirical research is not the only avenue to truth. He described the three basic paths to knowledge, and the corresponding tests of the knowledge, as follows: a) Thinking (logical); b) Sensing (empirical); and c) Symbolizing and intuition. Thus, he argued:

> In the analysis which follows I take the position that symbolism and intuition are legitimate ways of knowing, in spite of our ignorance about how they work, that they can be brought into play at any phase of the knowing process, and that they have, in fact, manifested themselves to some extent in all domains of psychological study, but that their greatest immediate relevance lies in the present

emergence of humanistic psychology.[4]

Royce cautioned that individual persons may tend to restrict themselves to one path of knowing at the expense of the others, thus failing to avail for themselves the full possibilities for gaining knowledge. He characterized psychologists as traditionally "super empirical." In particular, Royce argued that philosophers and psychologists tend to rely much more heavily on thinking and sensing than on symbolism/intuition that involves the metaphorical approach. The metaphorical approach is a subjective method that uses a word or phrase of one kind of object in place of another in order to support a similarity or analogy between them.

Royce cautioned that the empirical tests should not be abandoned, but welded to the metaphorical in order to temper our humanistic thought. A proposition should not be branded as useless simply because it is not immediately testable by empirical means. While rational and empirical sources of evidence are more important to the testing of theories, metaphorical knowledge is most important for the emergence of new conceptions, particularly for the more humanistic applications of psychology.

Smith joined the ranks of strong proponents of multiple approaches to psychological understanding. He said:

> One may entertain different grades of evidence without being misled—so long as one remains critically aware of its limitations. One may glean insights and hypotheses from many sources, including common human experience and its refinement in the arts, later to be tested by firmer criteria. I am convinced that there is no royal road to Truth, not even that of the experimentalist. Truth is elusive, and we do best to converge upon it from multiple perspectives... Given the aridity of much of our research literature, I think there is a legitimate place for armchair speculation.[5]

Le Shan argued that the shelves of books that describe the results of massive research efforts do not provide the answers to our most important questions about improving society.[6] Shoben similarly contended:

> While we have spilled ink by the hogshead in reporting studies of learning, we are only now coming to grips with the processes by which children acquire skill in language or an interest in biology, and the formal contribution of psychology to the improvement of race relations is small and far more dependent on the liberal spirit of psychologists than on the solidarity of the knowledge produced by their science.[7]

Thus, surely, there have been many voices advocating a more open view about what can be considered as acceptable evidence in behavioral science. There seems to be little justification for the cavalier assertions that casual observations and informal methods are inherently incorrect or useless. I have attributed this inordinate resistance to multiple avenues of evidence to a low tolerance of ambiguity by some psychologists that has been caused by the traditional methods of graduate training in psychology.[8] The training in science of psychologists has been constrained by fears of inherent inferiority relative to the perceived rigor of the physical sciences. As many have pointed out, this fear is based on an outdated conception of the nature of science.[9] Therefore, philosophical arguments about the nature of science are less important than the relative values of the results from different methods.

Faith

As a practical matter, we often cannot delay decisions until we have adequate proof for our beliefs. In our daily lives, we must rely on faith, which is belief without adequate proof. Even scientists are, on occasion, forced to rely on faith, because adequate evidence is not available. For example, consider psychologists who are consultants in human engineering, an applied field which considers how man can most efficiently work with machines. Because frequently there is not time to obtain a definitive research answer, the psychologist must make his or her best guess, or leave it to the engineer to make the guess. I have know engineers who are very good at what they have been trained to do, but patently awful at making guesses about psychological issues. The reason is that people usually do not act like non-sentient machines. Therefore, the behavioral scientist settles on a conclusion that is a basis for action, while knowing full well that he or she does not have adequate proof. But, he or she continues to look for proof with an open mind.

In truth, faith is always involved to some extent in beliefs about the nature of the physical world. A natural law is a verbal statement of the way events uniformly and consistently occur, supported by such ample evidence that it is not subject to doubt, unless substantial evidence to the contrary is obtained. Because there is no way to prove that contrary new evidence will never be obtained, there is *always* some doubt that a law will hold forever. But, we must have faith that the law will hold as we take action based on that law.

Each time our predictions of natural events are verified, we strengthen our faith that our beliefs are correct. An incorrect assumption ordinarily will not produce a correct prediction, and therefore will not be useful to us. This actually is the nature of an experiment. A presumed cause is manipulated in order to find out if a predicted effect occurs. If the predicted effect is obtained, we infer that the presumptions are correct.

This line of argument means that, in fact, I cannot establish beyond any doubt that my desk is truly a real object. I can, of course, see it, touch it and hear myself kick it. I feel pain from the kick, if I have kicked hard enough. To be sure, my imaginative desk "behaves" as a real desk should. I can write on it, and store pencils in its drawers. Indeed, my belief has survived a number of the most stringent empirical tests that I can devise and administer. To be sure, I ask my colleagues, and anyone else who is about, if they perceive a desk in front of me. I am encouraged if they agree. Until my presumed desk fails one of my tests—

until it disappoints my expectations—I feel secure in my belief—the conviction, if you will—that there truly is a desk before me.

Nevertheless, I still realize that the senses are fallible. I have indeed held false beliefs that have been proven, upon further examination, to be wrong. Consequently, my perception of my desk could be one of my perceptual mistakes, as well as a mistake of my colleagues. But I do not think so, and thus I go on.

In fact, as a practical matter, I have no choice but to believe, and to rely on my belief. I cannot run my life if I doubt that my desk exists—or my automobile, or traffic lights or my wife—after I have made reasonable empirical efforts to verify my beliefs.

I establish my beliefs in all scientific truths in basically the same way that I establish my belief in the reality of my desk. The empirical tests are convincing, but not absolutely infallible. Thus, the utility, not the absolute truth, of beliefs is the crucial criterion, once the person has performed adequate empirical and logical tests. Those tests should push the limits of the empirical science to its metaphysical boundaries.

The above argument is for—not against—the pursuit of scientific knowledge. Knowledge, a true belief based on sufficient direct experience, is more useful than other beliefs, which are based on less information. But where there is no knowledge, we must rely on simple beliefs in order to get on with our lives. We must have faith in what we cannot prove, but necessarily influences our actions. Thus, the difference between knowledge and a belief is relative to the amount of the information about the world on which they are based. A belief may indeed be true or not true. What works in our lives is probably true for us. Accordingly I have proposed what I call the Principle of Ultimate Practicality, as follows: "*In the absence of clear empirical or logical proof to the contrary, each individual person may conditionally believe whatever seems to work most harmoniously and effectively to achieve personal goals and to promote personal growth.*"[10]

Thus, the individual person is his or her own judge about what to believe. If the belief is objectively incorrect, it will not work for the individual. If it works for the individual, and makes him or her happy in life, the utility of it is sufficient to justify that belief. I go on to conclude that:

> Because the present view of science tends to minimize the differences between formal scientific methods and casual methods of studying nature, it follows that the same criteria for personal belief should be appropriate for scientific belief. Scientists also cannot suspend their activities because of ignorance. Assumptions must be made in order to mount research endeavors and must be corrected as contrary evidence appear; theories are only tentative explanations for a class of phenomena.[11]

Causality

This chapter now tackles the difficult question about the causality of human behavior. Why do some people doubt that they can control their own behaviors by a purposeful act of will?

It is the nature of humans to infer a causal relationship between Event A and Event B whenever the two events regularly change together in time and space. To say that two events co-vary is to say that a change in one occurs whenever there is a particular change in the other one. For example, we would observe that, if Event A is present, then Event B is also present. The obvious reason for the inference of a causal relation between Events A and B is that, if indeed Event A does cause Event B, then there must necessarily be such a co-relation between them. For convenience in speech and writing, psychologists use the word "correlation" to refer to such co-relation.

We know very well that we can make false inferences of causality in the case of superstitions. Event A can, by pure chance, be followed by Event B. For example, the baseball player has no clean socks to wear and so wears dirty socks. He subsequently hits three home runs. The tendency to draw the incorrect inference of a causal relation between wearing dirty socks and hitting home runs is powerful, though unjustified.

A bit of evidence for a false inference of causality comes from a demonstration that I used when teaching introductory psychology.[12] As I turned the crank on one end of a black box, a small flag on the opposite end of the box bobbed up and down in synchrony with the movement of the crank. I asked the students to infer what mechanism was at work inside the box. Most students, assuming that the cranking caused the flag to wave, guessed that there was some sort of gear arrangement between the crank and the flag. I then turned the box around to expose the truth that the crank was connected to absolutely nothing. In fact, I had secretly waved the flag by a hidden device with my free hand, timing it exactly with my cranking. Therefore, the two events were perfectly correlated in time, but clearly the one did not cause the other. Nevertheless, the causal delusion for an observer was powerful indeed!

The problem for determining causal relationships is that correlations alone do not *necessarily* indicate causal relationships. Clearly correlations between two events can occur for reasons other than a causal relationship between them. For example, some third event, Event C, could be responsible for producing *both* Events A and B. Therefore, before you can establish a causal relationship between Events A and B, you must rule out *all* possible alternative explanations for the empirical correlation between them. This process obviously requires the physical impossibility of proving a negative, that no alternative possibility has been overlooked.

The impossibility of proving a negative has led some psychologists to argue that we can never prove causality through an empirical correlation. I do not agree. You see, an adequate proof does not require the removal of every glimmer of doubt.

Truly, the philosophical problem of proving the causality of an event is truly formidable. One must prove to the satisfaction of the scientific community that there is no unidentified extraneous factor that enters into the causation of the event. To be sure, you never can prove beyond any shadow of a doubt that you have discounted every single other factor in a situation that could possibly have been a cause. Thus, the nature of proof is to convince ourselves and others by careful methodologies that the alternative possibilities are *not likely* to be correct.

Despite the difficulty of proving scientific causation, nevertheless in science we must assume that events are caused by other events. Indeed, an event may have many crucial causal factors, as Harré and Madden assert in their model of causality, called natural necessity, as follows:

> Cause is the whole set of necessary conditions sufficient for an effect. . . . A forest fire is caused by lightning striking the tree, dry underbrush and a prevailing wind. But why stop there? Oxygen in the air is also a necessary condition, but so is the presence of the planet itself, and so necessary conditions are sought *ad infinitum*, backwards in time and across all space.[13]

Thus, the problem of singling out one factor to identify as the specific cause of a particular behavior is obvious. Although we assume that every event has a cause, no matter how complex, the problem is in identifying the immediate, or efficient, cause. It may be a simple event, or a complex interaction of many causal factors extending back a very, very long time.

The philosophical approach of Harré and Madden fits well with the theory of chaos in physics, which proposes that major physical effects may be the result of apparently very minor antecedent events that occurred very early in a cumulative process.[14] For example, the flapping of a butterfly's wings in China a month ago may influence the weather in New York City tomorrow. Thus, when a tiny distant causal factor produces a critical difference, the result is typically called a butterfly effect.

Obviously, it is impossible to predict such an effect on the basis of understanding the detailed processes along the way. This does not say, however, that the weather—or human behavior—is therefore uncaused and thus completely unpredictable by its very nature. For example, psychological variables often interact such that a change in one variable in a total situation may change the way that some other variables affect that behavior. Therefore, the particular effect of that variable at one time depends upon which particular conditions happened to be existing in the particular environment. Or a manipulated variable may interact with some dispositional variable in the research subject such that all subjects will not respond to the manipulation in the same manner. Therefore, a psychologist may not be able to predict the behavior of a given person in a particular situation, saying, "It all depends." This phrase means that the behavior depends entirely upon the context of a situation, that the subject trait has not been specified or that its effects on the behavior are not known. Such an interaction effect may be relatively simple and understandable, or hopelessly complex, and thus not at all understandable (i.e., explainable).

Actually, the mechanism of causation may be so complex that we will never be able to understand the causation of all events. Long ago, Oppenheimer asserted, in fact, that the physical world cannot be predicted in detail, but only in general terms: "Physics is predictive, but within limits; its world is ordered, but not completely causal."[15]

The theory of chaos in physics parallels the "choices within limits" theory of Pollio and Henley with respect to human behavior.[16] Pollio and Henley propose that heredity and environment together place constraints on a person's behavior, thus producing some predictability. Within those limits, the person exercises a freedom of will that may produce inherently unpredictable results. Although Harré and Madden mention only physical causes, there is nothing in their definition to preclude a volitional factor.[17]

Cook and Campbell support this general argument. They asserted the reality of causes, but argued that we must base causal inferences "on procedures that reduce the uncertainty about causal connections even though this uncertainty can never be reduced to zero."[18] Cook and Campbell accept the modernity view of science, which says that some facts are merely necessary products of the particular theory that guided the research. But these authors also assert the existence of what they call stubborn facts, which are consistently obtained regardless of the theory that guided the research. Causal inferences can therefore confidently be drawn from them in order to guide behavior.

The crucial factor in proof is in the kind of truth that you seek, the kind of evidence that you accept and who you trust as the expert. The bottom line is defined by what you believe, whether your belief is based on overwhelming empirical evidence, or on intuition with little or no physical evidence. To be sure, some important facts about human behavior are so obvious that they do not need empirical evidence to convince the average student. We should seek scientific evidence when that is necessary or obtainable. But we do not need science to justify all our beliefs.

The issue therefore is philosophical and practical, not scientific. I agree with Buechner when he said, "I can't prove the friendship of my friend. When I experience it, I don't need to prove it. When I don't experience it, no proof will do."[19]

Causation of Human Behavior

In the following discussion of the causation of human behavior, the terms cause and causation refer to consistent empirical correlations between antecedents events (i.e., causes) and subsequent events (i.e., effects). We assume that all behavior is caused. Perhaps some behaviors are caused by factors that we cannot unmask, or identify by consistent correlations among events, such as voluntary acts of a human will.[20]

In the case of personal autonomy or freedom, our inability to discover a cause does not mean that there is no environmental cause, or that the causality is unknowable. If the cause cannot be discovered, we can attribute it to voluntary choice, or freedom, or we may attribute it to some extremely complex causal mechanism that is too difficult to find or to understand.

As Harcum argued, the concept of a hopelessly complex physical cause does not entail a scientific advantage over the free-will interpretation.[21] Because we cannot be sure which view is correct, the final conclusion must be based on the relative utilities of the two views.

It should be emphasized at this point that a theory is a guess about the explanation for a category of behaviors. It is necessarily an extrapolation from data, and therefore cannot be known to be correct. Moreover, many psychologists and philosophers have made different guesses about the nature and functioning of the human agent of action. The Behaviorists claim that it is merely the function of the physical mechanisms of behavior, while the Humanists claim that it involves a voluntary choice by a non-material spirit.

Doctrine of Determinism

One of the assumptions about the causality of human behavior is called the doctrine of determinism. Determinism states that for everything that happens, under those given conditions, nothing else *could* have happened. Therefore, this idea considers all human behaviors to be necessary consequences of present and past environmental experience, as both of these interact with the individual's inherited characteristics. The cause is simply the aggregate of purely physical mechanisms. Specifically excluded as a cause is any effect by a human volition system, or personal will.

According to the deterministic view, if we knew exactly what all of the environmental events were, including inherited structure, and how the two interacted with one another to produce their responses, we would have no uncertainty in predicting the behavior of the responding organism. This strict deterministic view was advocated and applied to human behavior in particular by the Behaviorist J. B. Watson,[22] and later by B. F. Skinner[23]. Because Skinner is probably the best-known of the Behaviorists, his arguments will be emphasized in this book.

The time lag between the causal event and the resulting action is not an issue in the deterministic view. The lag can be very brief, counted in very small fractions of a second. In fact, a stimulus event could continue in the nervous system even after a response to it was made. Or, the delay may be measured in years, decades or a lifetime. For example, one can consider the learning of emotions and cognitions in association with an earlier event which occurred during the person's childhood, and which persists in the form of some so-called personality trait or firm habit of the aged adult. In this case, the person may have the illusory feeling that he or she is making a free choice, because he or she may not consciously remember the causal event. Nevertheless, the person is in fact responding as he or she must, given these early experiences. These remote causes are what Lehrer called ancestorial factors, for which the particular causal mechanisms may be essentially impossible to unmask.[24]

To be sure, in some cases the causal experience may be known. A case from my own experience documents this fact. I have claustrophobia, which is a pathological fear of being confined in a small space. This fear can surely be traced to an experience that I had as a preschooler. Playing with other children, I was trapped for a few moments in a tunnel dug into a hillside such that I was in extreme fear for my life. A group of boys had dared each other to crawl into a narrow tunnel to see what was at the other end. After everyone else had failed, I succeeded. But when I tried to inch my way back out of the tunnel, my heavy coat caught on the sides of the tunnel and acted like Chinese handcuffs, preventing my escape. Unfortunately, by this time the other boys had gone home. Needless to say, I had a real fear of dying immediately. That fear of tight places has persisted unabated over 75 years.

But the experience had a positive side, because I am also convinced after 75-plus years that God was with me and saved me. If I had panicked and fought against the handcuffs, I surely would have died. God stilled my frantic tendency to fight my way out and inspired a pre-school boy to climb back into the tunnel, thus releasing the handcuffs. Then I could carefully pat down the coat as I slowly inched my way out of the tunnel. This Godly insight was entirely contrary to the natural basic instinct to fight out of the tunnel, which would have been fruitless and deadly. God saved me for a purpose which may be realized in the future lives of my grandsons. Probably the fear could be removed by psychotherapy, but I have not been willing to put myself through the discomfort of therapy because ordinarily it is not a major problem for me. Perhaps my greatest trial occurred when I was scheduled for an MRI examination prior to back surgery. When I was in place before the machine that would require confining my body in a small space, the nurse went to get me a tranquilizer, which I demanded. Meanwhile, I sat and contemplated the tight space into which my body was to be inserted. When the nurse returned I was no longer even in the building. By the way, as evidence for the effect of physical factors on the thought process, I should point out that, later, given a tranquilizer well in advance and blindfolded, I have been able to submit to several MRI examinations.

So, there is no doubt that the alleged ancestorial factors do exist. The issue is whether or not they can account for all behaviors for which the causal factors are not identified. For example, if I did not remember my youthful experience in the tunnel, I might think that I simply chose not to take the MRI examination.

The strict concept of determinism leaves absolutely no room for a domain of human will. Therefore, if we were to believe strictly in the doctrine of determinism, logically we could not also believe in the simultaneous existence of an intentional system that could influence behavior.

The problem with the deterministic view is that it is too restrictive. Of course, some behaviors can be understood and predicted from the person's genetic makeup, from his or her present physical surroundings and from his or her past history. But the causation of some other behaviors, I submit, are understood and predicted by reference to certain stable characteristics of the behaving organism—that is, from the very character of the person, as shown by his or her voluntary choices. Although some aspects of free will may be apparently capricious and unrelated to factors in the environment—the part that Harcum calls a Transcendental will—another part responds to physical factors in the environment—the part that Harcum calls a Responsive will.[25]

It should be emphasized that determinism is a philosophical concept, and not a religious one. For example, determinism is not, as Nelson claimed, the same as predestination, which is a religious concept. Nelson asserted that:

> Many Christians believe in the absolute sovereignty and control of God, which if carried to an extreme conclusion means that the lives of individuals are completely governed or preplanned by God. This doctrine of determinism or *predestination* is opposed by the *Arminian* position, which holds that individuals have free will, a view that is assumed by both Buddhism and Hinduism despite the doctrine of karma.[26]

Surely, as Nelson says, all Christians do believe in the absolute sovereignty of God. But, some do not believe in absolute control by God. For example, United Methodists believe that God can, at his pleasure, exercise complete control, but nevertheless he allows individual Christians some freedom to choose their own behaviors. In fact, our very ability to sin implies that we can make bad choices when we have the freedom to choose. Therefore, the assumption of human freedom to choose is contrary both to the principles of determinism and predestination. Nevertheless, the two principles are not the same.

Webster's New International Dictionary of the English language defines determinism as "The doctrine that all acts of the will result from causes which determine them."[27] This definition is supported by the World Book Encyclopedia Dictionary, as follows: "The doctrine that human actions are the necessary results of antecedent causes."[28]

In their comprehensive dictionary of psychological and psychoanalytical terms, English and English define determinism as "the doctrine that an event is completely explainable in terms of its antecedents."[29] They go on to say that, "In effect, if not in theory, some degree of determinism is postulated in all scientific, as well as practical, psychology."[30]

In his introductory textbook on psychology, Weiten indicates that determinism means "that behavior is fully determined by environmental stimuli."[31] It is noteworthy that Weiten does not use the word "predestination" in his psychology book.

In contrast to the dictionary definition of determinism, the Worldbook Dictionary defines predestination as, "An ordaining [establishing] beforehand."[32] In religious terms, it is "the action of God in deciding beforehand what will happen."[33] Similarly, Webster's New International Dictionary of the English language defines predestination as, "foreordination" and "to destine, decree, determine, appoint or settle beforehand."[34] English and English do not include the term "predestination" in their dictionary of psychological terms, although they do, of course, define the term "determinism." Thus, the term predestination does not appear in psychological sources, which nevertheless use the term "determinism."[35]

To be sure, neither the scientific principle of determinism nor the religious principle of predestination can be literally true if there is a valid principle of freedom of will. Freedom of will means that God allows the Christian to have a degree of influence on his or her fate in either a scientific or religious context.

Freedom of Will

Feinberg described indeterminism, the opposite of determinism, which states that some events are not completely caused by external events.[36] An extreme version of indeterminism is called libertarianism, which attributes human action entirely to the free responses of a personal will. As I said, this idea of libertarianism is inimical to the idea of a behavioral science because by definition a *completely* free will would be inscrutable, unpredictable and uncontrollable. It would actually eliminate the possibility of psychological science because there would be nothing to understand that could produce a behavior. The only causal explanation for a behavior would be, "The person just wanted to do it." Indeed, there could be no field of psychology.

Jeeves refers to this need for a deterministic orientation as "methodological determinism," and declares that it is shared by everyone. He says, in agreement with the present argument, that this assumption is necessary for the science of psychology, as follows:

> There is an important difference between what may be called a working orientation toward the world, what we have just called methodological determinism, and an inflexible and absolute ontological presupposition about the way the world is. Almost all scientific psychologists are determinists or near determinists in the sense of adopting methodological determinism. If they did not hope, and indeed expect, to identify regularities in human behavior that would enable them to explain, predict and control it, there would be little point in the whole enterprise in which they are engaged. What point would there be in undertaking an experiment on how school children learn mathematics or on the effects of particular drugs on the efficiency of the behavior of industrial workers or on comparing the efficacy of two competing types of psychotherapy, if the experimenter studying each of these, at root, believed that they were intrinsically capricious?[37]

But, the issue of free will is also critical among psychologists. Surely, Nelson was guilty of an understatement when he assessed the importance of the issue of free will in psychology, as follows: "The issue of free will posed by naturalistic determination and causal reductionism has also been a significant topic of discussion within psychology."[38] Indeed, it is a critical issue.

Weston says:

> Many of the issues that remain at the heart of contemporary psychological research and controversy are classic philosophical questions. One of these is whether human action is the product of free will or determinism. Those who champion free will follow in the footsteps of the seventeenth-century French philosopher Rene Descartes (1596-1650) who contended that human action follows from human intention—that is, that people choose a course of action and act on it. In contrast, proponents of determinism, from the Greek philosopher Democritus onward, assert that behavior follows lawful patterns like everything else in the universe, from falling rocks to planets revolving around the sun. Psychological determinists believe that the action of humans and other animals are determined by physical forces, internally by genetic processes and externally by environment events.[39]

To be sure, the issue is not really between free will and determinism, because no psychologists believe in a completely free will. Indeed, none deny that often environmental determinants are vitally important. No psychologist can believe in unrestricted choice, unhampered by physical events in the environment. Such a concept denies that human behavior is influenced by environmental factors. Such an idea is ridiculous.

Nevertheless, some psychologists do believe in freedom of will, or a limited free will. To be sure, a term like "limited free will" is an oxymoron, so the term "freedom of will" is preferred. Thus, there is some freedom of will, which is not completely free.

Even those psychologists called Humanists (e.g., Rogers) assert contributing causative effects of heredity and environment.[40] Thus, Humanists also embrace a science of behavior, although Humanists are often incorrectly accused of being libertarians.[41]

Soft Determinism

A mixture of the two absolute terms, determinism and free will, is not logically possible in a linguistic sense. For example, asking if a person has free will is like asking whether a person is telling the truth, is pregnant and so forth. Therefore, it might seem that we are left with the dilemma of choosing to follow the mutually exclusive principles of determinism or the concept of a completely free will. But a simple choice between two absolute views is not acceptable to many psychologists. Indeed, the Humanistic psychologists, Carl Rogers accepted an integrative view, called soft determinism, as follows:

> But responsible personal choice, which is the most essential element in being a person, which is the core of experience in psychotherapy, which exists prior to any scientific endeavor, is an equally prominent fact of our lives. To deny the experience of responsible choice is, to me, as restricted a view as to deny the possibility of a behavioral science. . . . We cannot profitably deny our subjective life, any more than we can deny the objec-

tive description of that life.[42]

Thus, psychologists and laity alike have two possible metaphysical choices about the causation of human behavior: determinism or soft determinism. We must reach a decision about which to follow on the basis of which makes the most logical and practical sense for running our personal and professional lives. We should choose the view which is of maximal use to the society as a whole in fostering helpful social responses. Because, as Rogers says, personal choice is the essential element of being human, and also the core experience in psychotherapy, the concept of soft determinism works better. My reasoning in accepting the concept and reality of freedom of will was forcefully expressed as follows:

> Among the reasons that I personally cling to the concept of a human will is that my religion requires it. It is generally accepted by contemporary theists that God permits man some freedom of choice (Salmon, 1981). This fact will not be a compelling reason for many, but for some it can be a powerful one. A conflict between science and religion is not necessary. If one believes in complete determinism, one can believe also that God made the rules. The situation is even easier if one believes in soft determinism: God made the rules and gives us the right to choose because the alleged scientific determinism does not have to be complete. We defy His rules at our peril.[43]

Other writers have supported the value of a belief in freedom of will. Moreover, Baumeister cited several empirical studies which indicated the value of a belief in freedom of choice. He asserted:

> I close by noting that those psychologists who deny the existence of human freedom may do significant harm. . . .
> The Judeo-Christian tradition has long emphasized human freedom in part as a way to promote socially responsible, virtuous action, and now laboratory data have confirmed the wisdom of that approach. People who are led to reject the idea of free will become prone to act in selfish, immoral ways that can harm others.
> Put another way, the Judeo-Christian view of human freedom is not just an idle theological opinion, but rather a form of social influence that can promote socially desirable behavior. Psychologists should be aware that rejecting that doctrine can harm society. From where I sit, nothing in the current research journals is compelling enough to justify taking that step.[44]

Alternative Terms

Because the absolute connotations of the terms "free will" and "determinism" add to the problem of choosing a compromise view, I have proposed alternative terms.[45] The term "Doctrine of Generativism" was suggested to replace the absolute term "Doctrine of Determinism." The word generativism is taken from the adjective generative, which means to have the power to originate or to produce. Thus, human actions can be produced, or generated, by environmental and hereditary factors. But, it also leaves open the possibility that such causality is not complete, thus arguing that internal personal factors can contribute, and even preempt—fail to consent to—the environmental and physical influences. The term generativism is exactly equivalent to the term soft determinism, without the oxymoronic character of that term.

To replace the oxymoronic term of limited free will, I proposed the term Viable Will.[46] The term Viable Will means simply full of life, active and workable. The viable will is active and vigorous in selecting responses, but nothing about the term implies that it is totally free from external influences and constraints. To be sure, in some cases, it may effectively be the sole factor in the selection of a response. In extremely opposite cases, the response may be solely determined by environmental factors or nearly so, in what is called stimulus-bound behavior. Thus, probably, most decisions are produced jointly by both the antecedent environmental events and an action of the viable will. Certainly, this is the belief of almost all lay citizens, as Harcum, Rosen and Burijon reported.[47] It is equivalent to the notion of choices within limits that was proposed by Pollio and Henley.[48]

Thus, instead of mechanically mediating a response, the viable will logically selects an appropriate one. Therefore, the viable will—as internal mechanism—has parity in causing behavior with, say, habit as an internal mechanism. To the extent that the will is responsive to the environment, its effects are not free, but explainable.[49]

Harcum's view of freedom of will is consistent with the view of William James.[50] Nevertheless, it entails greater flexibility in shifting to a different, incompatible belief state when that new incompatible state is more useful.

As a further elaboration, I incorporated within the generic term, viable will, two component parts. The first is the concept of a Responsive Will, which makes appropriate responses to stimulation from the environment.[51] It represents an aspect of the will that "comes to terms" and "acts for the sake of" the environment.[52] Whereas James conceived of such response as an attention to a stimulus, my view does not require attention.[53] Responses can range from automatic behaviors with virtually no attention to conscious decisions of acquiescence to an environmental press after extreme mental effort.

Because people can choose to be responsive to aspects of their environment, we can at times be sublimely confident in predicting the behavior of even perfect strangers. I proved this point to myself early one morning while I was sitting alone in a doctor's waiting room. I amused myself by predicting where new arrivals would sit. I was seated in one of six groupings of chairs. My group of chairs was against a wall and closest to the entrance door. As I predicted, the first person to arrive sat in the grouping of chairs farthest from my grouping, and therefore farthest from the entrance. The next three persons to arrive each sat, as I predicted, in different groupings of chairs. I could not predict which grouping each one would select, only that the selected seat would be in a grouping that had not been previously chosen.

After those other four chair groups had been selected, I now considered it an absolutely sure bet that the next person who entered would take a seat from among the remaining group of unoccupied chairs. Indeed, I was correct. Thus, I correctly predicted the behavior of a total stranger that was obviously voluntary by usual connotations of that term.

Undoubtedly, each new arrival was free of environmental constraints to select any unoccupied chair in the waiting room. But there were in fact internal restraints or limitations on his or her choices because of a general awareness of a certain convention in the society. Each person presumably understood that it would have been socially inappropriate to sit unnecessarily close to another person in the room because that would be a violation of the personal space of the stranger. In a word, each seated patient would have felt uncomfortable if someone had chosen a seat close to him or her when there were other chairs available at greater distances. Therefore, our best prediction of the behavior in a strange situation is probably what we ourselves would choose to do in that very situation. Obviously, we are better at understanding and predicting the behavior of people who are physically and culturally more similar to us.

Of course, my predictions would have been different if I had reason to believe that the new arrivals had been personally acquainted with someone already in the room. In such a case, the best prediction would have been that the new arrival would sit in the same grouping of seats as the one occupied by his or her friend.

A different aspect of the Viable Will does not routinely respond to the environmental press, although it may be influenced by it. For this aspect of will, I proposed the term Transcendental Will.[54] This aspect of will can initiate abrupt changes in the responding mechanisms, because it is responding primarily to internal personal representations. Although it may be influenced by the environmental press, it is not controlled by the environment.

By its very nature, the actions of the Transcending Will are thus virtually impossible to predict. Sometimes, the characteristics of the individual person provide a far better basis for prediction than do the conditions of his or her surroundings. Therefore, except in the simplest of situations, unless we know the person extremely well personally, or have studied his or her personality, we will be generally mystified about what he or she will do.

Arguments for Belief in Freedom

I have argued that, for practical purposes, the correct orientation for the freedom-vs-determinism issue must be in specific instances determined by practical successes.[55] Specifically, the reductionistic orientation is more useful for relatively stimulus-bound behaviors, and the voluntaristic orientation is more useful for less stimulus-bound behaviors, or those with more remote causation.

Figure 3-1. Example of a classic Rubin reversible figure

The above assertions mean that a successful solution of different psychological problems requires the practitioner to adopt different, mutually exclusive assumptions, called mental sets, at different times. A mental set is a predisposition to respond in a particular way. It is possible for a normal person to accept at a particular time, for practical purposes, a mental set that is completely incompatible with the set established at another time.

The concept of mental sets can be illustrated by the use of an ambiguous stimulus as in Figure 3-1, called a Rubin figure. Even though this figure remains physically the same over time, the perceptions by the observer reflect incompatible changes. Sometimes, the observer sees a white vase on a black background, and at other times the observer sees a pair of black faces as figures against the white background. Therefore, the true reality of the figure is in the eye of the beholder. The perception of reality changes more or less spontaneously over time.

Batson and Ventis point out that in effect, the reality of the picture is determined by the actual perception at the moment by that particular subject.[56] Thus, it is pointless to argue which description of the figure is objectively correct.

So it is with the issue of the reality of freedom of will. We admit that we cannot prove conclusively that such a thing exists, although we can supply arguments for it. In contrast, there is evidence for the value of internal origination when predictions of behavior are not verified by the expected outcomes based on observable aspects of the environment. Even if freedom of will did not exist, a mental set that accepts it is necessary for the survival of society. Evidence for the value of direct environmental influences on behavior is found when a behavior is successfully predicted.

The task before the Behaviorists, in order to prove the argument for determinism, is indeed formidable. The Behaviorists would be required to unravel the causal histories of many complex acts in exact detail. Because the generativism hypothesis in fact allows for at least partial success in predicting human behaviors, the Behaviorists would have to be essentially perfect. As Dennett argued, even complete success in unmasking the causes of simple specific animal behaviors is irrelevant as evidence for Skinner's argument against a voluntary agent in humans.[57] To be sure, Skinner categorically dismissed the arguments that he had not unmasked the learned mechanisms for complex responses, as follows:

> The commonest objection to a thoroughgoing functional analysis is simply that it cannot be carried out, but the only evidence for this is that it has not yet been carried out. We need not be discouraged by this fact. Human behavior is perhaps the most difficult subject to which methods of science have ever been applied, and it is only natural that substantial progress should be slow.[58]

Need I point out the frailty of this defense? All Skinner offered were his beliefs and hopes. This was merely a promissory note, not evidence.

Thus, in the absence of indisputable empirical or logical proof to resolve the free will/determinism issue, we are left with practical criteria. Which view is best for us personally and for society? Skinner identified as a good response the one that will assist in the survival of the species.[59] Because crystal balls are so unreliable in forecasting the future, we do not know how to apply this criterion for practical guidance concerning which is the more valuable response. Should we believe in a viable mechanism of human choice?

Is there survival value of a belief in a viable human mechanism of choice? I believe that there is, because we have in fact survived believing in a conception of some freedom of human choice. But, as Boring reminds us, it is always possible that false ideas can have survival value.[60] Thus we are left with predictions for the future that are based on a "faith" (i.e., Behaviorism) that all behaviors will be understood in terms of a few basic physical principles, including a most mysterious—but purely physical—human response selection mechanism, or that a spiritual essence is also needed.

Anecdotal Evidence

Toynbee argued that every human being has a creative spark from a spiritual source unrelated to other external causation.[61] Presumably, Toynbee did not achieve his belief in personal creativity on the basis of laboratory research. Like students in introductory psychology, he apparently based his conclusion on life experiences, with success based on a concept of freedom of will.[62]

The belief in internal control of our daily life is strong. For example, as an owner of animal pets, I have believed since I was a child that even the lower animals can reason. Surely, most of us who have conducted research with rats have endured the rather unhappy experience in the wee hours of the morning, stopwatch and clipboard in hand, of watching one of our research subjects taking a lengthy nap, instead of running about as hungry rats are supposed to do at night.

This is to say that even the behavior of animals is not entirely stimulus-bound, not fully controlled by the environmental situation. They too have semi-autonomous activity in the brain. As Hebb reminded us, this does not mean necessarily that there are not externally based causal mechanisms at work, but that the mechanisms necessarily involve a great deal of internally-based selectivity of the responses.[63] In other words, the animal can think creatively in order to adjust to varying stimulus complexities.

To be sure, household pets are a rich source of evidence for animal reasoning. The following true story provided, to my mind, totally convincing evidence for reasoning in animals. My dog had been very thirsty one evening, alternating frequent trips outside with drinks from the water bowl. We attributed her persistent thirst to alimentary problems because she had wantonly stolen and eaten half a Christmas fruitcake from the kitchen table the previous night. As I was sitting in my favorite chair in the family room, she came in from the adjoining utility room with her empty water bowl in her mouth. Keeping her eyes fixed on me, she walked up to me, placed her bowl on the floor before me, sat and waited. I dutifully picked up the bowl, took it into the utility room, filled it and placed it before her. She immediately drank enthusiastically from the bowl.

Although a strict behaviorist is not likely to be convinced by such evidence, I have no question that the dog's behavior was purposeful. My wife and I are confident that she had never performed such behavior prior to that night, nor had she seen it done. Any previous rewards for carrying her bowl would have been entirely accidental, inconsistent and very rare indeed. To the best of our knowledge and belief, this sort of behavior with the bowl was entirely novel. She had been observed on rare occasions to carry bowls in her mouth, usually just after she had been fed.

Therefore, her behavior was not an accident, nor was it learned. I submit that her behavior was the result of reasoning. Reasoning is typically defined by psychologists as "a capacity to solve problems by combining previously disparate experiences."[64]

Although this behavior was rather remarkable, this same dog had many times before given evidence of her high intelligence. For example, when she was still a puppy, she was observed to climb a woven wire fence, paw over paw, just like a human being would climb a ladder. I do not know how this dog might have learned to perform this act unless she had escaped from a circus. Admittedly, we cannot prove beyond doubt that no such experience existed. To be sure, Skinner, the Behaviorist, would characteristically argue that, because the behavior was actually manifested, the prerequisite background of learning it *must* have been experienced. That just-so proposition is more difficult for me to believe than the hypothesis of animal reasoning.

Evidence for reasoning in humans is even stronger. Dennett offered the following hypothetical example in support of an intentional system in humans:

> Suppose, to borrow one of Skinner's examples, I am held up and asked for my wallet. This has never happened to me before, so the correct response cannot have been 'reinforced' for me, yet I do the smart thing: I hand over my wallet. Why? The Skinnerian must claim that this is not truly novel behavior at all, but an instance of a *general sort* of behavior which has been previously conditioned. But what sort is it? Not only have I not been trained to hand over my wallet to men with guns, I have not been trained to empty my pockets for women with bombs, nor to turn over my possessions to armed entities. None of these things has ever happened to me before. I may never have been threatened before at all. Or more plausible, it may well be that most often when I have been threatened in the past, the 'reinforced' response was to *apologize* to the threatener for something I'd said. Obviously, though, when told, 'Your money or your life!' I don't respond by saying 'I'm sorry. I take it all back.' It is perfectly clear that what experience has taught me is that if I *want* to save my skin, and *believe* I am being threatened, I should do what I *believe* my threatener *wants* me to do.[65]

Of course, a very clever determinist could perhaps account for each of the above behaviors in terms of such common causal mechanisms as generalizations from previous experiences—inductions—and chains of learned associations, built one upon the other, all mediated by verbal habits. Thus, Skinnerians are convinced that even the most complex of human behaviors can be explained in terms of a relatively few such behavioral principles. In my view, such an interpretation is too much of a stretch. To be sure, science usually tries to avoid such stretches, and tentatively accepts the view that least stretches our credulity.

Classroom Demonstration

I had a favorite procedure to convince the students in my introductory psychology classes that human behavior can be predicted from a Responsive Will.[66] Early in a semester, just prior to a meeting of the class, I ask a student if he or she will upon request read to the class the contents of an envelope which I provide. At the appropriate time, I ask the student to stand and read aloud the contents of the envelope. The student rises and reads the following prediction: "Every student in the class is seated, except the one reading this prediction." Over the years my prediction about the behavior of every single one of the sometimes several hundred students in the auditorium has always been perfectly correct.

Typically, the students are not overly impressed with my feat, however. Ironically, their skepticism is based on the fact that the accurate prediction was so easy to make. And that is just the point! The situation is too familiar. So, we are contemptuous of such an obvious prediction. We tend to overlook such successes when we falsely assert that human behavior can never be predicted, just because we cannot predict it in some difficult cases.

To further my classroom demonstration, I ask how many students are seated in approximately the same area in the room as they were seated during the previous meeting of the class. Although seating is entirely optional, about three-quarters of the class indicate that they have been consistent in choosing a seat within the same small general area. Of these, a large proportion report actually occupying exactly the same seat for every meeting of the class. Such consistency of behavior surely suggests that the students' "free" choices are not entirely free of environmental influences. Actually, true freedom from external influences would probably show essentially randomness in seat selection. I argue that they are merely demonstrating the responsive aspect of their wills. Why would not a student voluntarily decide to be seated in a class, to take a habitual seat or to stand upon request by the instructor?

Many students still remain unconvinced by my demonstration, however. They agree with Buechner: "The fact that I know you so well that I know what you're going to do before you do it does not mean that you are not free to do whatever you damn well please."[67] This argument is, of course, entirely consistent with my notion of a Responsive Will. Usually a student will point out that he or she chose to be seated in a particular seat, and could even have chosen to be standing during class. In rebuttal, I argue that some basis in the environment must be involved in order to produce such a consistent choice of behavior in all students day after day. If I can discover that basis for a particular student, I can predict, to some level of accuracy that is better than chance, what seat that student will take.

Thus, the above illustrations are entirely consistent with the assumption that there is some measure of freedom in the selection of responses. Occasionally, students do leave the class if they become sick, they have buses to catch, the lecture is running overtime or some similar event or crisis arises during the class period. This surely represents a responsive aspect of the Viable Will.

I point out to the students that the predictions were easy to make, with great confidence, on the basis of my knowledge gained from observation of student behavior over many years. I know that the students have learned over their careers that, in the culture to which we are all accustomed, the proper student behavior is to be seated during class. This principle is different if some situation has occurred to indicate that the routine behaviors should be suspended. For example, what would you predict if the national anthem were played during class?

On any given year, my initial prediction of a seated class might not be correct, of course. A given student could have learned about my demonstration, and previously informed the entire class. Accordingly, every student except the reader might be standing. In fact, during one summer session, one of my classes made a game of adopting different seating arrangements for each class. This change in the basis of seat selection was no problem to my theory, however. I could predict that the seating would be different each day, to be sure, but not exactly how it would be different. Indeed, this procedure was quite reassuring to me, because the students apparently did not like the idea of being predictable.

To be sure, a devoted deterministic psychologist would stoutly maintain that the change in behavior was still predictable from knowledge of the environmental circumstances. My failure of accurate prediction, they would say, was simply caused by my ignorance of the circumstances of the student plot. The classic determinist explanation for any failure to predict behavior is that we are just not knowledgeable about the particular causation. But, that does not mean that we could predict behavior exactly if we *did* know all of the environmental and genetic causal factors.

Indeed, for other environmental settings, or other populations of students, the predictions about preferred seating might well be different. For example, during warm Spring days some professors move small classes outside to the lawn where it is perfectly acceptable student behavior to lie on the grass. Therefore, the behavioral scientist would predict that some students would lie down instead of being seated.

The task of predicting exactly which students would by lying, and which would be sitting, would be far more difficult. Unless the behavioral scientist knew very much about the specific characteristics of the individual students, he or she would avoid trying to predict the particular behavior of specific individuals. But the deterministic assumption of a scientific psychology holds that if they did study individual students they would have at least some degree of success in predicting which ones would be lying and which ones would be seated.

Now, consider a slightly different aspect of behavior. The behavioral scientist would probably have gratifying success in predicting, in any case, that individual students, lying or seated, would be physically closer to persons they knew well. This is what you would expect of Responsive Wills. Again, however, there is no evidence that one could become consistently perfect in this prediction.

My oldest grandson had a very good friend of college age who almost never wore shoes. Although I usually expect college students to wear shoes, for this lad I predicted no shoes, and I was almost always correct. Incidentally, he was also more likely to lie on the floor than to sit in a chair. Obviously, he tended to march to the beat of a different drummer. This fact had to be taken into account when making predictions about his behaviors.

Laboratory Evidence

I propose, in agreement with Viney, that a humanistic approach to psychological research is validated if a theory of human will can be used to understand and predict human behavior.[68] I did, in fact, accomplish this in a formal experiment.[69]

The behavior for my study was the choice of seat in an empty auditorium. This behavior was selected not only because it was simple, easily quantifiable and morally neutral, but also because it was potentially understandable in either voluntary or deterministic terms. Clearly, the subjects were free to select any of the theater seats in an empty auditorium. There was no compelling social value in selecting one seat over another. I already knew from casual observation that college students tended to take the same seat from class to class even though the seats were not assigned.

The study began when a research assistant met the subject outside the door to the auditorium in which each subject was currently taking a psychology course. The individual subject was handed a questionnaire, and told to take any seat in the classroom in order to complete it. Upon entering the auditorium, the subject found it empty, except for me, seated at the teacher's table in the front. I greeted the subject, and asked him or her to take any seat to complete the questionnaire. I then covertly recorded which seat was chosen.

In a second experiment, the subjects were told before entering the auditorium that the researcher was interested in which seat they would choose for completing the questionnaire. The experimenter could not predict what the effects of such knowledge would be.

The questionnaire asked if the subject typically took one particular seat during his or her regular class in that auditorium. Most reported that they did. The questionnaire then asked the student to go and sit now in his or her usual seat, or one as close to it as could be identified. The researcher recorded that usual seat, and then de-briefed and dismissed the subject. The de-briefing simply explained the purpose of the study, asked if there were any comments, explained arrangements for communicating the completed results and asked the subject not to discuss the experiment with other potential subjects.

Basically, the prediction for both experiments was that the nominally voluntary behavior of seat selection was to some extent influenced by the subject's seating habit in the academic course that was taken in that same room. This prediction was supported, but there was also substantial evidence for many other environmental influences on the behavior.

But only for the general population of subjects could the seat selection be predicted with any degree of accuracy. Specific predictions for particular subjects could not be very accurate, because the experimenter had no information about them, other than that they were students in courses that routinely met in that auditorium. Thus, initially, the only identified basis of seat selection was the seat that the subject might have routinely occupied during class. The researcher predicted that the subject would choose the seats they typically occupied in class, or seats closer to those seats than could be predicted by chance.

For the subjects who were not informed of the purpose of the study, the actual percentages of choices for different sections of the room differed significantly from the theoretical predictions on the basis of both totally habitual responses and random responding. For example, the subjects tended to favor the center sections of the room, seats near the entrance and the seats to the researcher's left. In addition, they greatly preferred aisle seats.

These subjects' choices could be explained easily on the basis of intuitively understanding a Responsive Will that directly responds to environmental factors. For example, common-sense interpretations are appropriate: taking the center seats caused the subject to sit directly facing the researcher, which was an entirely reasonable and socialized response. The seats on the left were reached by proceeding in a direct path from the entrance door, hence not requiring a change of direction in walking. The aisle seats were obviously more accessible, taken in accordance with a principle of least effort.

Some students made more personally relevant choices. During the debriefing after the experiment, the subjects often were able to give a reason for their choice of a particular seat. Some sat in the front, close to the experimenter, because they wanted to avoid the appearance of rudeness. One sat near the entrance door because of a personal injury to a leg, which made walking difficult. Obviously, if the experimenter had been in possession of the relevant knowledge of such factors prior to the experiment, he would have been accurate in his predictions for some individuals. The behavioral principle is clear: if you know something about the opinions, preferences and particular conditions pertaining to the person, you can have some success in predicting his or her behavior. This principle seems to be an equally powerful predictor of behavior as the person's history of rewards.

Most obvious from the data of the experiment in which the subjects were informed that seat selection was of interest was a large increase in the number of subjects who sat close to the front. This again makes sense on the basis of what the subject might anticipate the researcher to expect.

Another major effect of knowledge about the purpose of the experiment with informed subjects was a large decrease in the number of aisle seats taken. Many students passed up aisle seats in order to take seats that were directly in front of the researcher. Apparently, the subjects were now responding less to a need for least effort, and more to their cognitive appraisal of the demands of the situation—i.e., to appear more sociable. In a word, the knowledge that the choice of seat was important to the experimenter changed the basic motivation of the subjects. Presumably, they were now motivated to make a choice that the experimenter would admire, or at least accept as reasonable. Apparently, they did not consider the law of least effort to be a good social basis for the choice.

In both experiments, the subjects tended to sit closer to their habitual seat than would be predicted by chance. Chance was determined by assuming that the habitual seat was the one chosen as the habitual seat by the next subject in the experiment. Surprising to the researcher, this proximity effect was *greater* for the subjects who were told the purpose of the study. Although seven of the 136 uninformed subjects took their exact habitual seat in the 279-seat auditorium, 27 of the 128 informed subjects took their exact habitual seats. Ironically, this fourfold increase in the selection of habitual seats was not attributed to a strong increase in habit, but to a cognition by the subjects concerning what would be a reasonable basis for seat selection—i.e., what was demanded by the characteristics of the experimental situation. Presumably, the informed subjects were actively seeking to identify a rational reason to select a particular seat.

Actually, one subject in the informed group asked to sit in the seat that was at the time occupied by the experimenter. This most interesting response absolutely could not have been the effect of habit. It surely could not have been appropriate to a simple search for a seat to facilitate answering a questionnaire. But, it makes perfect sense as a response to the experimenter's implicit challenge to make a worthy response. *It was indeed a beautiful textbook example of a creative response.* The experimenter had not even considered this as a possible response!

The results for the informed group are thus loaded with paradox. For example, the experimenter was presumably enhancing the role of the personal agent by the emphasis on the subject's choice. The personal agent is a major source of individual differences. Therefore, one would ordinarily expect greater variability of responding—and thus less predictability of responding—for the informed subjects. That expectation was obviously true for the one very special subject who wanted the researcher's seat. But most of the participants were trapped into predictable responding by their presumed need to be sensible in the eyes of the experimenter.

Interestingly enough, the information about the purpose of the experiment led the subjects to make a response that the experimenter could predict. Attempts to coerce subjects into making a particular voluntary response would likely be effective in controlling the response, but for college students this would, I suspect, mean actually decreasing the frequency of the response that the subjects were pressured to make. Much would depend upon variables such as the actual strength of the coercion and the personality of the subject. Do we not know people who can be expected to make the diametrically opposed response to the one that we have strongly advocated?

I have argued, therefore, that the human will is responsive to environmental exigencies.[70] Thus, the action of the will can be predicted to that extent. For example, a person would typically choose to avoid being tortured. Such avoidance does not require an interpretation in terms of a learned avoidance response. Anyone would surely try to avoid being tortured in some land that he or she has never visited by a method that he or she cannot now imagine.

To be sure, a few people would voluntarily submit to such torture for compelling personal reasons. For example, a person might accept torture in order to save a loved one. Or, a person could desire torture to satisfy masochistic compulsions. Therefore, the human will is both responsive to the environment, or consents to it, and it also sometimes can transcend the press of the environment.

On the basis of the above arguments, it would be possible to make some common-sense predictions of the subjects' responses to the manipulation of certain variables in the seat-selection experiment. The predictions would be so obvious that the experiments could be considered "thought experiments:" the results would be obvious from just thinking rationally about the prevailing psychological principles in the situation. Suppose, for example, we tied each subject's ankles loosely together before he or she entered the room. On the basis of least effort, we would expect a greater frequency of seating near the entrance to the room. Or, suppose the subjects were required to enter the room from a door at the front instead of the rear of the room. Again, we would predict a greater frequency of seating at the front of the room. In either case, we have not made the responses less voluntary, even though they may have been made more predictable. We have merely given the responsive aspect of the human will a stronger reason for a particular rational basis for responding. To be sure, our prediction could be grossly in error for any given subject, because he or she was free to make an idiosyncratic cognition of the nature of the task, as one subject obviously did.

The basic conclusion from the study is that these behaviors can be understood either in terms of habit from experience in the environment, or in terms of a voluntary choice by a human will that is responsive to conditions in the environment. Which interpretation represents truth?

Readers of this book may by now be saying to themselves that my arguments seem to apply to the selection of seats in an empty auditorium, but they may not be relevant to, say, serious moral decisions. But the behavior in question is not the focus of the research. We are concerned with the psychological mechanisms that produce the behavior. Indeed, researchers can select a task for their research on the basis of practical, economic or moral reasons. Therefore, the specific behavior may not be particularly interesting, but the behavioral laws revealed by the performance may be extremely valuable. Perhaps most of us are not strongly interested in seating behavior in auditoriums, but the issue of the possibility of voluntary behavior is crucial to psychologists, and to our world.

Practical Value

There is a utilitarian gain from the use of humanistic theories. As Cook and Campbell believe, people want practical recipes that will lead to desired effects.[71] They want to identify cause and behavioral effect. We cannot postpone the flow of life until we obtain enough proof about the issue of intentionality to satisfy everyone. Because the truth is not known, we are free to accept any mechanism or conceptual agent that seems best to us for the mission that we have set for ourselves.

Admittedly, we cannot say that the assumption of a freedom of will is necessary for behavioral science. But, as Harcum said, "The concept of free will, on the other hand, also has a necessary social advantage. We need a conception of free will in order to develop a social conscience and to promote social justice."[72] For example, some kinds of psychotherapy would not even be possible without the assumption of human choice and responsibility.[73] And also, without the assumption of freedom of will, malfeasors could not be held accountable for their misdeeds.

Because the will may dominate the decision process, such that the response is relatively independent of the stimulus situation, the present view allows reference to both a principle of accountability, which attributes personal responsibility for an action, and also a principle of extenuation, which incorporates various degrees of extenuating circumstances in assessing ultimate credit or blame. The pertinent question is whether or not the person had the proper response available to him and just did not make a proper voluntary choice. This view also allows a dispersal of any culpability among more than one source. For example, the person could be guilty of making a poor decision, but with extenuating circumstances. With this view, we have both justification to forgive a person an undesired response, because it was influenced by external circumstances, and also to hold the person accountable, because the response was also influenced by an intentional choice.

Evaluation

There are several bases for evaluating the concept of freedom of will. They are the concepts of Extenuation, Accountability, Need Satisfaction and Morality, as well as the effects of incentives and the role in psychotherapy and information-processing.

Extenuation

The Principle of Extenuation holds that certain environmental events would produce much stronger tendencies for some responses than others. Therefore, the will of the responsible human might be overly influenced, or even overwhelmed, by the sheer strengths of the competing response tendencies. The term extenuation represents a familiar concept in the sense of extenuating circumstances. In the case of the overwhelming strength of the response tendency, we might refer to "an irresistible impulse," and therefore consider the perpetrators guiltless because their behaviors were not controlled by their own unfettered choice.

Many situations call for persons to be held responsible for their actions in spite of situational factors that make this difficult. As my division officer on my ship in the Navy said in reproof on many occasions, "Those are extenuating circumstances, but no excuse." I have used the same expression to students who have missed an exam, or were late turning in a paper without an adequate excuse. The point is that the offenders had a job to accomplish, which they failed to complete satisfactorily. Without the concept of a viable will, every circumstance that hinders completion of an assignment becomes an excuse, or reason for failure. Only with the concept of a Viable Will is the awarding of either blame or praise appropriate.

Jones and Nisbett propose that persons tend to attribute their own actions to environmental influences, but they attribute the actions of others to the behavioral traits of the other persons.[74] This actor-observer effect seems to be primarily the result of focusing on the different aspects of the behavioral situation. The actors focus on the environmental press to which they have responded, with less attention to themselves as an agent in the decision process. The observers cannot be as aware of the environmental press, and thus tend to interpret the action as flowing from the nature of the actors. Presumably, this effect would be most appropriate to situations in which blame, rather than praise, was relevant. In my theory, the observers have a more remote perspective than the actors on the causation of behavior in the situation.[75]

Accountability

The Principle of Accountability holds that people themselves should be held responsible for their acts, and therefore must answer for them, or explain them when justification is demanded. This principle is incompatible with the strict version of the Doctrine of Determinism. The crucial issue here is what Skinner called "the ultimate source of control."[76] In contrast to the traditional and popular conceptions of causality in terms of "self-control" and "personal responsibility," Skinner proposed instrumental habits developed through experience with the external environment, as follows:

> When a man controls himself, chooses a course of action, thinks out the solution to a problem or strives toward an increase in self-knowledge, he is *behaving*. He controls himself precisely as he would control the behavior of anyone else—through the manipulation of variables of which behavior is a function. His behavior in so doing is a proper object of analysis, and eventually it must be accounted for with variables lying outside the individual himself.[77]

The "he" referred to in the above quotation presumably is merely a non-sentient habit system molded by circumstances. Obviously, therefore, persons so conceived are in a fundamental sense powerless to change themselves, because their mechanisms of control were developed by mechanisms also outside their conscious control. If their behaviors are to be improved, they must rely almost entirely on the Law of Effect, and a little luck. In Skinner's words, "It appears, therefore, that society is responsible for the larger part of the behavior of self-control. *If this is correct, little ultimate control remains with the individual* (emphasis added)."[78]

The underlined sentence betrays the basic fatalism of the reductionist view. Who would actually use this point of view in supervising employees, educating college students or raising his or her children? If there is no control by a personal decision process, how can we hold people responsible for their behaviors? On the basis of the deterministic orientation, I can excuse myself by saying that someone did not say the right words, or give me the proper rewards, to cause me to behave correctly. If behavior is entirely caused by the environment and thus predictable, there can be no room for choices of good or evil. Therefore, a person could not be responsible for his or her deeds, good or bad.

Grunbaum claims that morality is possible in the framework of determinism because the persons do in fact make the responses, even though the causal mechanisms were beyond their control.[79] But to evaluate the behavior is not the same as evaluating the behaver, which is, of course, not a new idea. To be sure, it would be necessary to find the total network of causal agents in order to prevent a recurrence of the poor behavior.

The Law of Effect would suggest that under anything like normal conditions, a person would not learn to do things that are intrinsically aversive. Of course, we cannot rule out twists of habits, which are outside of anyone's control.

Need Satisfaction

Obviously, there is a persistent, strong need by the vast majority of us to believe that we are able to make voluntary choices. Brehm depicts human beings as desiring to see themselves free to respond as they wish, and showing a reactance or defensiveness to events that threaten this perception.[80] Whereas the perception of predictability in others can give people a sense of control over the environment, the consistent perception of the same dispositional traits within themselves implies a lack of freedom to choose their own actions.

Morality and Religion

If Skinnerians could convince us that we do not have dignity, or other humanistic attributes, then the one conflict would have been resolved. But new worse problems would have emerged. If my neighbor has no dignity and neither do I, I will help only for reasons that I perceive as practical in terms of my own goals and perspectives. These ultimately become translated into merely selfish motives.

A psychology that incorporates a belief in freedom of will, based on faith, is consistent with the Judeo-Christian religious tradition. It thus bypasses the debate between science and religion, and therefore opens the door to the belief in truth, in any way that a person can achieve it. It views science and religion as complementary enabling disciplines, and not as sources of constraint on the realization of possibilities.

Incentives

Skinner denied that there is "anyone or anything" that serves as a prime mover in the continuing flow of human behaviors.[81] This is a very pessimistic view of the causes of life events. In this view, each human endeavor is literally fully determined, and therefore can only be changed by accident. It is set to go as it was programmed unless some agent intervenes. The agent in the Behavioristic system has no true intelligence, being devoid of what we typically call reasoning ability. Even if this agent lies within a human being, a mutant thought might have happy or tragic consequences, with no possibility that the host organism could make a choice to recommend and execute the good ideas, or edit the bad. Therefore, the overt emission of good and bad responses would be equally likely, unless the owner of the thought had been somehow appropriately trained to handle the particular situation.

Certainly, we would not design a system that would produce an error rate of 50 percent, with a quality-control mechanism that would take years to find and correct mistakes. Although the bad ideas would eventually drop out, because of their long-term adverse consequences for human survival, the society would have to suffer through these adverse effects until those responses were finally extinguished. The good ideas would be retained only because of their positive survival value. The only basis of optimism would be a simple wish and hope for happy accidents, for undirected beneficial twists of response tendencies that could break through the established habit systems.

Thus, although the proposition of strict determinism might seem to solve the humanistic dilemma as a barrier to helping behaviors, it would surely create far more serious new problems. For example, there would no longer be any merit in helping another because the helping would not and could not be attributed to personal choice. This view of change would most probably add to feelings of hopelessness and depression about how one could change the world. Each person would start tomorrow concentrating on personal survival, because the rewards are more frequent, and certainly more tangible. They do not depend upon verbal mediation.

What incentives for performance are provided by the belief in voluntary responding? The immediately obvious value of the belief in a viable human will concerns the rewards for achievement. A specific achievement can be held out as a goal to be reached by voluntary effort. The later achievement serves to expand the ego, to build the self-esteem through success. For example, consider the following excerpt from an anonymous response, cited by Chiang and Maslow, written by a college student about a peak experience, one of the happiest moments in his or her life:

> Two years ago, while I was attempting to do some math problems in elementary calculus that I had for homework one night, I was following the long, involved procedure for finding the derivative of functions exactly the way my teacher had told me to do. I suddenly thought I saw a quick way of finding the answer. I tried my new method, which only required inspection rather than calculation, got an answer to the next few problems, then did them again the old way. I got the same answers, showing that my perceived relationships between function and derivatives were indeed correct.
>
> A day or so after this, going further in the math book, I found an explanation of the way that I had discovered for myself. Finding out that mathematicians had known this method before I stumbled upon it in no way marred my pleasure. Upon finding out that my method was correct, I became very excited. I felt very proud of myself, particularly because I had been having some trouble with math during the week or so before this experience.
>
> I ran around the house until I found my parents and showed them my findings. Then I sat down by myself and looked over my work again. I suppose I could say that I felt creative. I certainly felt as if I "belonged." I now saw myself as having a right to be in the advanced math class that I was in. I did not feel guilty any longer—there were no longer any nagging fears of inadequacy.[82]

How deflating and cruel it would be for this person now to be told that he or she had been merely programmed to perform as he or she did. Why tell him or her that this marvelous feat was just a result of a happy, chance combination of hereditary predisposition and life experiences?

Hall and Lindzey pointed out the practical value for man of Jung's view that human beings exhibit a quest for self-improvement, as follows:

> Jung points out that a purely causal attitude is likely to produce resignation and despair in man since from the standpoint of causality he is a prisoner of his past. He cannot undo what has already been done. The finalistic attitude, on the other hand, gives man a feeling of hope and something to live for. Jung's psychology is essentially an optimistic one.[83]

A belief in voluntary behavior thus permits the person to aspire to overcome apparent limits established by environmental circumstances, even to becoming a so-called over-achiever. History is full of instances of persons who have overcome pessimistic predictions for their futures.

Psychotherapy

Psychotherapy refers to using psychological means to help people correct personal problems or to feel better about themselves. Almost daily I hear researchers and clinical practitioners describe the principles for good social interaction and personal mental health, which are almost invariably corollaries of the Great Principle: Love one another. Everything from depression to ailing friendship appears to be ameliorated by behaving in a manner that is pleasing to someone else, as you would do naturally if you love that person. I have argued that a Christian connection to another person has a natural, though incidental, psychotherapeutic effect because it conveys unconditional positive regard and other personal characteristics that are crucial to the building of a successful therapeutic alliance.[84] A therapeutic alliance is a positive connection between the therapist and the client that is necessary for the success of a certain kind of psychotherapy.

Leichtman working with high risk, seriously disturbed children, considered his first goal was to establish a connection in the child's mind between that child's own response-initiation mechanisms and his overt maladaptive behaviors.[85] The child with behavior problems tends to see his behaviors as merely responsive to an external locus of control, for which therefore he bears no blame. The child must see that he or she is making bad choices of behavior that have bad consequences. Leichtman believed that the emotionally disturbed child must come to understand that the external world can exact retribution for transgressions. The reality of the world is that one cannot consistently respond selfishly and irresponsibly with impunity. Each person needs to understand that there are consequences of his actions that may in fact be unpleasant for him.

Lefcourt concluded that persons who perceived an internal locus of control of behavior were better able to withstand external manipulations of their behavior that did not conform to their personal beliefs.[86] Efforts for achievement tend to be greater when the achievement is attributed to an internal factor, such as personal effort. Personal psychopathology tends to be correlated with a perception of external control, probably because of a vicious circle of causality—a sense of helplessness generates defensive external attributions, which in turn adds to the feelings of helplessness. Lefcourt presented evidence that we must in fact learn to perceive ourselves individually as determiners of our own fates. It is the de-individuation brought about by group control that contributes to antisocial behavior of people in groups.

Information-processing

In addition to showing its usefulness in theories pertaining to social, moral and psychotherapeutic issues, the concept of freedom of will has also been useful in more specialized research problems. For example, Harcum employed the concept of personal choice in dealing with human processing of visual information and verbal serial learning.[87] In both tasks, the distribution of attention among arrays of stimulus elements was shown to be controlled by a chosen (voluntary) strategy of the subject, thus determining the relative numbers of errors in perception/recall of individual elements within the stimulus array. Indeed, the cognitive strategy of the subjects could be manipulated by such variables as verbal instructions, vividness and identifiability of individual elements of the array and previous experience with the same or similar arrays. Thus, the responsive aspect of the human will presumably selects a strategy that is most effective in perceiving and remembering a particular stimulus array.

Discussion

In his book, *Walden Two*, Skinner had the character Frazier, the fictional spokesman for the Skinnerian view, say, "I deny that freedom exists at all. I must deny it—or my program would be absurd. You can't have a science about a subject matter which hops capriciously about."[88] Here Skinner was using the exclusive argument about freedom as an absolute. The key point is that he denied any degree of freedom, and asserted gratuitously that this denial is necessary for a science of behavior. Of course, we know that a science cannot be totally capricious. But, it also does not have to be totally unambiguous either.

Mind-body Problem

We now come to the difficult problem of the nature and relationship between what we call mind and what we call body—the so-called mind-body problem. The assumption called monism is that mind and body consist of the same stuff of the universe. The assumption called dualism is that mind and body are composed of qualitatively different essences. There are several different sub-categories of each view, but only one view under each will be considered here.

The view of materialistic monism states that the one essence of the universe is material. This is the reductionistic view of the Behavioristic psychologists, such as Skinner.[89] It states that the entire person is physical, and thus the mind is merely a convenient term for the physical operation of the brain.

The view of interactionistic dualism states that there are two essences in the universe, one material and the other non-material (spiritual), and that these two essences influence, or interact with, one another. Therefore, there is more to the person than physical body, although the physical and spiritual parts work very closely together. For example, a wife may consistently develop a headache whenever the husband indicates a desire for physical intimacy, or a person with influenza does not desire to attend a party that would be very attractive if he or she were physically well.

According to Gleitman, Gross and Reisberg:

> We truly do not know how the physical events of sensation give rise to conscious experiences or how conscious decisions give rise to physical movements. We can surely talk about the correspondence between the physical and mental worlds—what physical events are going on when you experience 'red' or 'sad' or 'anxious'—but we do not yet have a cause-and-effect explanation for how these two worlds are linked.[90]

So we really do not have a solution for the mind-body problem.

Because we do not know the truth about this metaphysical issue, the Principle of Ultimate Practicality would seem to apply.[91] That is, the belief in a human spirit that can transcend physical constraints is more optimistic and useful. It also satisfies the human need to have a feeling of freedom.

Summary

This chapter argues that, although the issue of freedom of will (i.e., a feeling of making a voluntary choice) versus determinism (i.e., all events are caused by heredity and environmental experiences) cannot be resolved by empirical test, the issue can be resolved in terms of which assumption is of greater practical value. The chapter advocates the assumption, held by the great majority of psychologists and almost all laity, that a person's behavior can be caused both by internal intention of a personal will, which I call a Viable Will, and also by the interaction between environmental reward-contingencies and inherited factors. I have called this assumption of joint causality the Doctrine of Generativism.

A Viable Will accounts for much of the ambiguity in predicting responses. The Viable Will includes two components: a proposed Responsive Will that consents to routine rational responding to stimulation in the environment; and a proposed Transcending Will that responds primarily to internal representations, and therefore is not necessarily responsive to the existing environmental influences. The arguments for both aspects of will are supported by both anecdotal and experimental evidence.

It is further argued that the alleged ability of science to unmask the causation of certain simple behaviors in terms of environmental events does not prove that all behaviors can be similarly explained, especially in human beings.

In the absence of conclusive empirical evidence for either the Generative or the Deterministic view, we are left with only practical bases for deciding between them. The Principle of Ultimate Practicality states that we may believe whatever works for us in our daily lives, without withholding or delaying decisions until the truth or falsity of a proposition is finally established.

The first argument for the Generativism view is that it has all of the advantages of both the beliefs in the Principle of Determinism and in a Viable Will. Second, the belief in a Viable Will is virtually universal among people who are not professionally trained in psychology. Third, while it permits the concept of extenuation, so that a person need not be held fully accountable for all of his or her actions, it does entail a principle of accountability, which is absolutely essential for the survival of society. A society without the concept of a Viable Will becomes a conscienceless society. Fourth, a concept of Viable Will is optimistic, whereas the concept of determinism is fatalistic. Without the concept of will, the person has no incentive to try to improve his or her condition by personal effort. Finally, the concept of a Viable Will is indigenous to certain types of psychotherapy.

It is proposed that the Viable Will concept is most useful when the causation of the behavior is temporally, or psychologically, remote from the behavioral situation. The deterministic concept tends to be most useful whenever the causation is relatively contiguous.

Notes

1. B. F. Skinner, *Beyond Freedom and Dignity*. (New York: Knopf, 1971).
2. Horace B. English and Ava English, *A Comprehensive Dictionary of Psychological and Psychoanalytical Terms*. (New York: Longmans, Green, 1958).
3. James Deese, *Psychology as Science and Art*. (New York: Harcourt, Brace & Jovanovick, 1972). 31.
4. J. R. Royce. The present situation in theoretical psychology. In J. R. Royce, (Ed.), *Toward Unification in Psychology*. (Toronto: University of Toronto Press). 11-37, 1970, 27.
5. M. B. Smith, *Social Psychology and Human Values*. (Chicago: Aldine, 1967). 7.
6. Lawrence LeShan, *The Dilemma of Psychology*. (New York: Dutton, 1990.)
7. E. J. Shoben Jr., Psychology: Natural science or humanistic discipline? *Journal of Humanistic Psychology, 5*: 210-218, 1965, 218.
8. E. Rae Harcum, Defensive reactance of psychologists to a metaphysical foundation for interpreting different psychologies. *The Journal of Psychology, 122*: 217-235, 1988.
9. Sigmund Koch, The nature and limits of psychological knowledge: Lessons of a century qua "science." *American Psychologist, 36*, 257-275, 1981; P. T. Manicas and P. F. Secord, Implications for psychology of the new philosophy of science. *American Psychologist, 38*: 389-413, 1983.
10. E. Rae Harcum, *A Psychology of Freedom and Dignity*. (Westport, CT: Praeger, 1994). 38.
11. Harcum, *A Psychology of Freedom and Dignity*, 1994. 39.
12. E. Rae Harcum, A classroom demonstration of the difference between correlation and causality. *Perceptual and Motor Skills, 66*: 801-802, 1988.
13. R. Harré and E. H. Madden, *Causal Powers*. (Oxford: Basil Blackwell, 1975). 136.
14. J. Gleik, *Chaos: Making a New Science*. (New York: Viking, 1987).
15. Robert Oppenheimer, Analogy in science. *American Psychologist, 11*: 127-135, 1956, 134.
16. Howard R. Pollio and T. Henley, Empirical and philosophical reactions to Harcum's "Behavioral paradigm for a psychological resolution to the free-will issue. *The Journal of Mind and Behavior, 12*: 115-134, 1991.
17. Harré and Madden, *Causal Powers*, 1975.
18. T. D. Cook and D. T. Campbell, *Quasi-experimentations: Design and Analysis Issues for Field settings*. (Chicago: Rand McNally, 1979). 11.

19. F. Buechner, *Wishful Thinking: A Theological ABC*. (New York: Harper & Row, 1973). 26.
20. Harcum, *A Psychology of Freedom and Dignity*, 1994.
21. E. R. Harcum, Behavioral paradigm for a psychological resolution of the free-will issue. *The Journal of Mind and Behavior, 12*: 93-114, 1991; Harcum, *A Psychology of Freedom and Dignity*, 1994.
22. John B. Watson, Psychology as the Behaviorist views it. *Psychological Review, 20*: 158-177, 1913.
23. B. F. Skinner, *Science of Human Behavior*. (New York: Macmillan, 1953).
24. K. Lehrer, An empirical disproof of determinism? In K. Lehrer *Freedom and Determinism* (New York: Random House, 1966). 175-202.
25. Harcum, *A Psychology of Freedom and Dignity*, 1994.
26. James M. Nelson, *Psychology, Religion, and Spirituality*. (New York: Springer, 2009). 95.
27. William A. Neilson (Ed.), Webster's New International Dictionary of the English Language (2nd ed.) (Mayfield, MA: G & C. Merriam Company Publishers, 1994). 711.
28. Clarence L. Barnhart (Ed.-in-Chief), *The World Book Encyclopedia Dictionary*, L-Z, Vol. 2. (Chicago: Doubleday & Company, Inc., 1963). 543.
29. English and English, *A Comprehensive Dictionary of Psychological and Psychoanalytical Terms*, 1958. 147-148.
30. English and English, 1958. 148.
31. Wayne Weiten, *Psychology: Themes and Variations* (3rd ed.) (Pacific Grove, CA: Brooks/Cole Publishing Company, 1995). 489.
32. Barnhart, The World Book Encyclopedia Dictionary, 1963, 1530.
33. Ibid.
34. Neilson, Webster's New International Dictionary of the English Language, 1994, 1946.
35. English and English, *Comprehensive Dictionary of Psychological and Psychoanalytical Terms*, 1958.
36. J. Feinberg, Introduction to Part 4: Determinism and Free Will. In J. Feinberg (Ed.) *Reason and Responsibility* (5th ed.) (Belmont, CA: Wadsworth, 1981.)
37. Malcolm A. Jeeves, *Human Nature at the Millennium: Reflections on the Integration of Psychology and Christianity*. (Grand Rapids, MI: Baker Books, 1997). 213.
38. Nelson, *Psychology, Religion, and Spirituality*, 2009. 95.
39. Drew Weston, *Psychology: Mind, Brain and Culture*. (New York: John Wiley & Sons, Inc., 1996). 8.
40. Carl R. Rogers and B. F. Skinner, Some issues concerning the control of human behavior: A symposium, *Science, 124*: 1057-1066, 1956.
41. W. M. Baum, *Understanding Behaviorism*. (New York: HarperCollins, 1994).

42. Rogers and Skinner, Some issues concerning the control of human behavior: A symposium. 1956, 1064.
43. Harcum, *A Psychology of Freedom and Dignity* (1994). 38.
44. Roy F. Baumeister, Self and Volition. In W. R.. Miller and H. G. Delaney (Eds.) *Judeo-Christian Perspectives on Psychology*: Human Nature, Motivation and Change. (Washington, D.C.: American Psychological Association, 2005). 57-72.
45. Harcum, *A Psychology of Freedom and Dignity* (1994.)
46. Ibid.
47. E. Rae Harcum, Ellen F. Rosen and Barry N. Burijon, Popular vs. Skinnerian views of the relation between human freedom and dignity. *Journal of Psychology, 123*: 257-267, 1983.
48. Pollio and Henley, Empirical and philosophical reactions to Harcum's "Behavioral paradigm for a psychological resolution to the free-will issue, 1991.
49. Harcum, *A Psychology of Freedom and Dignity*, 1994.
50. William James, *The Principles of Psychology*, Vol. II (New York: Holt, 1890).
51. Harcum, Behavioral paradigm for a psychological solution of the free-will issue, 1991.
52. Pollio and Henley, Empirical and philosophical reactions to Harcum's "Behavioral paradigm for a psychological resolution of the free-will issue, 1991; Joseph F. Rychlak, Some theoretical and methodological questions concerning Harcum's proposed resolution of the free-will issue. *The Journal of Mind and Behavior, 12:* 135-150, 1991.
53. James, *The Principles of Psychology*, Vol. II, (1890).
54. Harcum, *A Psychology of Freedom and Dignity*. 1994.
55. E. Rae Harcum, The relative utility of complementary disparate views on voluntarism and determinism. *The Journal of Psychology, 125:* 217-228, 1990.
56. C. D. Batson and W. Laurence Ventis, *The Religious Experience*. (New York: Oxford University Press, 1982).
57. D. C. Dennett, *Brainstorms*. (Montgomery, VT: Bradford Books, 1981).
58. Skinner, *Science of Human Behavior*, 1953. 41.
59. Skinner, *Beyond Freedom and Dignity*, 1971.
60. Edwin G. Boring, When is human behavior predetermined? *The Scientific Monthly, 84:* 189-196, 1957.
61. Arnold Toynbe, Beyond Freedom and Dignity: An uneasy feeling of unreality. *The Center Magazine*, (March/April, 1972): 58-62.
62. Harcum, Rosen and Burijon, Popular vs. Skinnerian views of the relation between human freedom and dignity, 1989.
63. Donald O. Hebb, *The Organization of Behavior*. (New York: Wiley, 1949).

64. Norman R. F. Maier and T. C. Schneirla, Principles of Animal Psychology (enlarged edition). (New York: Dover, 1964). ix.
65. Dennett, *Brainstorms*. 1981, 67.
66. E. Rae Harcum, A classroom demonstration of determinism, prediction and control of human behavior. *Psychology, 23*: 41-43, 1988.
67. Buechner, *Wishful Thinking: A Theological ABC*, 72. 1973.
68. D. W. Viney, Williams James on free will and determinism. *The Journal of Mind and Behavior, 7*: 555-565, 1986.
69. Harcum, Behavioral paradigm for a psychological resolution of the free-will issue, 1991.
70. Harcum, *A Psychology of Freedom and Dignity*, 1994.
71. Cook and Campbell, *Quasi-experimentation: Design and Analysis Issues for Field Settings*, 1979.
72. E. Rae Harcum, *Psychology for Daily Living*. (Chicago: Nelson-Hall, 1979). 25.
73. E. Rae Harcum, Commitment to collaboration as a prerequisite for existential commonality in psychotherapy, *Psychotherapy, 26*: 200-209, 1989; E. Rae Harcum, Barry N. Burijon and Neill Watson, Client responsibility in the practitioners' operational definition of behavior therapy, *Journal of Human Behavior and Learning, 5*: 12-16, 1988; E. Rae Harcum, Barry N. Burijon and Neill Watson, Need for a theoretical justification of humanistic commitment components in behavior therapy, *Psychological Record, 39*: 493-500, 1989.
74. E. E. Jones and R. E. Nisbett, The actor and the observer: Divergent perceptions of the causes of behavior. In E. E. Jones, D. E. Kanhouse, H. H. Kelly, R. E. Nisbett, S. Valins and B. Weiner (Eds.) *Attribution: Perceiving the Causes of Behavior*. (Morristown, NJ: General Learning Press, 1972). 79-94.
75. Harcum, The relative utility of complementary disparate views on voluntarism and determinism, 1990.
76. Skinner, *Science and Human Behavior*, 1953, 240.
77. Skinner, *Science and Human Behavior*, 1953, 228-229.
78. Skinner, *Science and Human Behavior*, 1953, 240.
79. A. Grunbaum, Causality and the science of human behavior. *American Scientist, 40*: 665-677, 1952
80. Jack Brehm, *A Theory of Psychological Reactance*. (New York: Academic Press, 1966).
81. Skinner, *Science of Human Behavior*, 1953, 449.
82. H. Chiang and Abraham H. Maslow, *The Healthy Personality: Readings* (2nd ed.) (New York: Van Nostrand, 1977). 259-260.
83. Calvin S. Hall and Gardner Lindzey, *Theories of Personality*. (New York: Wiley, 1957). 97.
84. E. Rae Harcum, *Incidental Psychotherapy Within Christian Relationships*. (Lanham, MD: Hamilton Books, 2011).
85. H. Leichman, Personal communication, 1975.

86. H. M. Lefcourt, *Locus of Control: Current Trends in Theory and Research.* (New York: Erlbaum, 1976.)
87. E. Rae Harcum, *Serial Learning and Paralearning*. (New York: Wiley-Interscience, 1975.)
88. B. F. Skinner, *Walden Two*. (New York: Macmillan, 1948). 257.
89. Skinner, *Science of Human Behavior*, 1983.
90. Henry Gleitman, James Gross and David Reisberg, *Psychology* (8th ed.) (New York: W. W. Norton & Company, 2011.) 228.
91. Harcum, *A Psychology of Freedom and Dignity*, 1994.

Chapter 4

Methods

Methodology enters prominently into the schism between Humanistic and Behavioristic psychologies. The fundamental difference between these views is that the Behaviorists have insisted on an objective and rigorous conception of science, while the Humanists have advocated greater latitude in what is acceptable as evidence. As Harcum has pointed out, the advocacy by traditional science of rigorous methodology indeed sounds great, but such rigor also has some unwelcome connotations, as in *rigor mortis*, the stiffness of death.[1] Royce made the same point.[2] Hard scientists tend to think that the postulation of some sort of mysterious physical gremlin to account for creative responses in the human machine is superior to the postulation of a non-material ghost, or spirit, in the machine.

So far, the Behaviorists have appeared to carry the day in psychology. But, their narrow and rigid attitude has had unfortunate consequences for the field. As LeShan has argued, mainstream psychological research has unwisely insisted on adopting the conception of rigorous science, and thus the concept of mechanical man. In his view, this way of thinking about human beings has produced disastrous results for the discipline, as follows:

> Since no meaningful or important aspects of human life fit the mechanical model, we more and more studied the unimportant aspects of human life that did. Our other solution to the problem was to abandon studying human beings (our primary subjects) as such for the study of entities that we could study in mechanical ways and with mechanical assumptions. These included rats and pigeons in the laboratory and, lately, computers. Experiments that we did on human beings were designed to demonstrate their mechanical and rat-like characteristics—and were successful. We then claimed that we had experimentally proven that human beings were essentially rat-like and machine-like in nature.
> However, during this process, it became clear to the culture at large that if problems concerned the laboratory behavior of rats and pigeons, we *were* the experts to turn to. If, however, the problems were of the nature of how to stop killing each other, how to stop poisoning our planet, or how to stop our steadily increasing population growth, one had better turn elsewhere. Since this is a culture that sees science as the way to solve problems and the relevant science was clearly helpless to do so, increasing pessimism and hopelessness has spread through all Western society.[3]

Harman supports this view. He argued that traditional physical science does not have the answer to the truly important psychological questions. He proposed that we should be restructuring the concept of science, instead of simply calling science one thing and humanistic description another, as follows:

> What physicists have shown—and we must be grateful for this—is that when you push reductionist science to the limit, you encounter the need for something else, something more holistic. But to learn more about human consciousness, it is necessary to look not in the physics laboratory, but in the deeper recesses of the human mind.[4]

The advocacy of other methods and approaches does not require us to abandon the more rigorous methods. We need methodological pluralism in general psychology in order to take advantage of both rigorous science and humanistic methods. We must value empirical and analytic studies as well as intuitive and subjective ones.

As I have maintained, the validity of the different conceptions of how to test reality must be determined in terms of their utility to society.[5] Some Behavioristic tenets work well in some contexts, and should therefore not be abandoned. But, the Humanistic orientation is also essential for society, as many have contended.[6] In fact, Gelso cites the philosopher Kierkegaard as drawing an analogy between a deterministic philosopher and a man who constructs a fine castle, but dwells in his adjacent barn.[7]

Again, this is not to say that rigorous laboratory experiments and controlled observations are wrong or worthless. I merely say that rigorous science must be supplemented by insights from less rigorous approaches as well. A modern interpretation of the nature of science allows for the inclusion of the broader, more subjective attitudes. This is not an anti-scientific attitude, but rather a broadening and deepening of the scientific attitude, in keeping with the modernity view of science.

Types of Data

Different types of data are relative to different theoretical approaches to psychology, such that only some types of data are permitted by some theories. The Strict Behaviorists accept only third-person data, which is obtained from observations of overt behavior by a competent observer.

The Cognitive Behaviorists, Psychoanalysts and Humanists permit also second-person data, which is obtained by introspective reports of personal experience by a single observer. The observer tries to report the raw sensory experience without adding subjective interpretation. The possibility of subjective distortions makes such data virtually worthless in the eyes of some psychologists. For example, the founder of behaviorism, J. B. Watson, would accept such data only as a convenient way to arrive at data in the third-person category.[8] That is, an observer could report seeing someone scratch his ear or run through a red traffic light. Also, the actual report itself is, of course, observable by any competent observer, and thus is third-person data.

Finally, the Psychoanalysts and Humanists advocate the use of three types of data, adding first-person data. Such data is the personal experience of a single observer, and thus it is available only to that one observer.

The so-called hard-line scientists (i.e., Strict Behaviorists) are exemplified by Skinner, who was particularly vehement against the use of what he called "casual observation."[9] Therefore, he was suspicious of even third-person data when it was obtained in other than controlled laboratory situations by trained scientists.

The theorists of other, less rigorous, persuasions believe, however, that the most valid and useful observations are made in the uncontrolled life situations. For example, the inter-behavioral approach argues that no natural phenomena are outside of science, and therefore scientists can learn about human nature by examining all products of human endeavors, including artistic creations of all kinds.[10] Indeed, great writers have achieved their greatness partly because they have astutely observed and reported human behaviors in the first person. They have later transferred the inferred principles to the printed page by way of illustrations, characterizations and metaphors.

Therefore, despite the strong possibility for error, personal intuition and logic can be both a source of hypotheses and theories. These subjective factors can also be personally convincing to some individuals for the verification of hypotheses. Ultimately, of course, for final acceptance by the scientific community, such conclusions must converge with second- and third-person data.

Scientific Methods

The scientific approach to the understanding of behavior uses three basic methods, used singly or in combination: 1) Naturalistic, 2) Correlational and 3) Experimental. These methods describe how facts and principles of psychology are discovered. Methodology provides the very tools of the science of behavior.

Naturalistic

The first general approach of science is the naturalistic method. In this method the researcher attempts to describe and record the acts of the person in various natural settings. The student of behavior tries not to intrude into the subject person's perceptual environment, because such intrusion would destroy the natural characteristics of the setting. The goal is to make the research as relevant to real life as possible.

There are several variations of the naturalistic approach, representing varying degrees of reliability and usefulness. They are surely not mutually exclusive.

Anecdotal

The first, least reliable and thus most controversial, naturalistic method is the anecdotal method. This method involves the collection of brief stories, or anecdotes, about alleged instances of behavior. Each observation can potentially answer a question about a person.

An anecdote allegedly describes the behavior of a person in one particular situation. The researcher must assume that this sample is actually typical of the subject person's behavior. An example of such evidence would be the story about Sir Walter Raleigh placing his cloak over a mud puddle for Queen Elizabeth. Other examples would be George Washington telling the truth about the cherry tree, or Abe Lincoln walking many miles to return a few pennies of overcharge. If the story is true, you know something about that person. For example, if I tell you the true story about my brother-in-law getting out of bed one cold winter night to assist a stranger whose automobile was stuck in the snow in front of his home, you can make some strong inferences about his character. Do you feel that you know him better than if I had merely said he was a caring and helpful person?

I will give one final example of anecdotal evidence that is entirely true. According to my wife, it illustrates one of my stable characteristics. One day when our children were about four and six years old, my wife had taken me to work, keeping the family car at home. So, naturally she came to get me after work. Because I was not at the usual meeting place, we missed connections. She parked the car, and took the children up to my office to fetch me. Meanwhile, not remembering that I had not driven the car to work that day, I had left the office, found the car and driven home. Indeed, I was much surprised to discover that no one was home when I got there, although the telephone was ringing. The children were distressed thinking that the car had been stolen. My wife, on the basis of experience, reasoned exactly what had happened. Do you feel that you know me better after hearing this story?

To be sure, the anecdotal method is the weakest method of science. In fact, the behavior may not be either true or typical of the individual in different situations. There may have been some unusual circumstances, or the researcher may not have personally observed the incident described in the anecdote. Or, perhaps, the reporter may not have been trained in scientific observation and reporting. The story could, nevertheless, suggest some interesting hypotheses to be tested by more reliable methods.

Case History

The second naturalistic approach is the case history method. This is a comprehensive compilation of all information that can be obtained about a person's previous behaviors in many situations. Emphasis would be placed on information that would be relevant to a particular psychological issue. Generally, there would be information about such things as the person's age, medical history, general physical condition, family situation and behavioral symptoms.

An example of a case history is provided by the following edited version of a case study. This report was changed slightly to protect the identity of the child:

> George is a seven-year-old boy enrolled in special education. He is frail and delicate, resembling and acting like a five-year-old. He has limited motor skills. He lacks confidence in new surroundings, giving an overall picture of a dependent person. He has no playmates, and he amuses himself with television for hours.
>
> George is an only child, living alone with his mother and father. His father has steady work, but a low salary. Neither parent appears socially poised or intellectually alert. His mother appears disoriented occasionally, and has complained to the teacher that at times she cannot manage George. His grandfather, with whom he has much contact, initiated George's enrollment in the school.
>
> The home environment is not conducive to good personality adjustment. Signs of familial controversy and disharmony can be observed in George's role-playing. Several remarks indicated that George has observed the parents having sexual intercourse. The grandfather has been in a mental hospital.
>
> Physical characteristics are his small size and lack of good muscle control. Generally, he is not energetic in outdoor play and he falls occasionally when running. His slight, pale appearance raises questions of proper nutrition. He has many caries in his teeth, and some loss of hearing in both ears. Nevertheless, he speaks distinctly.
>
> The medical history shows no complications or abnormalities surrounding birth, and there is no mention of hereditary diseases. Yet some behavior may be interpreted as symptomatic of organic brain damage. George has been described as hyperactive at times. The teacher has observed his hands twitching during the daily marching exercise. There does not seem to be perseveration, however; he is usually ready to move on to other activity when the program demands it.
>
> George gets along well with his classmates. He is by far the most advanced mentally, but is hampered by his shy, dependent attitude. He finds it difficult to solve a conflict on his own, especially if there is physical violence involved. George also shows the classic symptoms of a child who does not share with siblings, exhibiting an excessive demand for attention.
>
> When George entered the program his reported IQ was 64. At the end of the first year, it was 63. While his shyness prevented much social interaction with the teacher, from time to time she caught glimpses of a fertile imagination. As he became more secure, he did show some evidence that he had the ability and need to imagine and to fantasize. Not only did he use the classroom toys, he was well able to substitute given objects and toys for other things. Therefore, the teacher doubted

> that the child was an uncomplicated case of mental retardation, suspecting that George could express himself more adequately if he were free from certain apparent emotional problems. His emotional development revealed some disturbing, if not neurotic, symptoms. He is sometimes overly concerned with insignificant details. George will not willingly mess his hands by spreading paste, by finger painting, or playing in the sand pit, and he finds chalk dust distasteful. On a field trip to the fire department, he was terrified at the sound of the siren, and begged to be allowed to leave. It took all his courage, plus continuous reassurance from the teacher for him to complete the trip.
>
> George needs the demonstration of affection; he chooses the softest blanket at rest time and takes comfort in its security. He requires reassurance and prodding to complete a task. He can manufacture numerous reasons for not helping with cleaning or putting equipment away. He may turn himself in his imagination into something different than himself, who naturally cannot do what is expected.
>
> George has a fantasy world and a real world. When he is in his real world, he is relaxed, his attention span is longer, and he gives evidence of readiness for an academic program. For example, he can read the names of the children at the school, and he remembers names easily.
>
> When George is in his fantasy world, he cannot concentrate for long on hand work, or finish a puzzle. Also, he is restless and irritable. He pretends so much about non-school material that it is impossible to accomplish anything. On a least one occasion, it was impossible for the teacher to elicit a real reaction for an entire school day. The teacher questioned whether George knew the difference between the real world and the make-believe, although later evidence indicated that he could make this distinction.[11]

Subsequent evidence bore out the suspicions derived from this case study. His psychologist concluded that George was not as retarded as the IQ score would indicate. The psychologist suspected that there were some very significant emotional factors that had depressed his scores on the intelligence test.

There is a need for caution also in using the case history method. For example, a case study of a person dropping out of school in the eighth grade may indicate intellectual or motivational weaknesses, but it may also have been forced on him or her by a death in the family, financial problem or other factors beyond his or her personal control. The researcher could discover what in fact was the cause by examining the teachers' comments in the school records, by interviewing neighbors, by studying the results of any tests that the person may have taken at the time of dropping out or even by asking the person directly.

Another potential problem is that the reader of a case history develops certain hypotheses and expectations about the person. These may blind him or her to the present truth that is readily available through observation. For example, some educators even propose that a schoolteacher not examine the prior school record of a new pupil. This would permit an independent judgment about the academic or emotional status of each child, because the new teachers would not be biased by the conclusions of previous teachers.

While there is some merit to this argument, the opposing one is far stronger: teachers or other guides need all of the evidence about the person that they can get. Nevertheless, they must always keep in mind that they are somewhat dependent upon the thoroughness and accuracy of the persons who actually compiled the case history. Factual information without the proper context may be misleading. It should not cause a guide to ignore the information that is currently available to his or her own eyes and ears.

The compiler of the case history must try to keep his or her own personal biases and judgments from distorting the factual information. For example, the person putting together a case history may decide that the subject's mother is domineering. But, this conclusion might be based on only brief observation by the compiler. Converging documentation for such a conclusion by reports from neighbors, or other sources, may be necessary.

Thus, some information in the personal history may in fact be misleading, or even false. But, other information in it may be absolutely essential. Examples of such vital information would be evidence of hearing or visual defects, brain damage or bad family situations. Without the case history, these facts might not be discovered by the teacher or counselor before some unfortunate incident has happened. Sometimes a child with a visual or hearing problem suffers through many months in a disadvantageous seat in the classroom just because the teacher was not informed of the disability. The teacher might either have carelessly failed to read the records properly, or just ignored what was written there. Perhaps, the important information was not even in the record because of lax recordkeeping, or some misguided principle favoring independent judgment. So, unfortunately, an uninformed teacher might give a sugared drink as a reward to a diabetic child.

Observation

A third type of naturalistic method is the observational method, in which the person is directly observed in selected relevant situations. For example, the supervisor or researcher might observe from the back of the room the behavior of a teacher in class. Better yet, the researcher might make observations through a one-way mirror. Because the observed person is unaware of the observation through the glass, he or she does not behave differently. Obviously, the researcher must take certain steps to ensure that he or she has not violated prescribed ethical principles in such research or evaluation.

Again, one must make allowances for the skill of the observer in recording facts. First, the observer must be instructed in exactly what behaviors are to be noted and recorded. Second, the observer must have awareness of the problems encountered in trying to record the true facts, in contrast to his or her subjective interpretation of the behaviors. People often misperceive or misinterpret scenes, even those that they see with their own eyes. Therefore, accurate observation is best accomplished by a trained observer.

A specific example of observation is used exclusively in psychological research. This is self-observation, or introspection. The person observes his or her own actions and feelings under selected conditions. The person introspects, or looks inside himself or herself, to determine what sensations, motivations and thoughts are present at a given time under known input conditions. The introspectionist attempts to report these experiences as accurately as possible, without elaboration or deletions. These reports are second-person data. In interpreting these data, we must remember that the actual data are the overt reports of the observer, and not the subjective experiences themselves.

A third type of observational evidence is the first-person data, which is the private experience of the observer. Because it is not observable by others, it is not considered valid by Behaviorist psychologists. The Psychoanalytic and Humanistic psychologists believe, however, that such data can nevertheless be useful, despite its private nature. It can contribute to the origin and development of theory, and to personal beliefs of individuals about different theories.

Indeed, the nature of proof is that it is ultimately a personal matter. The individual scientist has personal control over what kinds of evidence he or she finds convincing for acceptance of a given theory. To be sure, a theory requires general acceptance before it can be regarded as proved. But, nevertheless, the history of science has shown on occasion that the majority opinion was incorrect. For example, we can point to the false belief in a flat earth, and to the false belief in the rotation of the sun about the earth.

Survey

Another observational technique is the survey, which asks a large representative group of people about their attitudes and opinions on matters of interest. The questions can cover topics ranging over a virtually limitless array of topics: voting preferences, sexual habits, mother's nationality, the number of bathrooms and telephones in the house. These surveys can help to predict such things as the outcome of elections, the number of schools to be needed in the future, educational attitudes and the possible economic growth of an area. The economic growth would, for example, have an impact on where sewer lines will be needed, because it will influence where people will choose to build their homes.

The survey is useful to the extent that the answers that are obtained from a particular sample of respondents accurately represent the views and behaviors of the populations that the sample is thought to represent. If the samples are not representative of a given population, any predictions for that population based on that data probably would be faulty. For example, when only some members of the target population respond to the questionnaire, these respondents might be importantly different in some ways from the people who fail to respond. Therefore, the manner in which the survey questions are distributed to respondents is important. Survey questionnaires can be distributed in many different ways, depending upon the needs and ingenuity of the researcher. Often the questionnaires are sent through the mail, with stamped return envelopes to increase the likelihood that they will be returned. Another way to conduct surveys is through door-to-door or through telephone canvassing.

Regardless of the method of distribution, the survey researcher must make every effort to ensure that each member of the target population has an equal opportunity to appear in the survey. Otherwise, the survey is biased, perhaps in important ways. For example, if the sample of people returning questionnaires includes too high a proportion of Catholics, then the opinions on such matters as abortion and birth control probably would not give a true picture of the general attitudes of the total population in that region. If, for some reason, most of the questionnaires were mailed to a prosperous section of town, the answers on issues like guaranteed annual wages, or welfare programs or higher taxes might well be negative. If the same questions were answered by impoverished residents in a different section of town, the general tenor of the responses would likely be different.

The responding population also might be self-selected by their attitudes about the subject of the survey. The persons who take the trouble to complete and return a questionnaire must be different in at least this one respect from those who did not cooperate with the researcher. Moreover, the attitudes about, for example, sexual practices of persons who answer questions about sex on a survey might be quite different from those who refuse to answer those questions. Those persons who consider such questions to be personal and offensive could, for example, more likely be conservative in their attitudes about sex.

Often, several follow-up requests are given by the researcher to those who failed to return questionnaires, in serious attempts to increase the return rate. The researchers are vitally interested in any possible difference in attitudes or characteristics between the initial respondents and the reluctant respondents. Often the researchers find themselves in an ethical dilemma. Namely, they worry that even a telephone call to urge the potential subject to respond to a questionnaire may be coercive. Research ethics require that a researcher not coerce someone to serve as his or her subject.

We must be painstakingly careful about the possibility of this kind of nonrepresentative sampling when evaluating the results of surveys used for advertising. Say, the report is that 97 percent of the physicians included in the poll preferred Flimflam tongue depressors. One must be aware that the only physicians polled may have been those previously observed to have purchased Flimflams for their practices.

It is also important to analyze the specific wording of the questions and answers. A good example of misunderstanding a question comes to mind from a slightly different context. When conducting a research project on psychological stress, we asked the subjects questions about themselves in order to see whether or not persons with different personal characteristics had performed differently. One man missed the intent of the statement, "I frequently feel pain in the back of my neck." He replied that this statement did in fact apply to him. When questioned further, however, he reported that he truly did not often have such pain, but "I feel it every time I have it."

A good example of the problems of interpreting the meaning of responses on a survey is provided by one of my personal investigations, which was described in Chapter 1. It was an unpublished survey of introductory psychology students for the practical purpose of assessing the usefulness to the students of the reference list in their textbook. Whereas 129 of 131 students indicated that they never, or very rarely, used the reference list, one student said, "Yes, of course," and another said, "All the time." In a purely objective sense, these are both clearly "Yes," or affirmative, answers to the question. And that is the way they were *reported*. But that is not the way they *were interpreted*. How could an empirical scientist interpret an overt response of "Yes" to mean "No?" This is an extremely risky endeavor, of course. The researcher could in fact merely be swayed by his biases and expectations. But two other pieces of converging evidence supported the conclusion that these students truly did not use the reference list. First, there was the fact that no one else in the sample reported using the list more often than rarely. Therefore, to take the strong affirmative responses at face value, the scientist would have to see these two students as discretely and substantially different from everyone else in the sample. Then, there were the reports of these two individuals about the number of references on the list. Presumably, a student who routinely used the reference list would have a reasonable idea of the number of references in it. One student's guess was off by over 83 percent. The other student estimated that there were only six references in the book when there were over 40 references on *each* page of more than 40 pages of the reference list. Therefore, the responses of these two subjects suggest that they were merely being sarcastic.

This example indicates the difficulties often facing psychologists in interpreting data. Some would solve the problem by simply stating that a "Yes" response always means a "Yes," and should therefore without question be treated as such. But, that requires an assumption, too. So, in attempting to be scientific, we can make mistakes.

One point is, however, absolutely clear about the interpretation of these two atypical responses. The reader of the report of the study must be informed about the interpretive problem. The researcher *cannot* simply change "Yes" responses of a subject to "No" responses on the basis of a personal hunch or even a strong conviction. It would be professionally unethical, as well. The data language must be scrupulously accurate. Only the researcher's interpretation of that data is subject to error.

Finally, it is important to examine carefully the wording of the conclusions by the author of a research study. For example, there is a difference between saying that the respondents merely recommended the ingredients in Brand X, and saying that they actually recommended Brand X itself. Also, to report that none of the persons in a poll recommended another brand more than Brand X does not mean that the respondents recommended Brand X over the others, either. I like the ad in which the coach literally said that he could not say that the advertised product helped this team win the championship, but he was sure that it did not hurt their performance. The intended—but unwarranted—implication was, of course, that the use of the product did in fact help win the championship.

Clinical

A fifth classification of naturalistic method is the clinical method. This technique studies persons who have had certain, possibly abnormal, experiences or physical conditions, and therefore may show unusual behavior in some respect. An example would be to observe persons with traumatic brain injuries. Certain interpretations about the role of the damaged part of the brain in normal behavior can be made by noting and recording which acts remain, those which are changed or missing and other behaviors which are new since the accident.

Another illustration can be taken from the field of education. We can study a population of children with reading disabilities in order to find out why they are having problems, what they are lacking or what has been added to their lives. In this way, we can make judgments about what conditions are necessary for normal progress in learning to read.

The clinical method is also called the ex post facto experimental design. That means that it is like an experiment, and has been identified as such after the fact. In a formal experiment, some potential variable is deliberately manipulated and the effect of this operation is determined. Therefore, one can think of the clinical situation as an unplanned experiment, in which a variable was not manipulated by an experimenter, but by an accident, or an act of God. Although the experiment was not planned, the researcher seizes the opportunity to learn about the mechanisms of behavior from it, as if it were actually a planned experiment.

Often, the data could not, for ethical reasons, be obtained in an intentional experiment. For example, we could not ethically do an experiment that would damage parts of a human brain, or deliberately traumatize a child, simply in order to discover the effects of these experiences.

Description of Results

Results of the naturalistic method of science are often described simply by written narratives. This would be true especially for anecdotal and case history evidence. In other cases, however, some descriptive statistics would be possible in the form of frequency distributions, measures of central tendency and measures of the variability. A frequency distribution is a graph of the frequency with which each score of the dependent variable was obtained. The graph can be summarized by two measures: central tendency and variability. There are three measures of central tendency: mode, median and mean. The mode is the most frequent score. The median is the score which is at the middle of the distribution (divides the distribution in half). The mean is the average score, obtained by adding all scores and dividing by the number of scores.

The variability of scores in the frequency distribution can also be measured in three ways: range, mean deviation and standard deviation. The range is simply the interval between the highest and the lowest scores. The mean deviation is the average of the separations between the mean and each individual score, taken without regard to sign. The standard deviation is obtained by squaring the value of the separation (deviation) of each score from the mean, averaging that value and taking the square root of the result.

Ordinarily, a frequency distribution can be completely summarized by its mean and standard deviation. The other measures of central tendency and variability are useful for special purposes.

Correlational

A second general method of science is the correlational method. In this method, we relate the behavior of the individual to certain external or internal conditions that were present before or during the behavior. The aim is to find out which environmental or personal conditions were associated with certain acts.

Because a cause and an effect are correlated in time and space, we often infer causation from such correlations. We must do so with extreme caution, however, because alternative bases for empirical correlations must be ruled out before we can conclude that a given correlation did in fact indicate a causal relationship.

The correlational method is used frequently in a search for causes of education and emotional development. For example, suppose you did a study which found a positive relationship between the frequency of parents reading bedtime stories to their children and the language development of the children. Although a causal relationship is suggested, such an empirical correlation does not necessarily mean that language development is determined by verbal experience. In fact, part of this correlation, at least, could be produced by genetic inheritance because intelligent parents tend to provide verbal stimulation to their children. But they also pass along their own genetic bases for high intelligence.

The tendency to conclude that there is causation is very powerful when there is merely a temporal correlation between two events. But, the correlation could be an accident, or a coincidence, with neither event causing the other. Superstitions, for example, are developed through such accidental correlations. A superstition is born when a person notices that some event occurs immediately prior to some other event, and mistakenly concludes that there is a causal connection between them. For example, a baseball player may eat three eggs for breakfast, in contrast to the two eggs usually eaten, and hits two home runs in the game that day. Henceforth, he may eat three eggs on the mornings of every game day, at least until his batting average begins to wane.

Awareness of this strong tendency to infer causation from mere temporal correlation does not make a person immune to it. One of my psychologist colleagues tells the following story: he coughed as he was entering a room one day and the room lights dimmed briefly. The illusion that his cough had affected the lighting was so strong that he reported mustering all of his willpower, and conviction as a scientist, to resist the urge to cough again to see if his cough would dim the lights.

When teaching introductory psychology, I used a little demonstration of the difference between correlation and causality.[12] I showed the students a black box which contained a small flag on one end and a cranking device on the other. When I turned the crank, the flag waved. I asked the students what possible mechanism within the box was responsible for the connection between the flag and the crank. Most inferred a gear arrangement. When I turned the box around to expose the contents, it showed that the crank was connected to absolutely nothing. I had waved the flag by a device with my other hand. Hence, the waving of the flag and the cranking were correlated, but there was not a causal connection.

Simple correlations also provide one reason for the common belief in extra-sensory perception or ESP. This is an alleged awareness of some event through other than the known physical sensory systems. A typical example of alleged ESP would be something like this: a person dreams that a certain member of his family in another city has died, and then learns the following day that the very person died during the night. Believers in the existence of ESP would conclude that there was a causal relation between the death and the dream. They would say that the dream was achieved through some sensory mechanism that is different (extra) with respect to known senses, such as sight and hearing. Many scientists believe that there are such extra-sensory mechanisms. Many others doubt their existence, dismissing the correlational evidence as mere coincidence. Nevertheless, the number of stories that one hears in support of a causal relationship is amazing. Almost as soon as a person is identified as a psychologist at any social gathering, he is told of "true" instances of mental telepathy, clairvoyance and the like. Just to see how long it would take, I started out one morning to collect an example. Within ten minutes—from the first two persons I asked—I had two different alleged cases of ESP. Only one of them is given here, but the other was quite similar. The story is as follows: A woman's fiancé had been hurt in an accident, and immediately thereafter had received a phone call from his mother because she had a feeling that he had been in an accident. The fiancé concluded that the experience was paranormal because the probability that this was just a coincidence would be small indeed. The mother reported that she rarely telephoned her son.

It is therefore not surprising why so many people believe in such phenomena. The instances in which the dream does not come true are quickly forgotten. Indeed, in such a negative case, there is no interesting reason for remembering them. But, the dreams that come true are remembered forever because some importance is attached to them. Nevertheless, the crucial question remains: can all reports of ESP be dismissed for this reason?

The disbelievers in ESP point out that sometimes two events are correlated with one another because they are both affected by some third factor. For example, we notice a correlation between the height of the mercury in a thermometer and the stickiness of the tar on the street. The two events are related because they are both influenced by a third factor—namely, the ambient temperature.

Ambient heat causes the mercury in the thermometer to expand, and therefore rise in the tube. It also causes tar in the street to become sticky.

The correlation of the dream and the automobile accident described above could also be produced in such a way. The mother was perhaps aware that her son was about to take a dangerous trip on his motorcycle. She worried that an accident was likely, and therefore dreamed about one. Thus, the dream and the accident could both be traced to the perceived and real danger of the motorcycle trip.The plausible alternative hypothesis about the cause of the correlation does not disprove the ESP hypothesis, of course. The existence of ESP must, for now, remain a viable hypothesis.

A problem of current interest concerns the empirical relationship between the viewing of violence on television by a person and the number of violent acts perpetrated by that individual. A researcher discovers a correlation between the number of times a person has observed violent actions in television programs and the number of times he or she participates in a violent activity. Perhaps this means that the observance of violence produces violent behavior. But, perhaps a person already interested in violence would be likely to watch such broadcasts and also to participate actively in such activities.

Therefore, one would need more information before deciding whether or not this single observed correlation did in fact represent a causal relationship between the observation and the subsequent action. For example, additional data on the relations between viewing violent TV and engaging in violent behaviors could be collected a few years later. If the correlation between viewing violence on the first date and perpetrating violence on the second date is higher than the correlation between viewing and violence at either the first observations or in the later observations, then a causal relation is suggested. This very conclusion is, in fact, supported by empirical data.[13]

Examples of Use

If the researcher believes that some input or other condition may be producing certain acts, he or she may systematically collect evidence of possible connections between certain inputs and certain acts. Ordinarily, the social scientist does not, however, find a perfectly consistent relationship in true-life situations. Figure 4-1 represents a hypothetical result that one might expect to find in observing the relationship between the number of hours that students studied for an examination and their actual scores on that examination.

A situation of a less-than-perfect relationship (correlation) is represented in the figure. Each tally mark represents a single student classified according to the spent time (in columns) and according to his or her examination score (in rows). The empirical trend is for the students with better work habits— i.e., those who studied harder—to score higher on the test, and those with poor work habits to score lower.

		WORK HABITS			
		Poor	Average	Good	Sum
SCORES	High		卌 ||	|||	10
	Med.	卌 ||	卌 卌 卌 卌 卌 卌 卌 |	卌 ||	50
	Low	|||	卌 ||		10
	Sum	10	50	10	70

Figure 4-1: Illustration of a non-perfect correlation between work habits and scores on a test

The reason for the less-than-perfect relationship is that test scores are typically affected by many, many other factors in addition of work habits. For example, the intelligence of the student would also undoubtedly influence such behavior. An extremely intelligent student with average work habits might still perform among the top group of students in the examination, although probably not at the very top. On the other hand, a less capable student with average work habits might fall at the bottom of the distribution of examination scores. Thus, if you knew how hard a student studied for the examination, you would be able to make a more accurate prediction of examination score than if you did not have this information. Nevertheless, you could not predict the exact category of examination score.

If the input condition did in fact completely indicate the examination behavior, then a somewhat different result would occur. The actual relationship would then reveal a perfect correlation between work habits and performance on the examination, with all of the tallies falling in cells along the diagonal running from lower left to upper right. Then the researcher would know exactly in what category the examination score would fall if he or she just knew whether the work habits of the student were poor, average or good.

Yet another correlation result is possible, although not likely in the example that has been used. The actual examination may have been so poorly conceived, constructed and scored that the amount of studying by the student had no relationship whatsoever to his or her examination score. Thus, there would not be a correlation between the two variables, and no empirical basis for predicting examination score from knowledge of study habits. Then, there could be approximately one tally mark in each of the four cells at the corners of a matrix as in Figure 4-1, with eight scores in each of the cells between the corners, and 34 scores in the center cell. Therefore, there would be no differences in the distribution of these hypothetical grades for students in any of the study groups. Thus, the best guess about each student's performance would be the average examination score for the group, simply because most students made that score.

The previous discussion has been concerned with correlations that show direct, or positive, associations. That is, they show a higher value of one factor in association with the higher value of the other one. A similar situation could occur, however, in which a high value of one factor was associated with a low value of the other. Such a negative, or inverse, correlation is still used in the same general way for prediction purposes. Sometimes, the only difference between positive and negative correlations is merely whether the researcher reports scores in terms of correct responses or in terms of errors.

An empirical relationship can allow us to predict test scores from hours studied, but it still does not prove that hours studied causes better grades. There are viable alternative explanations. For example, the more intelligent students could spend more time studying. The longer study might not help their test scores, but their high intelligence would help.

Let us examine how the correlation technique could at least provide us with some hypotheses about the causal mechanisms for securing good grades. A hypothetical situation that would produce results as in Figure 4-1 is illustrated in Figure 4-2. The curve for the complete population (students in the course) is made up of students who showed, respectively, poor, average and good work habits—represented by the dashed lines in the figure. The two vertical lines in Figure 4-2 mark off the three divisions of examination scores—low, medium and high. To simplify this picture, the three curves are all made to be equal in size—the same number of students scored in the medium category on the examination as in the low and high categories—contrary to the specific tallies shown in Figure 4-1.

Obviously, the actual results of an empirical study are not likely to show such a neat pattern. The distribution of grades overlap for each group of students with different work habits because of other relevant factors, such as intelligence. Still, the better work habits tend to be related to better scores. Looking at only the group of students with poor work habits, we can see that about half of them

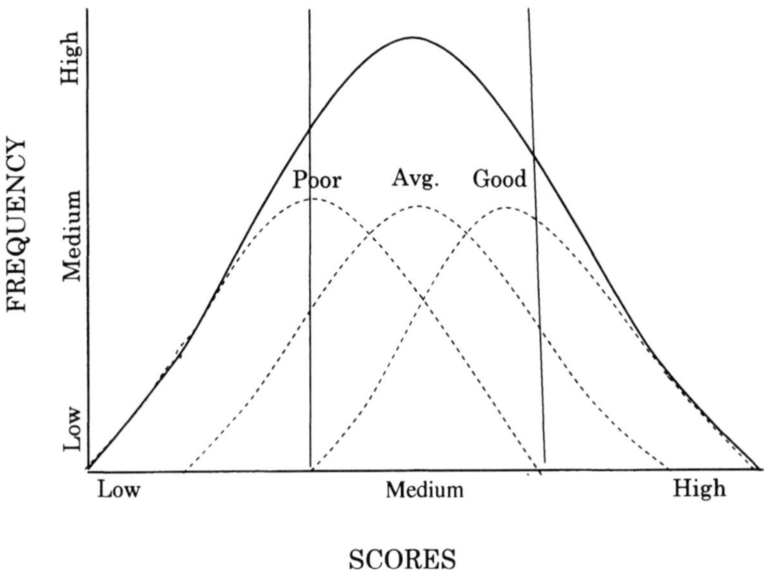

Figure 4-2: Objective situation that would produce results as in Fig. 4-1

in this example will score in the low category, and none at all of them will score highly on the test. The reverse is true in the example for the persons with good work habits. About half of them will score in the high category, and virtually none of them will score at the bottom. The students with average work habits score predominantly in the medium range, with relatively few in this example scoring either high or low.

This line of investigation might be pursued further to allow an even better prediction of the scores for individual students. We might ask why some persons with good work habits scored high on the examination, whereas most of them made scores at the upper end of the medium category. The answer might well be that these high-scoring persons were the most intelligent students in the class. Thus, the persons who made the high scores on the examination tended to be those who had good work habits and who were also the most intelligent.

The example can be made clearer by studying Figure 4-3. Suppose the largest curve represents the distribution of the scores on a test for all the pupils in a class. The smaller curve, shaded with diagonal lines, might represent those pupils with the best work habits. The smallest (blackened) curve might represent the most intelligent pupils from among that group of best workers. This situation

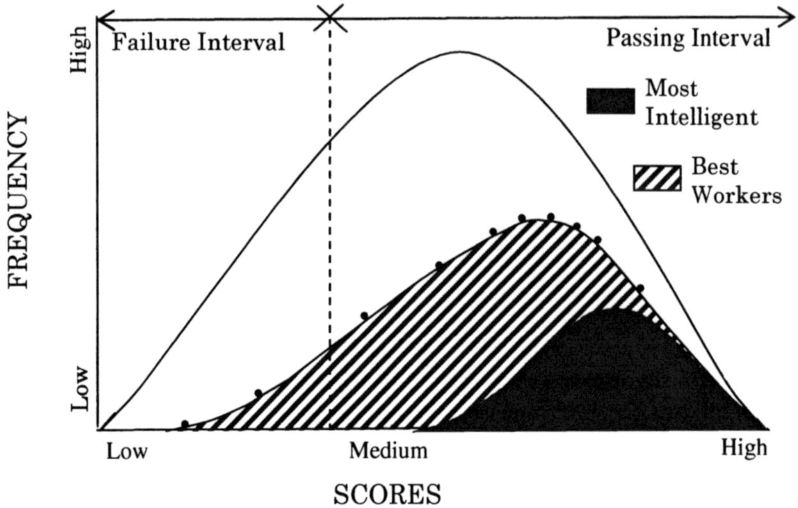

Figure 4-3: Illustration of the effects of two factors on scores of a test

indicates that both good work habits and high intelligence are correlated with a higher grade average. If the vertical dashed line represents a cut-off score to separate passing and failing averages, we can see that surely none of the hard-working pupils of greatest intelligence would fail the test.

To simplify Figure 4-3, the distribution of scores for the other categories of students are not shown. To be sure, prediction of the scores for the other groups would be made similarly. For example, the students of low intelligence and poor work habits would tend to occupy the lowest portion of the total distribution, such that the majority of them would not pass.

The analysis of other factors that influence the test scores could continue beyond the two-factor breakdown shown in Figure 4-3. For example, the highest scorers from among the group of most intelligent and best workers might be found to have had at least eight hours of sleep the night before the examination. Of these intelligent, hard-working, long-sleeping pupils, the ones with the very top grades might be those who had a good breakfast before the examination. Of these, the ones with the best penmanship might make the very top grades, and so forth. This search for the various correlates of good performance continues for as long as it provides useful data—i.e., the researcher obtains some appreciable correlation between a potential cause and the test score.

The above empirical relationships clearly suggest causal mechanisms between study habits, sleep, penmanship, etc., and good grades because all reasonable factors have presumably been examined. A researcher who was not convinced, however, could perform experiments, a research method to be described in the next section of this chapter. In an experiment, the researcher would, for example, compare the grades of a random group of students (not selected for a reason) who had been required to study for a certain number of hours with the grades of a group of students whose study had been restricted to fewer hours.

If a causal relationship for a behavior has been shown, the correlation can provide a basis for improving that behavior. In the example given, a student would be advised to improve study habits, get adequate rest, etc., in order to improve his or her score.

Figure 4-3 can be used to illustrate the danger of using "cut-off" scores to separate passing and failing performance. Suppose we let the baseline represent scores on a test that will be used to select people for, say, a particular job or for admission to college. Those selected are considered to be passing and those who are rejected are considered to be failing. The dividing line, or cut-off score, would be set according to the number of job positions or admission openings available. This selection ratio would be determined by the number of available jobs and the number of applicants.

But, the curve of performance is smooth, having no abrupt changes. Therefore, there is no clear behavioral marker of a division between "acceptable" and "non-acceptable" candidates. Persons who fell just slightly below the cut-off could possibly have fallen slightly above the cut-off if they had a little more sleep the night before the test, or a little better breakfast, or had not recently lost a $50 bet, etc. Thus, some rather tangential matters could influence who fell slightly below or slightly above the cut-off score. Perhaps some of the persons who were a little above the cut-off had a "good day" at the time of the test, in that all conditions for their performance could have been just right. Therefore, they performed slightly better than their normal level of ability. If selected, they could become what is known as false positives—those who are selected, but later fail on the job.

The persons falling just below the cut-off could become false negatives. They were not selected, but they could have succeeded if they had been tested under better conditions that would have permitted them to show their true (higher) level of ability. They could have suffered a so-called "bad day." It is more difficult to discover false negatives than false positives because they simply do not get the chance to prove that they could do the job.

This discussion shows why personnel and admissions officers do not like to make choices based on just a single test score, or indeed on any one criterion measure alone. This is true no matter how effective that test usually is, or the value of any other single criterion. To be sure, factors other than what the test is trying to measure can influence the performance. The more information that one has about a person, through different tests, personal interviews and letters of recommendation, the greater chance for eliminating the false positive and the false negative cases. But, the total elimination of errors is ordinarily not likely because the prediction of performance of individuals is usually based on less than perfect correlations. This point must always be kept in mind when interpreting test results, and certainly in making predictions from them.

It goes without saying that it is foolish to use a criterion that is not correlated with job performance. For example, factors such as race, gender, age and religion are not likely to be correlated with performance on most jobs, at least in ways that would indicate a legitimate causal relationship. To be sure, it might be reasonable to assume that, say, a coach of given race and gender could find it easier to gain rapport with a squad of primarily the same race and gender. But, no psychologist would argue that it was not possible for a coach of different race and gender to do as good or better a job of establishing rapport with his or her athletes. Thus, the law requires that an employer must prove, for any test used as a basis for hiring employees, that the test is a valid test—that the attribute measured by the test is crucial to performance on the job.

Experimental

The third and most powerful technique of science is the experimental method. For this, the investigator actually intervenes in the process of controlling or manipulating some potential causal factor.

Before-and-after Technique

The researcher may modify some input to the person and observe changes in the person's behaviors, as in the before-and-after method. For example, the investigator may observe the behavior of an individual before and after he or she has training in the use of a certain machine. The performance on the test machine is called the dependent variable. The experimenter adds to the experience of the person through training with that or a similar machine. The training would provide what is known as the independent variable, the one that was actually manipulated by the experimenter. Then, after the training was completed, another test on the dependent variable would be given to assess the subsequent performance. If the performance on the dependent variable is different (presumably better) after the training, then one might conclude that the training had influenced the behavior. Of course, the researcher must make the assumption—or verify it, if possible—that no other possible causal factors were involved.

Note that the experimental method absolutely requires the use of a standard, or natural, condition of testing, which is called the control condition, for which no independent variable is manipulated. For example, in the before-and-after case, the control condition would be the situation before the training. The condition for which the experimenter has manipulated or changed some factors is called the experimental condition.

The control condition is absolutely necessary in order to provide comparison data on the dependent variable to the performance of the dependent variable when the independent variable is manipulated. Indeed, without the control condition, there is truly no experiment.

The fundamental problem, particularly with this version of the experimental method, is that one never really knows whether or not something else happened coincidentally with the experimental manipulation, unknown to the experimenter. The problem is basically the same as with the correlational method: some other variable that influences the dependent variable might have changed when the independent variable was manipulated.

This other change of the experimental situation could have been truly coincidental, or actually a direct consequence of manipulating the independent variable. For example, the worker could have had an abscessed tooth pulled during the training period, thus improving his or her health and feeling of well-being. That would be a coincidental effect. Or, the training itself could have involved a different variable. For example, the training experience might have given the worker a more positive attitude or increased confidence about his or her job.

Another problem with the before-and-after technique is called regression to the mean. This means that those persons who score lowest on the test are likely to score higher on a re-test, and those who scored highest are likely to score lower. This occurs because those who scored lowest on the first test probably did so because many factors unrelated to the subject matter of the test unhappily worked against them on the occasion of the first testing. Because those persons would probably have better luck on the second test, their scores will be higher. Similarly, those who scored highest on the first test presumably experienced generally favorable circumstances, which would not be likely to be repeated on the second test. To assess this possible effect, a special control group of subjects would have to be re-tested without the administration of the independent variable. This actually involved a different method because the first test no longer provides the control condition. The control is now a group of independent subjects.

The experimenter can never be sure that some important source of error has *not* been missed. But, as we have said, you can never prove a negative. Therefore, the researcher never really knows for sure how the research subject would have performed without the experimental manipulation. In the absence of other information, the researcher would be forced to simply assume that the subject's behavior would not have changed at just that time. So, science can always involve an error.

Independent Groups

An experiment can also be accomplished by the use of two different groups of subjects. One group of subjects is given a manipulation, or change in conditions. It is called the experimental group; a different group is not given the manipulation, and is called the control group. For example, in studying the effects of training, as mentioned above, the control group of subjects would be given no training. The two groups would then be compared on the performance that is to be assessed—the dependent variable. If the only difference between the groups is provided by the training experience, then only the experience of the manipulated (independent) variable could create a difference between the two groups on the dependent variable.

Again, the assumption is that no other factor could have produced the change in the dependent variable, including some extraneous factor that was associated with the manipulation of the independent variable. This assumption must be supported by the fact that equal attention, other than the training itself, was paid to the control group of subjects. You see, if the two groups were alike in all relevant aspects prior to the experiment, and the training produced more attention to the experimental group of subjects, the two groups would now be different in two respects: the training and the attention paid to them. If the amount of attention affected the dependent variable, it would be a so-called confounding variable. The researcher would not know in such a confounded experiment whether or not an effect on the dependent variable was produced by the independent variable or by the confounding variable.

To control for the effect of attention, the control group must be treated in some way that will make them feel they had received the same kind of attention, but without the training on the task. For example, they may be shown a movie, or asked to fill out a questionnaire on some unrelated topic. Unfortunately, the researcher can never be sure that the perceived level of attention paid to them is equivalent for the two groups of subjects. This is the same problem as in the evaluation of psychotherapy.

Evaluating Differences

The problem in determining whether or not the acts of experimental and control subjects, or conditions, are the same or different is illustrated in Figure 4-4. This figure shows some possible results that might be obtained for three different groups of persons performing a given research task (i.e., dependent variable). The two groups of subjects at the left, called Control Group A (CA) and Control Group B (CB), illustrate what one might reasonably expect to find if two apparently equivalent groups of persons were given exactly the same task under identical conditions. That is, the groups are selected to be equivalent in all relevant aspects, and neither is given an independent variable.

Because of the variations that are usually expected among the individual persons in any two groups, the two distributions of results probably would *not* be exactly the same. Therefore, the average performance might be slightly different, as indicated by the dashed vertical arrows drawn from the tops of each distribution down to the baseline, indicating the respective mean of each distribution. This difference is produced by the problem of finding equal samples. A sample is a group of relatively few individuals selected from a larger population. For example, we could use some lottery system to select a random group of 25 persons out of a class of 300 students. The sample is random if our selection system literally gave each person in the population an equal chance of being selected for the study. If we did this selection twice, the two small samples of people selected from this same population probably would not show characteristics that will exactly duplicate the characteristics of the total population, or each other.

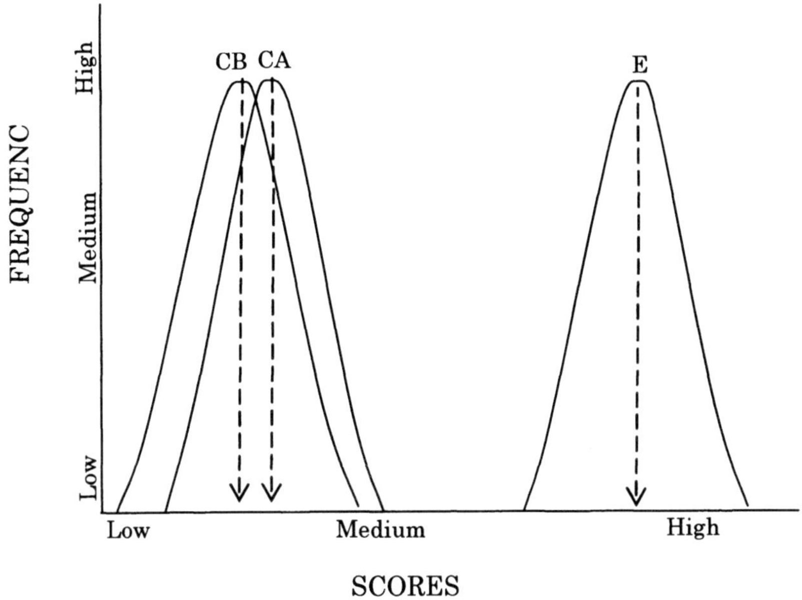

Figure 4-4: Illustration of significant and non-significant differences

To be sure, one would expect to find many instances of persons in the two different groups who perform exactly the same, but there may well be a few persons in one group that would perform slightly better or slightly worse. Therefore, there would probably be some slight differences, by chance in the sampling, between the two distributions of results. Thus, the odds would be very small that one could select subjects for an experiment at random, assign them randomly to different groups, and find that the two groups produced absolutely identical results on some research task.

One would not expect, however, to find a large difference from one group to another with respect to the degree of variability in performance for the persons within each group. As you see, the potential chance difference between two randomly selected groups becomes a critical issue in deciding whether or not an independent variable has had an effect.

Special statistical procedures are used to determine the probability that the performances of two groups are essentially the same, or are importantly different. These techniques are based on the comparison of the difference between the average scores of the two groups with respect to the variability of the scores among persons within each group. The smaller the difference between averages relative to the spread of the different scores within the groups, the smaller the chance that the difference is real. A real difference in groups is one that is not likely to reflect merely sampling differences in the selection of subjects. In fact, the difference between the means is small when the large overlapping of the two distributions is considered.

Basically, we would be likely to conclude that there are only sampling (chance) differences in the case of curves CA and CB in Figure 4-4, because the overlap in the two frequency distributions is great relative to the difference in the averages between the two groups. Statistical procedures beyond the scope of this book are available to perform this analysis in a more precise way. In fact, it is possible to make a probability statement of the likelihood that a given sample is different from some known population, or that two samples are different from one another.

In Figure 4-4, a third group (E), called the experimental group, is shown at the right of the figure. There is no overlap between the frequency distribution for this group and the distributions for either of the two control groups of subjects. Because this difference between the average of this group and the average of either control group is so large with respect to the variation of scores within each group, it appears that this group of subjects in fact reflects a real difference in performance from the two control groups.

Assume that this group was an experimental group that had been treated differently from the control groups (because it received an independent variable). Then, it follows that the treatment given this group caused it to be different from the other groups by an amount that was greater than could be expected by chance.

The difference would probably not have to be as large as the one illustrated in Figure 4-4 for the researcher to conclude that the E groups was different in performance from the other two (control) groups. The decision is based primarily on the calculated probability that the groups were different, with this probability value again coming as a result of certain statistical procedures that are beyond the scope of this book.

Basically, the relevant statistical procedures do in a more precise mathematical way what we have already done by our visual inspection. Specifically, the less the overlap in the two distributions, the less likely the differences between the means of the two groups could have occurred by chance.

When the experimenter concludes that the two groups actually did perform differently on the dependent variable, the difference between them on the dependent variable is then called a significant difference. As in the case of correlations, this interpretation means that the effect was judged not to be the result of chance.

The reader may have by now hit upon the real problem for the researcher. We can only make probability statements about whether or not an independent variable had an effect on the dependent variable. In some cases, as illustrated in Figure 4-4, we can be very confident of a difference, because the difference in means of performance is so large, actually with no overlap in the distributions. But, in other cases, we cannot be confident from the results of a single experiment. As a matter of fact, we could by chance actually obtain a difference as large as that between the E distribution and either control condition (CA or CB), but this obviously is not likely.

Our only defense against such chance errors is to repeat experiments and to do different ones. We continue research until we build a case that convinces us one way or the other. Nevertheless, new data at any time could convince us that our former conviction was incorrect. We should always keep an open mind to the possibility that we have made an error.

Problems of Interpretation

Problems with interpreting the results of experiments fall into two general categories: those related to internal validity and those of external validity. Internal validity refers to the design purity of the experiment. It allows valid conclusions within the conditions of the experiment. External validity refers to the degree to which the results can be applied to a real life situation—i.e., one external to the situation of the experiment.

As mentioned before, the experimental technique requires that every condition within the research situation be exactly the same for the experimental and the control group, except for the one factor that was manipulated—the independent variable. All other differences that could affect the performance must be eliminated, or they must be controlled so that they affect performance of the two groups equally. If these contingencies are true, we would say that our experimental conclusion had internal validity.

The assumption of initial equality between experimental and control groups is difficult to verify. Often, factors that the experimenter does not anticipate do intrude. For example, in some research on stress at a military base, we did not at first take a simple matter of pride into account. We were testing new recruits as they were going through basic training. A problem arose because we were working six days per week, but the testing unit to which we were attached was on a five-day week. Consequently, we had to make special arrangements to secure subjects on Saturdays. We noticed that on Saturdays our subjects seemed to be superior to those on Monday through Friday. After investigation, we discovered that the recruit leaders had been asked to send over a few men from their groups on Saturday for some tests. It turns out that they were hand-picking their best men so that their group would make a good showing. When we insisted that henceforth they should send us the first dozen men on their roster in alphabetical order, the proportion of talented men on Saturday took an abrupt drop to the Monday-through-Friday level.

Another source of potential error in experimental research is what is known as the placebo effect. This occurs when the subject in the experiment acts on the basis of his or her cognitive interpretations of how he or she expects the independent variable to affect behavior. This interpretation by the subject may cause the subject to perform differently from the control subjects, producing a confounding effect. Confounding occurs when there are two or more possible conditions that could be responsible for obtained differences between experimental and control groups on the dependent variable. In such a case, the experimenter does not know which of the antecedent differences caused the difference on the dependent variable.

The experimental control for this confounding placebo effect is to administer a placebo as part of the control conditions. This means to treat the control subjects exactly as if they were actually receiving the independent variable, although the experimenter does not actually administer the independent variable to them. Any effects of the subject's response to the placebo—the so-called placebo effect—will thus hopefully be the same for both the experimental and control subjects. For example, if the researcher wished to study the effects of a tranquilizing agent on the dependent variable, administered in the form of a pill, he or she would give an identical pill without the tranquilizing ingredient—a placebo—to the control group. To be sure, the tranquilizing effect must not be so great that the subjects would be aware of being tranquilized.

The technique of control for the placebo effect is rather straightforward whenever the researcher is simply administering a pill. But, it is by no means simple if the independent variable consists of a variable like training the subjects or giving them psychotherapy, or exposing them to the stress of some sensory bombardment. For example, the subjects surely know that they have received an environment manipulation, such as loud noise, high temperatures or psychotherapy.

The control for the placebo effect is necessary to preserve the internal validity of the experiment, but it produces a problem for the external validity of the experiment. A treatment in the real world may work only because of a placebo effect.

In fact, even in the case of a tranquilizer, as I have said, the subject may actually perceive that he or she has been tranquilized, particularly if the dosage is high. In testing the effects of anesthetics, a positive placebo effect could be produced by the expectations of the subject that he or she has been given something to ease the pain. Truly, the belief of the patient may reduce the pain, even though the alleged medication was just a placebo. There is really no practical problem if a client or patient has been made more comfortable, but there is a scientific problem in evaluating the potential effectiveness of a medication for a research subject.

The experience of one of my friends in graduate school illustrates this point. He had been serving as a research subject in a study on the effects of certain drugs on vision. He showed up one morning with a smashed face, having fallen off his bicycle the night before. It seems that the drug that he had taken the night before—obviously, in an experimental condition—had grossly disturbed his sense of balance. Therefore, the researcher had two problems of interpretation: 1) the subject knew that he had been drugged, and 2) the disruption of the sense of balance might have affected the performance on the research task.

The problem in the evaluation of psychotherapy is even more difficult. The control for the placebo effect in psychotherapy is to give the client an experience that he or she thinks is psychotherapy, but presumably is not. The problem is knowing whether or not your supposed placebo procedure is actually not therapeutic. Suppose the placebo consists of a friendly chat for one hour every afternoon with a ward attendant, covering any topic except the client's mental health problems. Suppose these clients show substantial decreases in their symptoms of psychopathology simply because of the chats. An interesting definitional problem ensues: if the procedure helps the client get better, is it not then psychotherapy? If the so-called control group also improves, but not as much as the experimental group, then the researcher can only interpret the results to mean that the one type of therapy is more effective than the other. If the experimental group does not improve more than the so-called control group, the researcher cannot conclude from such evidence that the supposed therapy given the experimental groups is not effective. It may merely be no more effective than the so-called placebo procedures used with the so-called control group. It is, of course, possible that the improvement in both groups was produced by some other factors, such that neither therapy was effective.

I have pointed out, for example, that a personal connection with a religious friend can have an incidental psychological effect.[14] That is, the relationship can be psychotherapeutic even though the friend is not attempting to practice psychotherapy. Therefore, such a relationship could not be used to provide control data for a program of psychotherapy.

A closely related phenomenon in experimental research is the unwelcome response of the subject to the demand characteristics of the study. The demand characteristics are the subjects' perceptions of what the experimental task requires of them. Because of it, the subject may respond according to how he or she thinks he or she should respond in order to be appropriate, or to present himself or herself in a favorable light. For example, I found in a previously mentioned study of so-called voluntary seating behavior that the subjects informed of the purpose of the study behaved quite differently from those subjects who had not been so informed.[15] The experimental behavior was the selection of a seat in an empty auditorium. The informed subjects tended to conform to their personal perceptions of normal standards of behavior in the situation, but their expectations were not the same as the behaviors of uninformed subjects.

Other sources of error are rather familiar to psychologists, and indeed obvious to most people. For example, the students could be responding on the basis of perceived social desirability of the response. The social desirability bias of a response is the degree to which it is perceived to be either personally enhancing or damaging to the person. It is well known that people like to give answers that make them look good to others, and to feel good about themselves.

These sources of error illustrate the problems of reaching conclusions from data. The very nature of science is to justify the conclusions from data. Even if we are justified in saying that our data do not lie, we can be very wrong about our conclusions from that unimpeachable data. That is why scientists do not always agree about conclusions of causality, and that is what theories are all about, and why we still have them.

Therefore, although the experimental method is the most powerful research techniques, it is most vulnerable to the charge of lack of relevance or applicability to true-life situations—external validity. Obviously, then, an experiment should be done in as relevant, or lifelike, a situation as possible.

Note that some procedures that are used to increase internal validity can have an adverse effect on external validity. As mentioned previously, a control group given a placebo now has a placebo effect as part of its presumably normal behavior. Thus, their responses may not be comparable to persons who have not been participating in psychological research.

Many psychologists have raised the issue of the external validity of laboratory research.[16] External validity refers to the relevance of results obtained in a laboratory to life situations outside the laboratory. As LeShan pointed out, there are usually two barriers to applying laboratory results to real situations in life.[17] The first is the artificiality, or possible sterility, of laboratory research situations with respect to genuine conditions of life. The second is the tendency of behavioral scientists to use animal subjects or college sophomores for much of their research.

The experiment may have to be conducted in a laboratory milieu so that other contaminating factors can be controlled or eliminated. This produces problems about the relevance of experimental results to so-called "true life situations." For example, the subjects may be responding to the demand characteristics of the laboratory study, rather than giving more natural responses.

Indeed, when I was doing research on stress for the military, a frequent criticism was that we could not produce stress that was equivalent to the subjects' belief that they could actually be hit by real bullets, or torn apart by a bomb or killed in a vehicular crash. The subjects in a laboratory study make the reasonable assumption that they will not be harmed psychologically or physically. Presumably, that belief places a limit on their possible stress, and thus erodes external validity.

The results of the experimental investigation apply, strictly speaking, only to the specific subjects who served in the experiment. Only if these subjects are representative of a larger population can the results be applicable to that larger population. A number of experiments have shown, however, that the persons who volunteer to serve in psychological experiments tend to have somewhat different personality characteristics than those who decline to volunteer. The volunteers are a bit more adventuresome, for example. This would not necessarily be important if one were doing research on, say, visual acuity or on memorization of meaningless material, but it probably would be important if the research involved risk-taking behavior, such as gambling, sky-diving or night patrol in a combat area.

Therefore, the results that are obtained in the laboratory tell us, strictly speaking, only about that laboratory behavior. These data may, or may not, tell us about the subjects' behavior in apparently similar true-life situations. This problem of the generalizability of results and conclusions from laboratory to real situations is *always* present.

Psychologists tend to use animal subjects because of the dual advantages of improved control of conditions and less expense. LeShan argued that mainstream psychology has used such advantages as excuses to study only those behavioral processes that lend themselves to easy laboratory control and less expense.[18] The use of animals is based on the assumption that basically the same principles of behavior apply to both animals and humans. Surely, some do, but clearly some do not. For example, factors such as verbal interpretation and communication are characteristic of humans and only minimally present in animals, if at all. Because most of the important problems in human life do not lend themselves to laboratory control, however, much of the psychological research literature is based on frequently irrelevant laboratory research with laboratory rats and college sophomores.

Le Shan cited a good example from the laboratory study of rat sexual behavior.[19] He pointed out that, while the female rat in the wild initiates sexual activity with the male by approaching him within three to four body lengths, ordinarily in the laboratory situation she cannot get that far away from him. Presumably, therefore, the male rat considers the female in the laboratory to be constantly interested in sex. Consequently, laboratory studies of rat sexual behavior probably generate exaggerated ideas of sexual interest in the male rat.

A major problem in interpreting data in the laboratory, with respect to what happens outside of the laboratory, is the existence of interactions. Interactions are contingent effects of variables that may change from one situation to another. The effects of a manipulated variable may be different if some other—presumed extraneous and unimportant—variable is changed. Such interactions occur even in physiological studies of behavior. For example, Cronbach presented the following example of an interaction that made predictions of physiological behavior difficult:

> Investigators checking on how animals metabolize drugs found that results differed mysteriously from laboratory to laboratory. The most startling inconsistency of all occurred after a refurbishing of a National Institutes of Health (NIH) animal room brought in new cages and new supplies. Previously, a mouse would sleep for about 35 minutes after a standard injection of hexobarbital. In their new homes, the NIH mice came miraculously back to their feet just 16 minutes after receiving a shot of the drug. Detective work proved that red-cedar bedding made the difference, stepping up the activity of several enzymes that metabolize hexobarbital.[20]

When the cedar bedding was replaced with the original birch or maple bedding, the original reaction to the drug returned. This is the physiological parallel of a contextual effect in social psychology. For a physiologist to know how long the effects of the drug will last, he or she must know also what type of bedding is being used for the animals. Similarly, a social psychologist needs to know the mental set of a subject in order to predict his or her response to, say, a request for help. The bedding is like the social context.

Similar problems with generalization of results also occur when humans are the subjects. For example, LeShan argued that the results of the classic Milgram obedience study were largely determined by the artificiality of the laboratory environment.[21] In that study, people were instructed to administer electric shocks to a person in a learning experiment whenever the person allegedly made a mistake. Actually, the true subject in the experiment was the person *giving* the shocks, because the alleged learner was actually a confederate of the experimenter. The stooge was only pretending to be making mistakes and receiving shocks. The interesting and disturbing aspect of the study was that the subjects administered, under specific instructions, supposed levels of shock that they had been led to believe were dangerously high. LeShan argued that these results were only relevant to the unnatural environment of the laboratory research, to which a different ethical rule was considered relevant by the subjects—the rule to obey the instructions of the experimenter.

Deese also emphasized the problem of assuming a particular belief state in the subject. Ordinarily, the subject must believe that he or she is not participating in the particular study for which the data is to be obtained. As Deese said:

> But belief is a complicated state, as even psychologists know, and it cannot be dismissed by asserting that a subject believes or does not believe, or is deluded or not deluded. . . .A subject may have to invent all sorts of myths, stories, or hypotheses to account for the remarkable series of events he faces in the psychological laboratory. These hypotheses may bear no relations to what the experimenter thinks is going on in the subject's mind. But they may have some relevance to what a subject does in the experimental situation. . . .In short, the subject does not always have in his head the conceptions that the experimenter thinks he has, yet the interpretation of such experiments often depends on that assumption.[22]

Therefore, even the so-called rigorous laboratory science in psychology entails a degree of intuition and supposition, despite attempts to imitate the ideals of the physical sciences. There is always a potential problem in inferring the cause of an event.

Data versus Interpretation

There is a story, presumably true, about the head of a prestigious women's college at about the time Kinsey published his reports on sexual habits. According to the story, the president gathered the student body into an assembly and asked all non-virgins to raise their hands. After counting hands, she declared in print that something over 95 percent of the women at her institution were virgins. This was obviously a ridiculous conclusion because there was apparently nothing in the situation to induce the students to condemn themselves in public. In fact, the college administrator certainly did not even deserve a truthful answer to such an outrageous, invasive question, asked in public.

She did have third-person (empirical) data, to be sure. If she had concluded that over 95 percent of her students *had declared* themselves to be virgins, her statement could not be disputed. She would have then been using data language which is merely a verbal or quantitative description of the data. Her error was that she failed to consider the enormous difference between declaring yourself in public to be a virgin, and actually being a virgin.

Data interpretation is the conclusion about psychological principles or processes that is reached by the investigator. This lady merely assumed her students would not lie. But she needed some independent corroboration, some converging evidence for that assumption. Thus, we must know when the reporting is actual data, and when the reporting is someone's personal interpretation of that data.

The Research Literature

Another problem in reaching scientific conclusions comes from the process of publishing research results. Basically, conclusions are reached from published results, although there are informal information networks and conferences in which research results are shared in verbal communications among interested scientists. Therefore, errors in the selection of articles to be published can produce publication of substandard work and failure of publication for meritorious work.

Publishability in journals for psychological research is usually determined by a two-tiered process, under the general rubric of peer review. Thus, the scientific merit of a research submission is judged by nominal peers of the authors. First, the researcher submits his or her research report to a journal that is perceived by the author as appropriate. If the action editor of that journal considers the content and merit of the report to be appropriate for that journal, he or she refers it for evaluation to several reviewers, selected for their presumed expertise. The reviewers submit their comments and recommendations about the publishability of the research report to the action editor, who then accepts or rejects the submission, or asks for revision and re-submission.

Because the action editors and peer reviewers are successful products of the system—namely, highly published authors—they can be guilty of perpetuating its products. According to Mahoney, the system tends to be biased in favor of topics, terms, methods and authors that are familiar to the evaluators.[23] Such personal and professional biases are, of course, not in the best interests of behavioral science. Mahoney documented some of the questionable factors that actually increase the likelihood of acceptance of an article for publication, as follows: a) authors' prestige, b) institutional prestige, c) self-citation, d) avoidance of direct replication, e) achievement of statistical significance, f) reporting results that are consistent with the particular viewpoint of the journal and g) *unintelligible* writing, which means to deceive the reviewer into thinking that a report must be truly profound if he or she cannot understand it. The major categories of advantage seem to be the authors' prestige, the institutional prestige and writing to the incompetence of the reviewers.

Unfortunately, none of the factors listed by Mahoney contributes directly to progress of the science, because they mean that the best empirical research on a topic is not available to the scientific community. The unavailability of some research reports produces what Rosenthal has called the file-drawer problem.[24] That is, the researcher who is unable to publish his or her work consigns it to a personal file, rendering it unavailable to other researchers.

Thus, the published literature tends to be biased in favor of popular theories, methodologies, results and authors, particularly those authors from more prestigious institutions. Moreover, the unpublished studies may be endlessly repeated by other researchers, particularly those who are not connected to an informal communication network of prestigious researchers. The problems of peer review thus indicate that science cannot be devoid of subjective influences because it is conducted by fallible human beings.

Indeed, many accounts of alleged biases in peer review have appeared in the psychological literature. A particularly egregious case was described by Harcum and Rosen.[25] They reported great editorial opposition to their repeated attempts to report a series of studies that attempted to open a new line of research, which proved that an important proposition by an eminent psychologist was absolutely incorrect. In fact, the major journals in the research area refused to publish their work, prompting Harcum and Rosen to review in print the work of the editors and the reviewers in a most unflattering light.

The subject of the Harcum and Rosen research was a proposition of the eminent psychologist, B. F. Skinner.[26] This proposition was promoted over several years and eventually provided the thesis for his celebrated book, *Beyond Freedom and Dignity*. Skinner attempted to explain why society opposed progress in science, particularly the thoroughgoing deterministic science of behavior that he advocated.

The first point Skinner proposed, and no one disputed, is that the members of society tend to award dignity, or worth, to those individuals whom society perceives as having performed credible deeds voluntarily. Skinner's second point also has not been disputed: science can discover hereditary and environmental causes for behaviors that were previously attributed to voluntary choice. But, Harcum and Rosen disputed Skinner's final conclusion: that society fears that a continuing successful science could eventually destroy the concept of voluntary choice, and thereby eliminate the very possibility of according dignity to human beings.

In opposition to Skinner, Harcum and Rosen argued that our society also accords an unlearned, or intrinsic, dignity to its members, which therefore would not in any way be threatened by scientific progress. This argument destroyed Skinner's proposed practical reason for society to abandon its cherished belief in voluntary choice.

Skinner provided no empirical evidence for his assertion. This is ironic in view of Skinner's long and distinguished track record in empirical science, and strong advocacy for data. No one had called attention to this lack of data. Surely, only a person of Skinner's stature could have published such strong conclusions without data, and without immediate complaint. This circumstance is, unfortunately, most damaging to the lofty claims for the reliance on objective science of psychology. It should give pause to anyone who wishes to place the future of our civilization on the hallowed shoulders of science alone.

Indeed, ancient and modern literature, not to say the culture about us, is replete with references to intrinsic human dignity. Surely that literature is not limited to religious authors.

Nevertheless, Harcum and Rosen reasoned, obviously correctly, that the Behaviorists would not be convinced without laboratory evidence. Accordingly, they attempted to document the popular belief in intrinsic human dignity. In a series of experiments, they employed several methods, all of which consistently indicated that various groups of subjects do believe in an intrinsic (innate) dignity of all human beings. For example, they showed that newborn babies, who surely have not had the opportunity to earn dignity, were in fact reported by many subjects to have it.

The stated reasons for rejection of the Harcum and Rosen submissions fell into two categories: a) their data did not prove that society believed in intrinsic human dignity, and b) the belief in intrinsic dignity had nothing to do with any arguments of B. F. Skinner. The authors subsequently charged that the evaluations of their work were hindered by the evaluators' unwillingness to concede that a prestigious standard bearer for scientific rigor had promulgated a thesis on the basis of no data, and, moreover, that his thesis had actually been proved to be incorrect.

There was really no consistency among the comments of the editors and evaluators who read the submissions, except for the negative recommendations. The general absence of scientific objectivity was starkly revealed by one editor, who did not think the particular research report of Harcum and Rosen even merited a referral to reviewers, and so rejected it outright himself without referral to reviewers. The following is an excerpt from his comments:

> I have to admit that I wasn't quite sure what point you wanted to make with your paper. In a way, you take on a straw person in Fred Skinner. I suppose there are those who still take his pronouncements seriously, but I haven't encountered any recently. That is not to say that his work (and that of other behaviorists such as Hull) has not had an impact on our field, some good and some bad, but that is not the same as saying that his particular (and somewhat peculiar) notions about dignity have any currency. While I haven't read *Beyond Freedom and Dignity* in years, I would be very surprised if he meant that all forms of human dignity have to be earned. Skinner was (and remains), whatever you may think of his theory, an acute observer of human behavior, and would not likely have missed the obvious point that in this and other societies we accord the old, the young, and the helpless some forms of respect and dignity.[27]

To be sure, a reader may be excused for thinking that this review could be taken as support for the Harcum and Rosen submission, rather than a reason for rejecting it. These comments support several of the negative conclusions of Mahoney about the reviewing process.[28] Surely this editor did not consider himself or herself to be a peer of the authors. Does this represent a science that should be allowed to rule our lives?

Several years after the above editor pronounced Skinner's arguments dead, Baum published a book strongly supporting the strict deterministic approach.[29] Therefore, one conclusion seems inescapable: if behavioral science is to be the savior of the world, it must be, first, scrupulous in following its own good principles; and, second, it must be broadened in concept to permit more inclusive acceptance of different forms of data. Science itself must embrace objective thinking, but it must deal also with subjective data.

Indeed, the cavalier comments of the editor quoted above soundly condemn the very concept of the peer review, and give credence to those who say that psychology represents fad and fashion, and not the ideal of objective science. Surely, the above quotation does not have the sound of one researcher writing to a peer—meaning a colleague of equal skill and experience. This editor is not quite sure of the facts (namely, had not read the relevant work in years), but nevertheless, if these lesser authors say that Skinner is wrong, then they must surely be wrong.

To be sure, some may say that science triumphed because the authors persevered until their results were ultimately published. But, the costs to truth and science were incalculable. First, there was an unnecessary and inordinate delay in dissemination of the research results. Second, there was an inordinate waste of professional effort and resources in re-writes, re-submissions and multiple evaluations. Third, the eventual journals of publication were not the best for the particular research topic. And, finally, the researchers were thoroughly dissuaded from pursuing further a promising line of research. This is not a failure of scientific philosophy, but of the actual practice of science. So, the lesson for the neophyte scientist—indeed, to all of us— is clear: do not believe everything you read.

Discussion

After hearing descriptions of all of the pitfalls in conducting and interpreting psychological research, some college students complain that psychologists therefore are not sure about any of their conclusions. But that is an overreaction to my words of caution. Given the sensibility and importance of psychological information to our society, I would rather err on the side of caution. It is all a part of giving psychology away. Science must be treated like a loaded gun—necessary for the right purposes, but deadly in the wrong hands.

Psychologists do know a great deal about the causation of behavior. Even the conventional introductory books in psychology present only a selected sample of what we know. To be sure, all psychologists are trained to recognize and to deal with these pitfalls of interpretation. Nevertheless, mistakes are made, in terms of research published that should not have been, as well as meritorious research that was denied publication. You must learn to identify the errors for yourself.

Science is Open-Minded

The goal of science is to establish principles and laws of behavior. A principle is a statement of a uniformity in nature that can be used to guide behavior. The evidence for a principle is not strong enough to consider it a law, although such confirming evidence may be found in the future. A law is a principle supported by such strong evidence that it is not subject to doubt, *unless new disconfirming information about it is obtained.* Note that even a law can be modified or refuted by new evidence.

An example of a law in physics is the law of gravity. While we do not doubt it, nevertheless we cannot know with certainty that it will never be modified by some new unanticipated evidence. Indeed, in my personal experience, a reversal of established principles is possible. I learned in high school physics that the atom was the irreducible substance of matter. In graduate school, I learned that color television was not physically possible.

An example of a well-established principle in psychology is the law of least effort. It says that, all things equal, the individual will perform the behavior that requires the least physical effort. But, as I showed in my study of seating behaviors, the need to enhance personal esteem can at times overpower this principle when these motivations are made to compete.[30]

Another well-established law in psychology is the law of effect, which says that a response followed by satisfaction of some motivation (is rewarded) tends to be repeated. Although this law is a verity in psychology, and actually familiar to everyone, it does not tell us that the repetition of the rewarded act is inevitable. The reason lies in the possible effects of a host of other relevant variables, personal and environmental. For example, you are not very likely to increase a helping behavior by a friend by giving him or her a monetary reward for the help.

The neophyte students of psychology must understand that not everything they read or hear about the field or its principles is true, or can be literally applied. They need to develop for themselves skills for evaluating specific allegations. The danger in the universal adaptability of psychological knowledge is that many half-truths and exaggerations abound. The reader is therefore cautioned to beware of overgeneralizations. In fact, almost all firm declarations about the specific causation of behavior should be qualified. Often, to be sure, the qualifications are not mentioned in order to avoid being tedious. For example, we say in general that thinking occurs primarily in the cerebral cortex of the brain (the so-called gray matter), but we must not ignore the role of such factors as human motivations and emotions in the thinking process. These factors involve other areas of the brain.

Science Has Value

The analytical approach to the study of human behavior has general value for daily life. One individual trying to understand the acts of another may perform very simple experiments, or correlational or naturalistic studies. To do this, he or she obviously must know something about the tools of science. This will help him or her to know which factors to observe, or to correlate, or to manipulate in an experiment.

In the case of naturalistic observation, the student would observe the behavior of a person over a period of time to determine what behaviors appeared most frequently. In the case of the correlational approach, they would observe what inputs were present, or what internal conditions existed at about the time the person produced certain acts. On the basis of this first information, he or she might even try to manipulate inputs to the person to see what acts were forthcoming. Once the student of behavior found the correct input to produce the desired act, he or she could help that person to make the correct act by attempting to establish the appropriate conditions for it.

The scientific method is thus a problem-solving approach. It attempts to discover the conditions that bring forth certain acts in a person. Therefore, training to do research is training in problem-solving. Development of this analytic skill is unquestionably necessary for a person to become fully educated.

Some humanists of an extreme sort argue that such use of behavioral science is improper because it is dehumanizing, treating human beings as objects of study, like guinea pigs. To me, the question of morality hinges on the attitudes, mind sets and goals of the practitioners. If the goal is to show concern for fellow human beings by trying to help and to improve the human condition, how can it be evil if it is done with sense and good taste?

Morality of Scientists

Finally, I raise a most disturbing question: is behavioral science too important to leave to behavioral scientists? Given the number of scientists who deny the undeniable presence of value and moral judgment in science, how can we leave the final decisions about the morality of conclusions about society to them? Therefore, science must also be monitored by men and women who are dually trained in science and in morality. Ironically, only those who understand morality can truly be objective about their science.

Summary

The various basic methods of psychological research are listed and described in this chapter. The first of these methods is naturalistic observation, in which the behavior of a subject person in some situation is merely described. This method includes anecdotal (in which stories about instances of behavior are collected), case history (systemic gathering of information about a person), observation (direct observation of behavior), survey (questioning a sample of people on selected topics) and clinical (study of persons with unusual experiences and behaviors).

The second basic method is correlational, in which the relationships between certain acts and input factors and other conditions are observed and recorded. It was emphasized that a correlation between two variables does not necessarily mean that one caused the other. In order to reach the conclusion of causation, supporting (converging) evidence is needed.

The third basic technique, which determines the effect of actually manipulating a potential factor, is the experimental method. The procedure is to have a control condition that provides a reference point of usual performance. A variable is manipulated to produce an experimental condition that is compared to the performance under the control condition. If the results of the two conditions are different—and only the manipulation of the research variable makes the two conditions different—the manipulated variable is accorded responsibility for the difference.

The advantages and disadvantages of each scientific method were discussed. Interpretational pitfalls were discussed. Examples of sources of interpretational error were placebo effects (subjects respond as they interpret the manipulation) and demand characteristics (subjects respond as they perceive the situation requires). The new student of psychology is also cautioned about believing uncritically what appears in the literature of psychology, because science does not produce an error-free product.

The problems of generalizing results of research from a laboratory or controlled environment to "true life" situations are discussed. The critical factor is the degree of psychological similarity between the research environment and the real environment to which the research results are to be applied.

The reader is cautioned to make the distinction between a presentation of empirical results, or data, and the interpretation of those results. Interpretations can be in error because they are the result of subjective evaluation of the empirical results.

The general value of the scientific approach for daily living is then discussed. Use of various methods to solve the numerous problems that arise from the daily interaction among people is discussed.

Finally, the author raises the issue of morality in science. He asks whether or not behavioral science is too important to leave to the scientists. Perhaps crucial social decisions based on behavioral data should be reached by behavioral scientists who are also trained in moral reasoning, and are monitored by the people of God.

Notes

1. E. Rae Harcum, Parity for the theoretical ghosts and gremlins: Response to Pollis/Henley and Rychlak, *The Journal of Mind and Behavior, 12*: 151-162, 1991.
2. J. R. Royce, Heretical thoughts on the definition of psychology, *Psychological Reports, 8*: 11-13, 1961.
3. Lawrence LeShan, *The Dilemma of Psychology*. (New York: Dutton, 1990). 158.
4. W. W. Harman, The transpersonal challenge to the scientific paradigm: The need for a restructuring of science. *ReVision, 11*: 13-21, 1988, 13.
5. E. Rae Harcum, The relative utility of complementary disparate views on voluntarism and determinism. *The Journal of Psychology, 125*: 217-228, 1990.
6. E. Rae Harcum, *A Psychology of Freedom and Dignity* (Westport CT: Praeger, 1994); C. J. Gelso, Two different worlds: A paradox in counseling and psychotherapy, *Journal of Counseling Psychology, 17*: 271-278, 1970; Rollo May, *Psychology and the Human Dilemma* (Princeton: Van Nostrand, 1967); Irvin D. Yalom, *Existential Psychotherapy* (New York: Basic Books, 1980).
7. Gelso, *Two different worlds*. 1970.
8. John B. Watson, Psychology as the Behaviorist views it, *Psychological Review, 20*: 158-177, 1913.
9. B. F. Skinner, Beyond Freedom and Dignity (New York: Knopf, 1971). 19.
10. D. W. Zimmerman, A note on the completeness of the scientific method, *Psychological Record, 34*: 175-179, 1984.
11. Phoebe M. Harcum, personal communication, January 2, 2000.
12. E. Rae Harcum, A classroom demonstration of the difference between correlation and causality, *Perceptual and Motor Skills, 66*: 801-802, 1988.
13. I. D. Eron, L. R. Huesmann, M. M. Lefkowitz and L. O. Walder, Does television violence cause aggression? *American Psychologist, 27*: 253-263, 1972.
14. E. Rae Harcum, *Incidental Psychotherapy Within Christian Relationships* (Lanham, MD: Hamilton Books, 2011).
15. E. Rae Harcum, Behavioral paradigm for a psychological resolution of the free-will issue, *The Journal of Mind and Behavior, 12*: 93-114, 1991.
16. James Deese, *Psychology as Science and Art* (New York: Harcourt, Brace and Jovanovich, 1972); LeShan, *The Dilemma of Psychology* (New York: Dutton, 1990).
17. LeShan, *The Dilemma of Psychology*. 1990.
18. Ibid.

19. Ibid.
20. Lee J. Cronbach, Beyond the two disciplines of scientific psychology, *American Psychologist, 30*: 116-127, 1975, 121.
21. LeShan, *The Dilemma of Psychology*, 1990; Stanley Milgram, Behavioral study of obedience, *Journal of Abnormal and Social Psychology, 67*: 371-378, 1963.
22. Deese, *Psychology as Science and Art* (1972). 25.
23. Michael J. Mahoney, Publications, politics and scientific progress, *The Behavioral and Brain Sciences, 5*: 220- 221, 1982.
24. Robert Rosenthal, The "file-drawer problem" and tolerance for null results, *Psychological Bulletin, 86*: 638-641, 1979.
25. E. Rae Harcum and Ellen F. Rosen, *The Gatekeepers of Psychology* (Westport, CT: Praeger, 1993).
26. Skinner, *Beyond Freedom and Dignity*, 1971.
27. Harcum and Rosen, *The Gatekeepers of Psychology* (1993). 55.
28. Mahoney, Publications, politics, and scientific progress. 1982.
29. W. M. Baum, *Understanding Behaviorism* (New York: HarperCollins, 1994).
30. Harcum, Behavioral paradigm for a psychological resolution of the free-will issue. 1991.

Chapter 5

Models of Behavior

Models of behavior are often confused with theories. The difference is that a model is an analogy to help us understand the function of a psychological process, whereas a theory is a serious proposition about the true nature of the process. Thus, a model is definitely not intended to reflect exactly how the behavior is produced. This is what a theory tries to do. A theory is like a hypothesis, except that a hypothesis attempts to explain a particular behavior, whereas the theory tries to explain a grouping or category of such individual behaviors. The theorist believes that the behavior is produced literally in the way described by the theory. Thus, the theory is a guess at the truth. Accordingly, a theory may be falsified by reference to disconfirming data.

In contrast, a model cannot be falsified. It may merely be deemed inappropriate as an analogy, and thus not useful. If the person who constructs an alleged model believes that his or her construction actually describes the mechanism by which a behavior is produced, then he or she has crafted a theory, and not a model. Therefore, we do not ask whether a model is correct. We merely ask whether or not it is useful to us in organizing our thinking about the principles of behavior.

A psychological model is also not to be confused with a replica or reproduction of a thing, either as full-sized or in miniature. Therefore, it is not like a model airplane, for example, which accurately depicts the original airplane on a smaller scale. Also, it is not like a model home which is a literal actualization of the architectural plans for a particular home. Both of these uses of the term imply an actual reproduction, perhaps on a different scale, rather than a symbolic representation.

Psychologists construct models of behavior in order to help us direct our thinking about the principles that determine the behavior. A model provides a useful way to represent the relationships among those variables. It offers an easily understandable mechanism that could produce a given behavior so that the principle determining the behavior can be more easily understood. For example, I can use the functioning of a thermostat on a furnace as a model for the principle of homeostasis, which reflects the maintenance of a constant internal environment for the body. This model indicates that too much, or too little, of something within the body, detected by sensors, causes certain structures to modify the output of that thing. This process continues until the need is corrected. But, to be sure, there is no need or intention to assume that the heat adjustment device in the thermostat works in exactly the same way that the heat sensor and controller works in the body.

Another example of employing a psychological model would be to say that a human being is like an automobile. An automobile needs fuel to move, like a person needs energy to behave. Thus, a person needs motivation to propel, or drive, actions if he or she is to move at all in any direction—that is, merely to behave in some manner. The automobile also needs a gear shift and a steering wheel to determine in which direction it will travel, once there is power to move the wheels. The person also needs some internal mechanisms to determine in which direction the energized action will take. In other words, a person requires some mechanism to control what particular response will be used to satisfy the prevailing motivations. Thus, some mechanism of human anatomy acts like a steering wheel to select behaviors. But, to be sure, no one would suggest that there is literally a steering wheel within the human anatomy. Therefore, the automobile represents a model, not a theory.

We can also say that human beings are like computers in that they take in information and refer it to some memory storage bank in order to select a response. Then, they select an appropriate response routine on the basis of the way the individual person has been programmed. In a human being, the programming is produced by the joint effects of the genetic inheritance and personal experiences. Thus, the computer can serve as a model for certain human behaviors.

Although both of these models—automobile and computer—are indeed useful ways to think about human beings in some contexts, obviously they have limitations. For example, there are obvious ways that human beings are not at all like automobiles or computers: namely, they are not composed of metal or microchips, and do not need to be oiled or plugged into a power source.

Indeed, there also are obviously some things that automobiles and computers can do that humans cannot do. And there are some things that humans can do that automobiles and computers cannot. Although the computer can perform feats of memory and calculation that are far beyond the capability of a human brain, computers cannot read between the lines of an instruction in ways that they have not been programmed. They cannot correctly interpret instructions that represent obviously wrong, or silly, errors. They cannot recognize tongue-in-cheek comments, or sarcasm. They cannot perceive other relationships that people can interpret easily, such as reading maps. They can be programmed to simulate human thought, of course, but a programmed computer can be tripped up by simple tricks that humans can handle easily.

Throughout this book, there are many other analogies to help the student understand a given psychological mechanism. For example, we can say that selective human attention works like an auditory filter, which blocks some sounds, but lets other sounds through. Physiological arousal is like putting a coin in a jukebox, which turns the machine on, thus enabling it to function. Bottling up tension is like putting a tight lid on a kettle of boiling water, causing the kettle to explode, or, as we say, to "blow its top." To produce a thinking disorder through stress is like giving a machine conflicting inputs that it is not designed to handle, causing it to jam, or to respond inappropriately in gross ways—to go "haywire."

Models can have varying degrees of complexity, of course. The level of complexity for a given model depends upon both the need for complexity in a particular context, and the skill of the model builder at capturing a sufficient number of the properties of the entity. To be sure, any model of human behavior that I can produce will be far too simple, no matter how complex the model. What Joyce Kilmer said about describing a tree in a poem is equally true of describing a person through a model of a person. Models and theories are made by fools like me, but only God can make a person.

Let us now consider some existing models of human behavior. These models range from one that is appropriate for very simple reflex operations to one that is appropriate for the most complex of human behaviors. Some psychologists would employ each of the models as it was appropriate for a given situation, while others (the Behaviorists) would consider only the simplest (S–R) one as appropriate and complete.

S–R Model

The simplest model of behavior is the S–R model, which is merely the letters S and R connected by a dash or an arrow. The S represents an observable stimulus, and the R represents the overt response that has been produced by that stimulus. This model indicates that the only important relations in psychology concern which stimuli evoke which responses.

A machine-like version of this model would be a child's piggybank, in which the deposit of a coin in the slot at the top causes the pig to tip his hat. Because a direct mechanical arrangement in the bank forces the hat to tip whenever a coin in inserted, the relationship between the two events is necessary and constant. Therefore, this would be an appropriate model for stimulus-bound behaviors.

The psychologists who are called Strict Behaviorists are satisfied with such a simple model. They are satisfied because they are basically, or nominally, atheoretical. They do not want to guess or theorize about what is going on in the organism between the input stimulus and the output responses. They just want to discover and describe the empirical relationships between the stimulus (coin insertion) and the response (tip of the hat).

The direct mechanical arrangement is built-in by the nature of the nervous system of the species, and modified by learning experiences. The behavior is stimulus-bound because no ambiguity in response selection is added by some other mechanism. This approach has been called atheoretical in content. Indeed, however, arguably it is a kind of theoretical approach because it asserts that there is nothing to theorize about, or no profit in theorizing at this time because we know so little about the actual mechanisms of causation.

To be sure, most psychologists would agree that such a simple S–R model is sufficient for the so-called stimulus-bound behaviors. A scream of pain is surely likely if a person accidentally sits on a hot curling iron. But, only the Strict Behaviorists believe that this model is sufficient to describe fully the most complex behaviors.

There are cases, of course, in which behaviors cannot be unambiguously attached to a particular stimulus. For example, figuratively the coin may not always produce a tip of the hat, or the hat may be tipped when there has been no prior insertion of a coin. In such a case, the Strict Behaviorists argue that the problem for understanding is produced merely by the difficulty in discovering the fact or actuality of the relationships. In other words, the mechanism within the piggybank may be more complicated, but it is still basically a mechanical arrangement. To be sure, the critical stimulus event could have occurred even years before the response. Nevertheless, the lingering trace of the experience could still be currently effective. In any case, there remains the problem for these psychologists of identifying exactly the natures of the alleged stimuli and the alleged responses, and to describe their relationship. While this argument provides a reasonable excuse for failure to verify the theory, it also provides a justification for failure to falsify the theory. Therefore, this theoretical issue cannot be resolved at this time.

S–O–R Model

Most psychologists would insist on at least one modification of the S–R model. That modification is the S–O–R model, which adds an O between the S and R to represent specific characteristics of the behaving Organism (O). The reason for this addition is that there are usually things going on inside the organism that have major effects on the particular response that will be produced by a given stimulus. The addition of the O indicates the presence of mediating and moderating mechanisms between the S and the R.

The organism itself mediates or moderates, and thus often changes the effects of the stimulus. The organism therefore produces ambiguity in the response, often preventing stimulus-bound behavior. The organismic factors include such processes as attention, arousal, mental set, motivation and emotion.

We may ask how the proponents of the S–R model explain the effects of mediating or moderating variables. For example, how do they deal with the fact that an aroused—say, angry—person responds differently from a calm person? The Strict Behaviorists simply refer to observable antecedent variables. They go back to the observation of the annoying stimulus; the response of a person subjected to that particular stimulus responds differently compared to a person who was not subjected to that earlier stimulus.

The Cognitive Behaviorists accept the S–O–R model. Cognitions occur within the organism.

S–O–R Cyclic Model

The S–O–R model is still too static and restrictive because it isolates a stimulus-response event from the continuing flow of events. Specifically, the response to one stimulus typically has an important influence on later stimulation. For example, if you respond to the desire for food by running into a fast-food restaurant, you now find yourself in a different stimulus situation than if you had resisted the original urge, and had followed the urge to go instead to the library. Consequently, you are now expected to read and probably prevented from eating. Therefore, an improvement in the S–O–R model is as follows: S–O–R–S–O–R–S–O–R–S–O–R, etc. The sequence of Ss, Os and Rs would stretch from the present time in the person's life backwards to the birth of that person. This holistic description is consistent with the natural necessity conception of causality, which says that any prior event can be a part of the cause of a particular response.[1] So, in a sense, the first S in the series could be the first stimulus to which the person responded as a neonate.

In a practical sense, a series, such as above, is impossible to reproduce and to use. Therefore, for convenience, we typically shorten it by drawing an arrow from the R back to the S to produce the S–O–R Cyclic model. In such a case, the arrow from R back to S is called the feedback from the response, indicating that the response feeds back to influence the stimulation for the next response. Nevertheless, it truly is a feedforward mechanism because a response cannot, to be sure, actually influence events backward in time. Indeed, an S–O–R sequence is embedded in a much longer sequence of Ss, Os and Rs.

Simple Functional Model

A bit more complicated form of the S–O–R cyclic model, modified from Harcum, is shown in Figure 5-1.[2] This model, called the Simple Functional Model, adds a general description of the three major functions, or processes, that take place inside the O (organism) in the S–O–R cyclic model. They are: Believing, Directing and Selecting. These functions are complexly interrelated, and surely not discretely different from one another.

In Figure 5-1, the circle represents essentially the organism, the part that is responsible for idiosyncratic responding. It includes the personal agent and other control processes of memory, emotion and motivation that are intimately associated with it. These are the most important sources of individual differences.

The model in Figure 5-1 is slightly different from the one proposed by Harcum.[3] Specifically, the three internal parts of the personality are converted from things (i.e., views, desires and decisions) to processes (i.e., believing, directing and selecting). These terms are a bit broader in scope. Therefore, they are more comprehensive and dynamic.

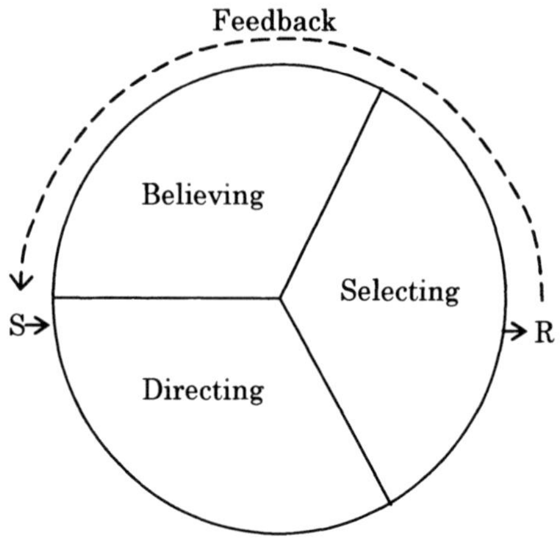

Figure 5-1: A simple functional model of a person

Believing

The believing process begins with interpreting the input that the individual person receives through sense organs. The interpreting mechanism makes sense out of the input stimulation by referring it to the memory bank developed from previous experience. The person assesses what the input means to himself or herself. For example, the person asks whether or not the input represents a perceived threat to personal safety. Or, the person asks if the relevant adaptive behavior conflicts with his or her conception of right and wrong. Or, it may be that the input is perceived at the time as just not worthy of any coping response at all. In short, this process reflects how the person views and understands the way the world works, and what it means to him or her.

Directing

The directing function leads the organism toward different responses according to different learned and unlearned motivations and emotions that are prevailing at the time. Suppose, for example, the stimulus is provided by a hot fudge sundae. The response to eat or not to eat could be determined by the person's uncontrollable passion for fudge and ice cream. Or the response could be controlled by his or her craving for a thinner body, or by an allergy to chocolate or milk. The person may not eat because of a commitment to religious fasting, or by the need to rush off to class to keep from being late, or by a need not to appear to be a pig in front of friends. Indeed, all of these motivations, and surely more, could be present at one time, producing ambiguity in the response.

Selecting

The overt response is thus a resultant of many response tendencies of different strengths. The one response that ultimately wins out depends upon the relative strengths of the various pushes that are simultaneously aroused. To be sure, the ultimate selection of a response from among them may not be difficult. If there is really no contest among the various response tendencies in the particular situation, the decision is made quickly and easily—the familiar "no-brainer."

On the other hand, the selection of the actual overt response may require an anguished and lengthy consideration of all possible consequences, in the style of Prince Hamlet. This dynamic model thus emphasizes the possible multiple causation of behaviors. The final response is likely to be the resultant of many different forces pushing in different directions.

A given motivation might be satisfied by several possible overt responses. For example, a need for dessert could be satisfied by choosing any of several sweet items. A need for aggression against a person could be satisfied by verbally insulting, hitting, stabbing or shooting. Similarly, a given overt response might be used to satisfy more than one particular motivation. For example, a verbal insult may be aggressive, or it may be a way of bolstering self-esteem, or part of a behavioral strategy to humiliate or to subjugate another person.

Response selection thus represents the blocking or suppression of some response tendencies, and the passage of others. Consequently, there is passage or facilitation of some particular response tendency, or possibly several others, if they are not incompatible with one another.

Because of the multiple causation of behaviors, a concept of a final common path (FCP) is necessary. This concept considers the response-production process to be like a channel, or conduit, through which only some response tendencies can pass at one time for the ultimate overt responding. The ones that pass will be ultimately manifested in overt behaviors.

One model that could accurately describe this selection process would be a handful of marbles dropped into a funnel. All of the marbles cannot pass through simultaneously. The marbles would represent response tendencies, and the order of passage would represent the final selection of overt responses. Thus, two or more marbles can mutually block passage through the funnel. In such a case, it would be difficult to predict which marble, or which response, would get through. In fact, no marble could get through—absolute inaction of any behavior. To be sure, total inaction is actually an action. Sitting absolutely still, without moving a muscle, is still a response.

Another appropriate model for this competition process among response tendencies would be a group of people trying to exit a room by a single narrow doorway. The first persons to begin the exit prevent, or preempt, the others from leaving until the early birds have passed. As we know, too many people trying to exit at the same time may block the exit for each other and for all others, such that no one can leave.

In the behavioral situation, the tendency to respond to each stimulus may prevent the expression of all others, so that no active response at all can be made. Tragically, this is a familiar result when there has been a fire in a crowded dance hall. In the case of a single person, because of response competition he or she may be frozen in inaction, with completely passive behavior, just when some immediate response is vital.

Thus, this analogy shows that in some crisis situations no adaptable response tendencies may survive. That is, if a person experiences the push of too many strong response tendencies, he or she might not be able to respond at all appropriately. Ironically, sometimes the greatest stress to respond produces the least capacity to cope with the situation.

The doorway model would describe how the response of not eating a chocolate sundae is incompatible with the response of eating the sundae. Or, the avoidance response from the fear of rejection could block the eager request for a date with an attractive person.

Elaborated Model

The functional model in Figure 5-1 is admittedly very general. Therefore, it is useful regardless of the theoretical bent or methodological preferences of the psychologist, except perhaps the Strict Behaviorist, who theoretically ignores the internal mechanisms. The model will be elaborated as appropriate for the specific applications to be considered in the remainder of the book. This final version should serve in all of the psychological approaches, except Strict Behaviorism.

The Elaborated Model in Figure 5-2 is entirely consistent with the functional model in Figure 5-1. It merely expresses the same components in more detail, along with particular models for some other processes.

As has been said, a model is merely an analogy to represent in a symbolic way the relationships among parts of a system. Nevertheless, it may also help develop some clues about how the function might be accomplished. For example, surely there is not a physical funnel in the nervous system, but I do think that the nervous system sometimes acts like a funnel. Thus, the model in Figure 5-2 cannot be a theory because it represents the function of nerves and neurohumors by symbolic devices.

The Elaborated Model in Figure 5-2 obviates the need to provide theories for all of the processes that mediate responses to certain stimuli. This book does not attempt to describe the mechanisms producing all aspects of human behavior, for two reasons: a) such descriptions are not necessary for achieving the goals of this book, and b) such discussions are easily found in any conventional introductory book in psychology.

The present book does engage, however, the one fundamental issue that is not typically discussed in the conventional books: human agency. The proposal for such an agent requires the best theoretical explanation that we can devise. A

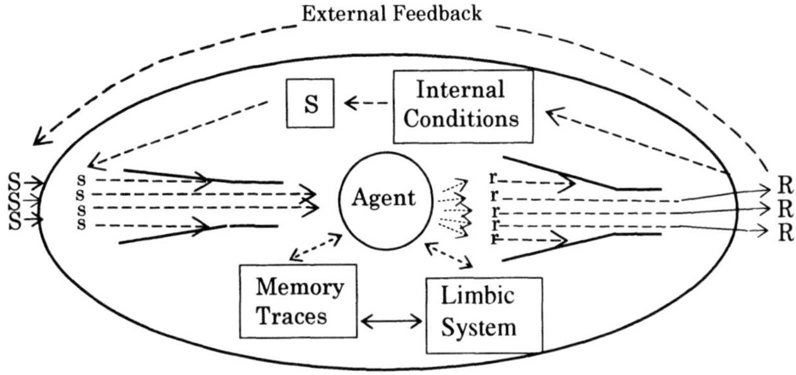

Figure 5-2: An elaborated model of a person

theory will be offered in the next chapter.

In the Elaborated Behavioral Model in Figure 5-2, the large ellipse represents the skin of a person. The three components at the center of the ellipse represent the same mechanisms as the entities within the circle of the Functional Model in Figure 5-1. In general, the agent corresponds to the selecting process, the memory traces correspond to the believing process and the limbic system corresponds to the directing process.

Ss and Rs

The capital Ss outside the skin represent observable stimulus events. These are called distal stimuli. The large Rs represent overt responses, most of them observable, although some require special apparatus for viewing.

Not all of the Ss and Rs are outside of the body, however. For example, stomach contractions are responses, and they produce sensations from inside the body. There can be a dry throat, a full bladder, a stomachache, etc. Examples of other internal physiological responses that would change the internal environment would be sweating, secretion from other glands, change of heart rate, constriction of blood vessels and so forth. Such internal responses are represented by the small box, called Internal Conditions, at the top right within the ellipse.

Those events that lie outside of the body are usually observable through simple visual inspection. For example, the subject steps on the brake pedal in response to a red traffic light. The red light is an easily observed stimulus.

Stimulus Selection

Immediately to the right of the distal stimuli , within the body, are the small letters s, which refer to what are called proximal stimuli. These are the changed or processed internal forms of the distal stimuli. The proximal stimuli are the neural impulses that impinge ultimately on the neural representations of the thought processes, or mind, in the brain of the central nervous system. They are the result of the transduction of the physical stimuli into neural impulses by the receiving organ.

As I said, the rectangle at the top of the figure (Internal Conditions) indicates the conditions within the body as a result of previous stimulations and responses. For example, if the previous responses to the perception of an empty stomach resulted in the ingestion of a hot dog, the stomach would now be at least partially filled with hot dog, bun and mustard. This would produce new distal stimulation (an internal S) for the sensory system to pass on to the central agent—called the Executive. This new distal stimulation then produces proximal stimulation—the small letter s. Later, as the hot dog is digested, there are different neural messages to the Executive—first distal, then proximal.

Psychologically, there is ordinarily no important difference between the external and the internal stimuli. In any particular instance, of course, one or the other may have greater effects on the behavior of certain individuals. Therefore, for the remainder of the book the references to external environment refer to the conditions external to the central nervous system. For example, perceptions of the so-called external world would include perceptions of the various states within one's own body. To be sure, the distal stimuli, whatever their particular location, are converted to proximal neural messages before they reach the mind (brain).

The arrows in the figure indicate the potential pathways of the inputs. To be sure, not all pathways are followed on each administration of a given stimulus. Therefore, the convergence of the arrows at the left in the figure indicates that several proximal stimuli are likely to interact to produce a result that is different from a simple sum of individual inputs. This reflects the field or configurational characteristics of the stimuli, which have been emphasized by the Gestalt psychologists.

The funnel shape at the left in the figure represents a mechanism that allows only some of the proximal stimuli to pass through for further processing. This mechanism is called selectivity of sensation and perception. This mechanism means that the person may not respond to all of the original distal stimuli, which basically represent the real world. The agent must respond to the proximal stimuli that have been massaged by the contextual stimuli. Thus, they have been changed by the transduction mechanism, which has converted the distal stimuli into proximal stimuli. Then, some of them pass through the selectivity mechanism, and some do not. Therefore, the neural representations that reach the Executive for interpretation are drastically changed from the original physical stimuli in the external environment, with possible changes in the information transmitted about the external world.

The possibility that the Executive can perceive distal stimuli directly, bypassing the sensory/perceptual mechanisms represented in this figure, is discussed in the next chapter. Such possibility remains a highly controversial issue in psychology and philosophy.

Semi-Autonomous Central Process

The circle and two rectangular boxes in the center of the figure together indicate symbolically the central nervous system of the person, primarily the brain and certain associated internal organs. These parts are generally equivalent to the circle in Figure 5-1. The memory traces are primarily responsible for the believing process. The limbic system is primarily responsible for the directing (arousal) process. And the Executive Agent is primarily responsible for the selecting process. But, again, these processes are not cleanly separable from one another.

Observation of the internal responses would often require special apparatus. For example, different areas of the brain would become active because of the stimulation by a red light, as opposed to a green light. Similarly, particular motor areas of the brain would become active before the person could operate the muscles that engage the brake of the automobile. Specialists are enjoying continuing success in inferring mental content from physiological recordings of brain activity.

To be sure, some internal responses could be inferred rather directly from their results. For example, one could read the heart beat from the pulse, infer sweating from a wet T-shirt and infer dilated blood capillaries from a blush on the face.

The three components at the center together make up the Semi-Autonomous Central Process (S-ACP), as proposed by Hebb.[4] The mutually connecting (two-headed) arrows in the S-ACP indicate the intimate and complex interrelationships among the three central parts. Hebb proposed that there must be some mechanism within the brain, continuously active, which both massages and interprets the proximal stimulation. Thus, this mechanism is continuously interacting with incoming proximal stimulation as long as the person is alive. It is reflected in the continuous activity of the brain—so-called brain waves, which are the changes in electrical activity in the electroencephalograph (EEG).

The process is called semi-autonomous because it can function partly independently (autonomously) of the stimulus input. For example, the person may be essentially unaware of the sensory stimulation from the environment. This could happen if he or she were concentrating on some fascinating or worrisome idea. Then, we often say that the person is "lost in thought," or that his or her "mind is a million miles away." In such a case, the person may even fail to respond to strong stimulation that would ordinarily achieve an immediate response.

At the other extreme, the behavior may be largely stimulus-bound. This is the way it is likely to be with, say, a severe toothache. In such a case, the person may actually be unable to think of, or react to, anything else. In the case of stimulus-bound behaviors, the so-called personality characteristics of the individual have little to do with controlling the ultimate responses.

More commonly, of course, the two processes of stimulation and central neural activity mutually influence each other. Then, the central activity changes somewhat the character of the incoming stimulation. In turn, the incoming stimulation influences somewhat the particular state of the central activity.

Memory Traces

The Memory Traces component in Figure 5-2 represents the lingering traces within the organism from earlier stimulations. This includes the long-term effects of habits that can be measured in years. It also includes the transient effects of the immediately preceding stimulation, possibly measured in microseconds. The Memory Trace component is represented for convenience in Figure 5-2 by a rectangular box. The most appropriate model of the memory system, a Library Model, would be a library filled with various types of documents in storage, to be accessed by some sort of card or computer indexing system. Some of the documents could be figuratively "carved in stone," meaning essentially fixed and unchangeable, more or less permanently stored. Others could be less permanently stored, as in books, notebooks and computer disks. And some records could be very temporary, like writing with a stick in the sand at the beach, to be eroded by the next wave, or rendered illegible by further strokes of the stick.

The librarian, representing the Executive in charge of the storage system, may have been so busy with other work, that he or she has not always faithfully reproduced the actual events in the records. In fact, the keeper of records has not always used totally unambiguous accession codes. Moreover, documents that are filed later can partially replace some of the earlier documentation of similar events, or replace them entirely. Sometimes the librarian simply misplaces or forgets an accession code. The result is that the librarian cannot always be sure that a record can be recovered from the storage files. Or, if it is recovered, it may not be an accurate record of a previous event.

This Library Model reflects the gross gaps and falsifications that a person may sometimes experience in perception and memory. Experiences are not only lost from memory, but the experiences that are remembered can be greatly distorted from the original events.

Limbic System

The part of the S-ACP that is called the Limbic System generally represents the directing, or arousing, part in the model shown in Figure 5-1. The limbic system in the brain mediates and organizes emotional and motivational arousal and performance. This is not to say that the limbic system is entirely responsible for personal desires, but it does have a central role.

For convenience, this system is indicated in Figure 5-2 also by a rectangle. A good model for the system would be a compact-disk audio system. The first crucial component of this Compact Disk Model would be a connection to some source of electrical power. That is, the system must be plugged in and turned on. This connection to power provides the energy to perform certain tasks that are within the capability of the system. In the case of the disk, the function of the system is to perform, or to reproduce, various sounds. The music that is heard depends upon which disk is inserted in the system, and the location of the receiving head on the disk. Only those disks receiving power would produce their sounds, of course. The quality, or fidelity, of the resulting sounds would be determined by certain characteristics of the CD system. Various imperfections and maladjustments in the system would produce distorted and unpleasant results. The limbic system would not produce sounds, of course, but a variety of responses, and some of the responses activated by the limbic system will produce pleasant hedonic tones, and others will not.

The Agent

The Executive part of the personality in Figure 5-2 represents the primary agent of action, primarily the selecting part of the person in Figure 5-1. This agent chooses the final responses. The Executive or Agent within the S-ACP may add the most ambiguity in the response-selection process, depending upon the degree of the involvement into the overall picture. It can intervene a very little bit, or it may not even enter at all, thus producing completely stimulus-bound behaviors. At the other extreme, it can completely control the system, and thus produce extremely idiosyncratic behaviors, independent of the environmental stimulation. Thus, the Executive or Agent is the major contributor of the organismic variables.

A good model for the Executive would be a CEO Model. This model represents the CEO of an organization dealing with an in-basket and out-basket on his or her desk. Inputs would be reflected by informational messages and various requests for action dropped in the in-basket. The activity by the administrator, in relating the input to past inputs and to the new information and deciding upon a course of action placed in the out-basket, is analogous to the activity of the Executive within a person.

An entity of freedom of will would reside in the Executive. This location is reasonable because the Executive is the agent that typically makes final decisions about behavior. To be sure, the CEO is not completely free in selecting his or her response. There are limitations set by, for example, company policy, strong personal habits and limited resources. Similarly, there are limitations on the actions available to the human will. The body is not prepared for or capable of making any possible response, regardless of the dedication of the will. For example, without proper training, I cannot now play the piano no matter how much I will myself to do so.

Response Selection

The small forms of the letter r to the right of the Executive in Figure 5-2 indicate that the S-ACP can produce many covert response tendencies. Not all of them will ultimately be manifested in the array of overt behaviors, because of the Final Common Path (FCP). The funnel at the right within the figure thus indicates a response-selection mechanism. The various response tendencies can interfere with one another, particularly if they are mutually antagonistic. Indeed, they can be edited or blocked by some other response-production mechanism. Therefore, as indicated by the funnel shape at the right of the figure, only some response tendencies may pass through the selection process to become overt behaviors.

The overt responses then affect the stimulus input for subsequent responding, as indicated by the internal and external feedback (cyclic) loops in the figure. For example, the particular prior response may cause the person to find himself or herself in a totally different environment, both externally and internally. It may produce a satisfying state of affairs, and thus invoke learning through the law of effect. In any case, the particular nature of a person's responses in a given situation is very likely to affect the next stimulus-response connection.

Discussion of Model

The model in Figure 5-2 is just one of many possible models that could be used for organizing our conceptions of the processes and functions of behavior. Thus, the model does not purport to reflect objective truth in the sense of faithfully describing actual physical mechanisms. We ask only if the model is useful to us. The model is useful if the person acts as if this were a correct description of the processes and functions controlling his or her behaviors.

Actually, we can be certain that the model in Figure 5-2 is not a literal representation of how the system actually works. The very separation of the various components tells us that. The various components in the model describe functions rather than mechanisms of how those functions are accomplished. For example, the stimulus-selection funnel at the left of the model obviously cannot be a separate and distinct entity from the Agent. In fact, a major part of stimulus selection is the attention of the Agent. The attention is, in turn, influenced by the prevailing motivations and emotions, and so forth.

Other psychologists might prefer different labels for the components of Figure 5-2. But, few of them would argue that this model was a useless representation of the relationship among the parts, or that the parts did not reflect real psychological processes and functions. Therefore, this model might be considered a universal or generic model of general behavior, or of personality.

Summary

The use of models, as opposed to theory, is discussed. A model is merely an analogy, used to describe the production of behavior in a simple way that illustrates the relationships among the various parts of a system. Its value lies in its usefulness, not in its reflection of some absolute truth or objective reality.

The simplest model, S–R, is most suited for describing so-called stimulus-bound behaviors. The Behavioristic psychologists who follow this model merely seek to discover empirical functional relationships between stimuli and responses.

The S–O–R model incorporates more complex behaviors. Because it considers what is going on inside the organism, it permits the use of theory.

The S–O–R Cyclic model adds a consideration of contexts, including the context of a flow of events. Specifically, an overt response of the organism affects future stimulation.

The Simple Functional Model is an expansion of the S–O–R Cyclical model. It incorporates the different functions of the O component, which includes believing information about the environment, directing the organism toward specific responses and selecting the particular overt responses. The cyclic nature of the model is indicated by a feedback mechanism.

An Elaborated model of behavior represents more completely the major processes lying within the organism. It includes mechanisms for selective attention and selective responding. It includes a Semi-Autonomous Central Process, which contains components to reflect experience, motivation, emotion and decisions about appropriate responses. Therefore, it incorporates, in addition to stimulus, response and feedback components, internal mechanisms of central processing of the input information: systems of memory traces, motivational/emotional factors of the limbic system and a mechanism of human agency, called the Executive. It is proposed that the Executive can be directly aware of the environment, effectively by-passing the known mechanisms of sensation and perception. The Executive is assumed to have freedom of will and therefore can make responses independent of heredity and environment influences. Nevertheless, the Executive also can be faithfully responsive to such influences.

Notes

1. R. Harré and E. H. Madden, *Causal Powers* (Oxford: Basil Blackwell, 1975).
2. E. Rae Harcum, *Psychology for Daily Living* (Chicago: Nelson Hall, 1979).
3. Ibid.
4. Donald O. Hebb, The semi-autonomous process: Its nature and nurture, *American Psychologist, 18*: 16-27, 1963.

Chapter 6

Theories of Behavior

Suppose one day you found your mail scattered over your front yard, instead of neatly tucked into the mailbox as usual. What would be your first reaction, your first question? Very likely, you would simply ask how such a thing could happen. When you seek an explanation for such an unusual physical event, then you are acting like a professional psychologist and scientist.

Next, you will very likely begin to make guesses about possible answers to your question. If so, you are making some hypotheses, or tentative explanations for the event. Such crafting of hypotheses is the start of theorizing. To be sure some scientists do not believe in theorizing, being content with sheer description of events, but most scientists prefer to use theories.

Included among your original hypotheses could be that a high wind toppled the mailbox and blew the mail about the yard, or some prankster could have considered it humorous to scatter the contents of the mailbox. Thus, the first hypotheses are likely to follow the Principle of Parsimony, which says to look first for the simplest explanation. Therefore, you would check the weather reports, the condition of the mailbox, whether or not the neighbors had a similar problem on that day, etc.

Other hypotheses will be based on your own experiences with the letter carrier. It could be that the carrier had become mentally disordered, that the carrier was angry with you for some reason, that the post office changed its regulations, that the carrier was participating in some mysterious psychological experiment and so forth. The number of possible hypotheses is virtually unlimited, constrained only by the variety of your experience, and your skill and creativity in generating hypotheses. Your understanding about the relative plausibility of the hypotheses will cause you to undertake a general ranking of their likelihoods.

The kinds of hypotheses would also be dependent upon your preference for certain kinds of explanations. In fact, some hypotheses will naturally seem to you at the outset more likely than others. For example, if you were a voluntarist, a believer in complete freedom of the human will, you would simply presume that the mail carrier just felt like doing what he or she did.

That is not really an explanation, of course. And, it actually marks the end of theorizing. Moreover, such an explanation would not satisfy most of us. It would certainly not satisfy a scientist. A scientist would then ask what situations or conditions caused him to feel that way. That is why the assumption of some degree of determinism of behavior is necessary for a science of behavior. We look for some element of efficient causation.

Of course, you may simply consider the behavior too trivial even to try to understand it. Surely, some behaviors are just that trivial. But, still psychologists would not concede that they did not actually have causal explanations.

Whereas a hypothesis is a possible explanation for one particular bit of behavior, a theory is a proposed explanation for a whole class or category of behaviors. For example, suppose your investigations revealed that postmen frequently scattered the mail in such a manner. Then, you might find it reasonable to develop a theory of postman behavior to account for these actions.

Now, let us consider a more realistic example of a complex behavior: reading the printed page. This simple task actually represents a complex category of different behaviors, including appropriate eye movements, the identification of words and the comprehension of meaning. A theory of reading would be complex indeed, generating many different hypotheses to explain the cause of specific responses that form parts of the general act.

By the same argument, a general theory of all behaviors of a human being, including all sub-categories, must be far more complex. To be sure, ideally we would like to have one global theory of behavior that could potentially account for all possible human behaviors to some satisfactory degree of confidence, and was generally accepted by professional psychologists. It would in fact, be a theory of personality, defined as the totality of stable characteristics within a person that determines his or her behaviors over time. Alas, we do not have as yet such a universally accepted theory.

Theory in Science

An important issue concerns the general role of theory in science. A theory is not known to be correct, although it must be consistent with facts. If a theory were shown to be correct, it would lose its tentative nature, and thus no longer be a theory.

In practice, theories are not likely to be entirely correct, or entirely incorrect. So, if the theory is not necessarily correct, what good is it? The good theory is beneficial because it has a practical role in the development of research, as Hebb asserts.[1] Theory gives us ideas about what to study, and how to study it. But, the guidance should not be so firm as to restrict the research. As Hebb advises:

> What we need from a theory is that it should hold together long enough to lead us to a better one. . . . We must take it seriously, but not be dominated by it; bend every effort to making it as good as possible, but still avoid having our experiments limited to it.[2]

To be sure, a viable theory must be plausible and useful. Obviously, if a theorist commits himself or herself so completely to a theory that he or she is truly unable to evaluate it, or to accept disconfirming evidence about it, then the theory is not useful.

A theory must be based on valid evidence. Indeed, some psychologists would undoubtedly say that, for example, my present speculations about the nature of the human agent are too far removed from data even to be called a theory. Nevertheless, I will consider it at least useful if it succeeds in encouraging other psychologists to break out of the confines of reductionistic thinking—to thinking only in physical terms. Too many psychologists have argued that only the reductionistic perspective is truly scientific. By breaking the shackles of reductionism, we will also show the new student that psychologists are willing to tackle the really tough ontological problems that face us all.

A belief in such an indeterminate mechanism removes the blinders of logical positivism, which says that if you cannot measure it, it does not exist or is nonsense. Such a position is stifling to theory development, and disastrous to social and moral progress.

Wolman proposes three criteria for a good theory, as follows: 1) it must contain immanent truth, which means that the theory does not contain self-contradiction in logic or inference; 2) it must have transcendent truth, which means that the theory is consistent with the facts; and 3) it must be heuristically useful, which means that it must be a helpful guide toward the acquisition of new truths.[3] Whereas the transcendent truth affords an immediate practical usefulness, the heuristic usefulness produces future benefits. A heuristically useful theory directs the search for modification or elaboration of the original theory. For example, a belief in God has heuristic usefulness because it keeps the mind open to the discovery of new truths, different laws of nature, different realities and different concepts of causality.

My Principle of Ultimate Practicality, mentioned previously, is consistent with the above criteria for a good theory.[4] It says that, unless there is proof to the contrary, each person is free to believe whatever works to achieve his or her personal goals and welfare. Note that this principle does not give license to believe just anything in a whimsical way. Undoubtedly, an incorrect belief will naturally create problems in prediction and in controlling behavior. It reminds us that one may not reasonably believe what is contrary to fact, or generalizations directly based on those facts. But the derivation of theory to account for those facts allows much latitude for the individual in drawing personal conclusions. The principle does say that the individual is the ultimate judge of his or her own satisfaction with a theory for achieving personal goals.

If an individual's conclusions are not consistent with the empirical facts and accepted as laws of nature, the person will run into difficulty because his or her system will not work. For example, if I believe that I can fly like a hummingbird if I just flap my arms fast enough, and test this belief by stepping off a roof, I will find that my belief is not practical. If I believe that I am happy and successful because of God's favor, I can easily maintain that belief as long as I am happy and successful. If I must endure hardships like Job in the Bible, I face a challenge to by belief. Then I must decide, like Job, what works for me. Thus, the individual is the ultimate authority on what he or she can and should believe.

But, there is a danger in following this dictum. The individual must be prepared to become a martyr if he or she holds on to a belief that conflicts strongly with the cherished beliefs of society, particularly if society cannot accept or tolerate the deviance. Then, there is a strong multiple approach-avoidance conflict between conformity and guilt on one hand versus conviction and persecution on the other.

Harcum also contended that personal beliefs are based upon the same criteria that are appropriate for scientific beliefs.[5] Scientists must often made assumptions without adequate evidence in order to carry out their research. Those assumptions are corrected as contrary evidence is obtained. Because theories are always tentative, they are subject to change as the evidence comes in.

Three Psychological Theories

The three major theoretical approaches to the general theory of personality are shown in the first column of Table 6-1. They are Behaviorism,[6] Psychoanalysis[7] and Humanism.[8] The Behaviorism approach is subdivided into two categories: the Strict Behaviorism of Watson,[9] and the Cognitive Behaviorism of Hebb.[10] The three major theories are distinguished primarily by their positions on two significant issues: the type of data allowed and the philosophical issue of determinism vs. free-will.

The theories in Table 6-1 are called general theories of behavior because they attempt to explain all human behaviors, and not just some certain smaller class or sub-group of behaviors. Obviously, the different approaches are not equally effective in accounting for all of the different types of behaviors. These different approaches were derived by theorists who studied and emphasized different behaviors in their researches. For example, Behaviorism was developed primarily by research psychologists studying animals in laboratories. Psychoanalysis was developed by psychologists and psychiatrists studying persons with abnormal mental processing—thinking disorders. Humanism was crafted by psychologists studying normal human adjustment to life circumstances.

The first major issue among the theories is described in the second column of Table 6-1. It represents the type of data that a given theory considers legitimate for behavioral science. The second issue, described in the third column, concerns the different stances of the theories on the philosophical issue of freedom of will.

Types of Data

The categories of data represent three types. They are: a) perception of public events, called third-person data; b) reportable subjective experience, called second-person data; and c) unreportable subjective experience, called first-person data. The subdivision of Strict Behaviorism permits only third-person data.

Approach	Data	Philosophy	Key Concept
Strict Behaviorism	Third Person	Determinism	Association
Cognitive Behaviorism	Third + Second Person		Belief
Psychodynamic	Third + Second + First Person		Fixation
Humanism		Soft Determinism	Agent

Table 6-1: Major theoretical approaches

The subdivision of Cognitive Behaviorism permits second-person data as well as third-person data. The second-person data represent introspection. Introspection is the report of private personal experience—looking inside oneself.

The Psychoanalytic and the Humanistic categories permit also first-person data: the private and unobservable responses of the individual. Humanistic psychologists are still trying to work out additional ways for using such data, which basically means to convert this data into more objective form.

Free Will vs. Determinism

The second fundamental difference among the three theoretical orientations is their views on the free will vs. determinism issue. Whereas the Behavioristic and Psychoanalytic theories are deterministic in philosophical orientation, Humanistic Psychology reserves a role also for some freedom of the person to choose behaviors by an act of personal will or intention. Thus, Humanism presumes some sort of personal agent that is not exclusively responsive to environmental and genetic control, thus reflects what we ordinarily call voluntary control of behavior. As I have said before, the will is not completely free, but it does have some freedom of voluntary choice.

The Behavioristic and Psychoanalytic theories presume causation in terms of environmental experience and heredity. The Humanistic approach adds the causal agent of a personal spirit that possesses freedom of will.

Constructs

The main theoretical construct for each theory is given in the final column of Table 6-1. A construct is a hypothetical entity, because it has not been empirically proved to exist. The theorist assumes and alleges that the thing does exist, and builds his or her theory around that assumption. In brief, the Strict Behavioristic approach proposes that there are bonds or associations between stimuli and responses. These connections are produced by inherited structure and they are modified by learning.

Cognitive Behaviorism emphasizes that the mechanisms of learning produce beliefs within the person, which provide a mediating basis for responding—a basis for a connection to a response. These beliefs are internal responses that represent propositions about the nature of reality, and thus guide the response.

The Psychoanalytic approach proposes that anxieties over whether or not pleasurable urges can be satisfied cause a stoppage or fixation of emotional development at a stage of development that is short of mature responding.

The Humanistic approach proposes that there is a viable agent within the person that is responsive to conditions in the environment in ways that he or she thinks will best promote the personal welfare of the individual. The agent is presumed to have the ability to make a voluntary choice of behaviors within certain limits.

Other Differences

The different theoretical approaches are also distinguished from one another by more superficial differences. For example, they differ in the type of language preferred, and the metaphors and analogies that are used for explanation and clarification of the guesses about the causation of behaviors. Often, these preferences are related to the personal backgrounds and experiences of the theorist.

They are also related to the theorist's preference for emphasizing certain processes, and the specific behaviors in which he or she is most interested. Therefore, a language of biological mechanisms and learning situations is used by the Behaviorists. A language of unconscious threatening urges is used by the Psychoanalysts. The Humanists tend to use a language of self-esteem and self-fulfillment.

Behaviorism

The Behavioristic approach to psychology was developed by John B. Watson as a reaction to the prevailing use of subjective experience as the subject matter of psychology.[11] Watson proposed instead to study only observable responses, and to use strictly objective methods. The specific approach of Strict Behaviorism even declared that all subjective terms, such as consciousness and intention, were irrelevant to a science of psychology. Therefore, the Behavioristic approach has all of the characteristics of a rigorous science, including the denial of any place for voluntary choice by a transcendental agent of action.

Behaviorism is basically a theory of learning. Learning is defined as a process inferred from durable changes in behaviors as a result of experience. Therefore, according to the theory of Behaviorism, a behavior is the result of the interaction of genetic structures and learning experience.

Strict Behaviorism

As shown in Table 6-1, the key concept in Strict Behaviorism is association, which is the presumed connection between a stimulus and a response as a result of the joint affects of heredity and the learning process. Strict Behaviorism considers the personality of an individual as solely the result of particular individual experiences (learning) as it has been controlled or influenced by the genetic endowment of the individual. The founder of Strict Behaviorism was J. B. Watson. Other leading proponents of this general view of Strict Behaviorism were Hull, Spence and Skinner.

Cognitive Behaviorism

In contrast to Strict Behaviorists, the Cognitive Behaviorists concede a role for cognitive awareness. Therefore, they permit the use of more subjective, second-person data. They argue that the behavior of an individual can be understood in terms of the beliefs about the environment, learned through the interaction of heredity and environment. Therefore, the beliefs of a person can intervene between stimulus and response, thus mediating or moderating a rich variety of potential responses. Although this approach is also strictly deterministic, the approach entails greater ability to predict ambiguous responses because of the cognitive concepts.

Major proponents for Cognitive Behaviorism have been Albert Bandura, D. O. Hebb and Robert Rescorla.

Psychoanalytic Theory

Psychoanalytic theory was developed initially from the clinical practice of Sigmund Freud.[12] Therefore, it is a psychology of abnormal behaviors caused by disordered thinking. Because the theory is biological in nature, it assumes progressive changes of both biological and psychological mechanisms as a result of normal growth, if indeed the environment is benign. If the environment is not benign, then certain abnormalities of thought and action are produced. The theory is thus entirely deterministic.

A key part of the theory is the presumption of a general motivation to satisfy a basic biological need for pleasure, called the libido. Freud referred to the libidinal impulses as sexual, although he did not mean the adult sexuality that we think of today. He meant a broader, more inclusive, concept of pleasurable activities, which included such actions as a baby sucking a mother's breast, or the elimination of wastes from the body.

The exact ways the needs of the libido are satisfied are shaped and directed by life experiences. Therefore, in a sense, the pleasure—or its equivalent in terms of an absence of pain and guilt—must be achieved in different ways as one grows.

Ultimately, the various ways of achieving personal satisfaction may conflict in different situations, leading to internal conflicts. The id is the part of the personality that is concerned with the basic libidinal need for physiological gratification. It responds in accordance with the pleasure principle, which is the demand that the libido be immediately gratified. This principle conflicts with the demands of the ego, the part of the emerging personality concerned with rational assessments of reality on the basis of practical experience. This assessment is a response to the reality principle, which is a response to the realities in the environment which can modify the demands of the pleasure principle in order to ultimately meet the needs of the individual.

The id may also conflict with the demands of the superego, which is the part of the mature personality structure that is concerned with learned issues of right and wrong. It is developed through imitation of the same-sex parent. At different times, coalitions between the three parts of the personality change, with the consequent changes in the type of internal conflict, and possibly the resulting behaviors.

The internal conflicts themselves are troubling to the person, producing fears and anxieties. Moreover, if they are not resolved, or mitigated by so-called defense mechanisms for that particular purpose, they can lead to various psychological problems and symptoms. Thus, in the Psychoanalytic approach, all behaviors are assumed to have a cause rooted in the overall quest for pleasure, and freedom from the anxiety which comes from doubts that the pleasure can be achieved.

Some of the conflicts among methods of achieving psychological pleasure or comfort are available to conscious experience, but many are not. They are unconscious and are kept that way because they are unacceptable consciously to the person. Therefore, many of the causes of behavior, though determined completely by intrapsychic events, are not available to conscious experience, and certainly not under voluntary control.

The adult personality is understood in terms of certain personality types related to characteristics of a person at various stages of his or her psychosexual development. The order of the stages and the approximate durations of the various stages are determined by the biology of the organism. Each of the first three stages is characterized by the part of the body that is relatively most important for pleasurable experiences at that given stage: mouth (oral stage), anus (anal stage) and penis (phallic stage). Next, the latency stage is characterized as a preadolescent transition phase with masked sexuality. Finally, the genital stage represents adult sexuality. The general timing of the stages are as follows: 1) oral, ages 0-1 years; 2) anal, ages 2-3 years; 3) phallic, ages 4-5 years; 4) latency, ages 6-12 years; and 5) genital, age 12 and on.

If certain environmental factors, such as excessive gratification or excessive thwarting of pleasure motivation, occur at any given stage, then fixation occurs. This means that the person continues a lifelong quest for satisfying the pleasure motives with behaviors associated with that stage of development. Therefore, for example, an adult may be characterized as an oral personality because he or she is preoccupied with oral activities such as smoking or overeating, presumably due to fixation at the oral stage of development. Fixation is the key concept in the Psychoanalytic theory.

The Psychoanalytic approach is dissimilar to the Behavioristic approach because it de-emphasizes the role of learning, and emphasizes motivation. The Behavioristic approach emphasizes learning and de-emphasized motivation. Also, research in Psychoanalytic theory tends to be more oriented toward intuitive interpretations of clinical cases, and correlations among naturally occurring events rather than objective, controlled laboratory experiments, as is true of Behaviorism.

The sexist nature of the psychoanalytic theory is a weakness that has been seriously criticized. The proposed process of development of the personality from latency to the genital stage is anything but straightforward for the male child, and even more tenuous for the girl.

Sigmund Freud was the founder and pre-eminent name in Psychoanalytic theory. Other leading proponents of this general theory have been Erickson,

Fromm and Horney.

Humanism

The movement of Humanisitic psychology was developed as an alternative to the Behavioristic and Psychoanalytic approaches. Therefore, it has been called the "Third Force in Psychology."[13] The major point is a denial of the deterministic view of the other approaches. The Humanistic psychologists believe the human beings can, by intentional acts of a personal will, change their behaviors in creative ways. Also, the Humanists employ all three categories of data.

Taft listed the views of Humanistic psychology as follows:[14] 1) *Humanistic psychology emphasizes wholeness and uniqueness of persons.* The meaning of wholeness is basically intuitive. Wholeness implies the possession of mental health and the general personal development of intellectual, ethical and social capabilities. A whole person is productive and successful; 2) *The humanistic approach accepts the reality of behavior, instead of trying to reduce it into something else.* Therefore, a behavior is considered an act designed to achieve a purpose, rather than a mere manifestation of physiological responses to some environmental stimulation. For example, love is not just a reflection of neurophysiology or hormones; 3) *Humanistic psychology describes psychological events in terms of personal experiences rather that behaviors.* Thus, mental events intervene between a stimulus and a response; 4) *Humanistic psychology explains behaviors in terms of what it means to the particular person.* The person is responsive to the way he or she understands the situation. The conditions of understanding become a moderating variable in affecting the response; 5) *It attributes the responsibility for behavior to persons rather than to environments, emphasizing pro-activity or purpose rather than reactivity.* The person is conceived as a personal agent that sometimes has the capacity to exercise a voluntary will independently of heredity and environment. This agent can anticipate and plan, as well as respond to existing stimulations; 6) *Humanistic psychology considers the basic directedness and themes in people's lives, stressing growth and realization of potential, rather than objective standards of achievement.* Thus success is defined in terms of achieving one's potential for wholeness, rather than garnering extrinsic rewards.

The key concept of Humanistic psychology is the personal agent, conceived as a part of the individual organism that drives, leads and otherwise causes the total person to act. It can on occasion respond independently of heredity and environment, but it does not have to be independent of environmental influence. Thus, the individual agent can voluntarily choose among responses, and also initiate responses spontaneously. The basic goal of the internal agent is to achieve personal growth and self-actualization for the person.

According to the Humanistic view, the Behavioristic approach does not deal adequately with the problems of purpose, intrinsic choices, meaning in social groupings, creativity, concept of the self and certain so-called paranormal phenomena, such as extrasensory perception. In agreement with LeShan,[15] Harman argued that the goal of Behavioristic psychology has been to predict and control objectively, rather than to gain insight about the causes of human action in real life situations.[16] Whereas the prevailing conceptions of science were characterized by objectivism, positivism, determinism and reductionism, Harman proposed that a desired restructuring of behavioral science would involve more holistic approaches. He advocated expanded alternatives for seeking the truth, because no particular approach grasps it completely. The growth of important personal values can be controlled by the persons themselves. This growth is conceptualized in terms of personal fulfillment, or wholeness, rather than the learned acquisition of societally approved responses, as the Behaviorists would argue.

LeShan, supporting Harman's views, pointed out that some years ago he encountered strong and consistent resistance against his attempts to provide psychotherapy for seriously ill cancer patients using spiritual methods.[17] His work subsequently showed that psychological and spiritual factors could have substantial effects on progress in healing cancer.

The Humanistic psychologists object to the Psychoanalytic view because it overemphasizes the role of sex in affecting behaviors. They also object to the Psychoanalytic emphasis on thinking disorders instead of the role of normal thinking in mental health.

To be sure, there is nothing in the Humanistic orientation to psychology that conflicts with religious teachings. As a psychological theory, it emphasizes growth and development of the individual person, instead of service to others. Therefore, the people of God need only add a spiritual dimension to it to justify helping behaviors.

Because many theorists have been prominent in the development of the humanistic approach, I do not identify one person as the founder. Among the leaders in this approach have been Maslow, May, Rogers and Pollio.

Eclecticism

The existence of the three major theoretical divisions in psychology, more or less neatly described in a table, does not mean that all psychologists can be cleanly placed within one of these divisions. Psychologists can also be categorized according to the ease or difficulty of placing their personal theoretical orientation into one of these major divisions. Indeed, the psychologists who are called doctrinaire do fall nicely and consistently into one given category. A very doctrinaire person confines his or her theorizing to one orientation, and finds little or no use for other views.

The Behaviorists are doctrinaire. For example, when Wertheimer assessed the status of theories in psychology some years ago, he concluded that the other theories had yielded to the tenets of Behaviorism. He said, "Behaviorism, although its extreme Watsonian form no long exists, characterizes most of today's psychologists, and its definition of psychology as the science of behavior has won the day."[18] Today, over 30 years later, many psychologists would strongly disagree with that bold statement. Although the Behaviorists are, I suspect, outnumbered by advocates of other theories, nevertheless they undoubtedly have an influence on the profession far beyond their numbers.

Those psychologists who are called eclectic do not adhere to a single theoretical position. They shift from theory to theory as each seems useful or appropriate to them. For them, practicality is more important than theoretical purity. This is particularly characteristic of clinicians, who must give their first priority to the welfare of their clients.

Usually, the eclectic psychologists have a preferred theoretical orientation, although they do not restrict themselves exclusively to it. For example, a therapist might classify himself or herself as being "more comfortable" with one theory than another. But, depending upon the perceived utility of doing so, the therapist would be able to shift to a different approach. Just as different therapies were developed on the basis of different presenting problems, they are thus likely to be more useful in handling those particular problems.

Discussion

Although some psychologists claim not to theorize, I truly doubt that the actual search for causal stimuli would ever be purely random, or even haphazard, as a lack of such a guiding theory would imply. Presumably, there would be a hierarchy of the various guesses according to some preference or plan. For example, the investigator would decide which possible stimulus conditions to check out first, requiring at least some low level of guesswork, or hypothesis-making. Thus, the only true value in avoiding theory is that the investigator is not blinded from a consideration of relevant data by his or her infatuation with the original guesses.

Other Theories of Interest

Several other theories are important primarily for their historical, and specialized interest. Therefore, they do not appear in Table 6-1.

Structuralism

The first attempt at psychological theory, Structuralism, attempted to account for behaviors in terms of the structure of the mind, inferred from an observer's conscious experience. Its founder, Wilhelm Wundt, used the method of introspection (second-person data). In this method, trained observers of controlled stimulus inputs were asked to describe the content (structure) of their conscious experience. From these descriptions, Wundt attempted to understand the content, or elements of sensation or conscious experience. A sensation is defined as the immediate conscious experience of a person in response to a stimulus input. Therefore, it is presumed to be raw, unprocessed and relatively meaningless—thus, not interpreted in terms of any meaning attached to it by the person who experiences it. For example, in Wundt's studies, the subject would be asked about such things as the duration and intensity of the sensation, and how strongly or vividly it stood out in attention.

Thus, in theory, a sensation is entirely stimulus-bound, meaning it is produced by, and therefore is a response only to, the stimulus input. Although nominally a sensation is entirely caused by the stimulus, that is probably, strictly speaking, never true. It is very unlikely that the effects of a stimulus can pass through a complex brain without somehow being affected to some extent by the brain mechanisms.

The method of introspection can be demonstrated by simply slapping the back of one hand hard enough to elicit pain. You can report the severity of the pain, how long it lasts and something about its quality. For example, is it sharp or dull or aching?

Now, slap your hand again, but a bit harder this time. Now the pain will be more intense. It will cover a larger area of the hand. It will last longer. Is it qualitatively different?

Now, dig one knuckle into the back of your hand. The type of pain now probably will be qualitatively different from the pain of the slap. Are there other differences? Thus, the conscious contents of the mind are related, so some extent at least, to certain different characteristics of the stimulation.

Structuralism failed to survive because of the basic subjectivity of the method. The subjectivity necessarily involved added input from the personality characteristics of the subject, producing an unreliability of the method. To be sure, introspectionists were presumably trained not to make interpretations of the stimulus input, but most modern psychologists doubt that such training can be entirely successful.

Functionalism

Later, a related theory, Functionalism, used the same basic methodology. But the observers were asked to describe the functioning of the mind instead of its content. The observers were asked to describe the mental operations that they went through as they performed prescribed tasks, or functions. For example, suppose I ask you how many saw cuts would be necessary to divide a 12-foot board into three equal pieces, each four feet long. You could imagine yourself wielding a saw and counting the cuts as you made than. Or, you might prefer to visualize, or to verbalize, a mathematical formula. Thus, the mind is described in terms of how it functions to produce a practical response.

The theoretical approach of Functionalism also failed to survive because of the inherent subjectivity of the methodology. Although the introspectionists attempts to report private experience, it is essentially impossible to report isolated experiences without altering them somewhat through personal interpretations. Probably, also, the content and the functioning of the human mind is too complex to be captured directly by such a simple methodology. Some modern psy-

Figure 6-1: Illustration of a Gestalt principle

chologists do believe, however that we gave up on the basic method too soon. These investigators are developing more sophisticated ways to use the basic method.

Gestalt

The specific theory of Gestalt Psychology was proposed by Wolfgang Köhler.[19] Before the theory itself is described, its main principle will be demonstrated in Figure 6-1. Try to identify what this figure represents. When asked to report their perceptions of the object in the figure, most observers report such things as ornamental spears and fish backbones. Few see the word "summers" included within the figure. The word is clearly visible in cursive writing, however, when a sheet of paper is placed over the bottom half of the figure, which is just a vertical mirror image of the top half. To see the word within the total figure requires the viewer to analyze, or abstract, a part of the overall figure from the total. According to Gestalt theory, such analysis of parts cannot occur when the complete figure is visible.

Thus, Gestalt is actually a theory of perception, not truly a general theory of behavior. Nevertheless, it does have broad applications. It emphasizes the roles of the form and configuration of a stimulus in the way it is perceived. The word, Gestalt, is the German word for form or figure, and thus is always capitalized.

The Gestalt theory says that the perception of the whole is more than, or different from, the sum of its component stimulus parts. For example, the particular arrangement or configuration of a group of stimuli entails an emergent quality that literally produces a different stimulus event than the very same group of objective stimuli arranged in a different configuration. For example, constellations of stars suggest certain figures. Therefore, they are given appropriate names, such as Orion and the Big Dipper.

According to the theory, certain configurations of stimuli, called good Gestalts, tend to be more easily perceived, and better recalled. Such good forms tend to be symmetrical figures that are more easily described verbally.

Although some (physiological) aspects of the Gestalt theory have been clearly disproved, nevertheless parts of the theory persist in terms of some important truths that are emphasized. Because the main premises of the theory are generally valid, some relevant Gestalt principles have been incorporated into the body of basic psychological knowledge. Indeed, a certain configuration of stimulus elements can produce an emergent, or new, stimulus, which is indeed not reducible to its component parts.

But, the argument that a figure can never be perceived in terms of its component parts has been proved incorrect. In fact, it is possible to construct a figure from isolated perceptions of its component parts. For example, suppose you can see, through a break in a fence, a horse running behind the fence. You can identify the horse, even though you have seen only a part of it at a time, as each part appears through the gap in the fence.

Moreover, the physiological mechanisms that were proposed for how these Gestalt principles actually operate in the brain have also been shown to be incorrect. Thus, the evaluation of Gestalt theory illustrates an important truth about theories: they are rarely totally correct, or seldom totally incorrect.

Executive Agent

This next section of the chapter will tackle the formidable task of proposing a central mechanism by which creative behaviors are produced. Specifically, this section presents a theory about the nature of the mind. To be sure, this elaboration of theory is necessary in order to complete a Humanistic orientation for the causation of behavior.

The major issue in the theoretical description of the causal agent in the control of behavior is whether or not it originates behavior in a purposive way—through freedom of will—or is it merely a label for the actions of an undirected and uncontrolled, presumably neural, mechanism.[20] To develop a theory about how the Executive works is to attempt to resolve the mind-body problem.

I submit that the causal agent within the human being is part physical and part non-physical, or spiritual. Admittedly, this is an extremely radical view among psychologists. The alternative theory reduces the human being to an array of purely physical mechanisms, which would not have a freedom of will.

Reductionistic Conception

Reductionistic approaches to theories of causal behavior have been worked out in detail.[21] These approaches reduce the causes of behavior to a few innate mechanisms and learned habits, with or without attempts to speculate about the underlying neural mechanisms.

Skinner's view is most familiar.[22] It asserts that the basic factor controlling behavior consists of learning based on inherited structure moderated by reward contingencies. Therefore, the person simply performs innate acts and new ones that have been rewarded in the past. Any disjunction, or lack of connection, in the response acquisition or retention process is attributed to a behavioral "mutation" or "twist" in the response production process. This abrupt change is related to unspecified complex relationships and interactions among the verbal habits. Therefore, it is unguided and surely not intentionally directed toward a desired goal.

Some scientists feel comfortable with this reductionistic approach, because it allegedly does not go beyond objective data. But that appearance can be misleading, because no one has actually observed a behavioral "mutation" or "twist," only the alleged result of one. Harcum argued that such proposed reductionistic explanations of creative behaviors are no more scientifically acceptable than the mentalistic or spiritual conceptions.[23] Namely, a mysterious mechanistic gremlin in a machine ("mutation") is not a better explanation *a priori* than a non-materialistic ghost or spirit in the machine.

Indeed, the non-materialistic interpretation has the advantage of being more useful. A belief about a person's purpose is often a better predictor of that person's future responses than are his or her history of rewards and punishments. Indeed, the history can not in any manner predict particular mutations of habits.

Other reductionistic theories are not so restrictive. For example, Hebb's cognitive theory uses terms like attention and expectancy.[24] Nevertheless, Hebb suggests only purely physiological mechanisms. Still, the theory is of the "just-so" variety: whatever the adaptive response, the physical conditions were allegedly just right to produce that particular response.

Transcendental Conception

In proposing a transcendental agent as a cause of voluntary behavior, I begin with the deterministic theory of Hebb and add to it parts that Hebb would surely not support.[25] To refer to the internal causal agent, I have used the term "the Executive"[26], a term taken from Neisser[27], although my meaning is critically changed from Neisser. Again, I assert that the Executive has a spiritual component, rather than being exclusively neural. The spirit part interacts with the neurological mechanisms in an unknown way. The hypothesis of such an entity constitutes a radical departure in psychology. Nevertheless, it is an obvious logical consequence of the concept of freedom of choice.

A theory of the Executive is again much more elaborate than can be illustrated within the single circle in the Elaborated Model in Figure 5-2 of Chapter 5.[28] It consists of two parts: a responsive part, called the Responsive Will, which rationally responds to the environment, and a second part that is called the Transcendental Will, which is not limited by the environment.

In Chapter 5, I proposed the CEO model to describe the functioning of the Executive. Like the CEO of a large corporation, the Executive examines the sensory information in his or her in-basket, reaches an administrative decision and places an executive response in his or her out-basket. To describe the decision process, I propose what I call the Customer Theory of the functioning of the Executive. The model for this theory is a customer selecting a flavor of ice cream or sherbet from among the many specific offerings available at the ice cream parlor. The customer must select a product that is available at the shop. The limitations of the store's inventory thus prevent the customer from making some selections that he or she might otherwise have chosen. The Responsive Will of the Executive accepts the limitation.

A person's repertoire of available responses is like the store's inventory. The inventory includes memories of experiences of the person as they interact with his or her genetic endowment. For example, some experiences may produce lingering traces which are available in the array of available responses, and some are not available.

The customer can, of course, freely select from among those flavors in the inventory. But, the customer ordinarily does not choose randomly from among the available alternatives. For example, he or she may dislike chocolate. Or the customer may have an allergy to strawberry. There may be a special craving for raspberry. The customer may prefer sherbet to ice cream. The choice of the Viable Will may be rational and responsive, or it may be capricious and creative. This is not to say that the customer is limited by the particular packaging or organization of the inventory in the store. The customer can create new combinations that are not listed, but still possible with that inventory. For example, the customer can request scoops of chocolate, vanilla and strawberry in order to create a Neapolitan dish that was not on the list of available dishes. In fact, a very large number of new dishes can be similarly created. So, the Executive can make an enormous number of different responses, within the array of responses that are possible or available. The limitations are placed by the hereditary disposition of the individual, by the experiences of the organism and by the grace of God. The Reductionistic Theory would explain the behavior of such novelties as accidental mixtures (mutations) in the normal course of events.

The Customer Theory fits the conceptual principle of Soft Determinism, which says that the particular response is the joint result of environmental and hereditary determinants and the limited choice of the Executive. Again, the Executive cannot make choices that are not available to it through the interactive effect of heredity and environment, although there is freedom of choice within those limits. This fits the concept of choice within limits as proposed by Pollio and Henley.[29] But, always there is the guiding hand of God.

The Mechanism

Now it remains for the theorist to suggest the actual psychological mechanisms by which the Customer Theory is executed. We will go as far as we can go, knowing that ultimately we must finish with mystery.

Some speculations about the actual mechanisms responsible for intentional behavior can be borrowed from Hebb, although Hebb strongly emphasized that such mechanisms must be purely physiological.[30] I accept no such limitation. The proposed theory overlaps substantially the theoretical orientation of Connectionism, which proposes complex neural networks as the mediators of response selection. But, the present proposal differs critically from all of the previous views because of the ultimate injection of a spiritual component.

The basic concept in Hebb's theory is the cell assembly, which is a configuration of neurons in the major association areas of the brain that fire in a reasonably consistent temporal-spatial pattern. Activation of a given cell assembly corresponds to the arousal of a conscious perception within the person. Therefore, the memory of a prior stimulus situation involves the reactivation of a sufficient proportion of the neurons in the original pattern of neural firing in the cell assembly.

Another major Hebbian concept is the phase sequence, which is a temporal series of cell assemblies. At first, the specific assemblies follow one another because of the consistent objective relations among stimulus events in the real environment. For example, as you enter the front door of your house and walk through it, certain perceptions naturally follow certain other perceptions. It is likely that you will first perceive the living room, as that cell assembly is activated, followed by consistent changes in visual perceptions as you perceive the feedback from your muscles for walking and for glancing about the room. If your muscles for walking now take you into the dining room, you will perceive the dining table, dish cupboard, etc. because those cell assemblies are thus activated. But if your muscles for walking take you into the family room, you will experience different cell assemblies—namely, for the television set, easy chairs and fireplace. So it is that, as you walk through the house, certain perceptions of scenes and experiences (cell assemblies) naturally follow others. Because the temporal relations among the cell assemblies corresponding to these individual perceptions are sufficiently consistent, they become associated. Therefore, activation of the prior assemblies, and thus the conscious perceptions, increases the likelihood that they will activate the subsequent neural patterns, with their associated assemblies (conscious perceptions). The chain of cell assemblies in the phase sequence is therefore like a train of thought that can itself arouse a perception later in the train, sometimes independently of the immediate existing stimulation from the external environment. In such a case, we would say that the very consistency of the series of perceptions (produced by the activity of the appropriate assemblies) leads the person to expect that certain perceptions (from the appropriate assemblies) will follow certain other perceptions. In effect, a mental set—a predisposition to respond in a certain way to experience a particular assembly—is established by the immediate past experiences. Thus, in common language, such a train of thought is like a series of conscious mental pictures (from their cell assemblies) that influence the later thought (other cell assemblies) because of the consistent associations between them. Thus, future thought is initiated and constrained by the prior thought processes.

In this theory, the phenomenon of attention is explained by the facilitation or priming effect of one cell assembly within the phase sequence on another assembly, increasing the likelihood that the facilitated assembly will now become a part of the sequence to be established. Whereas attention implies a rather transient state of central facilitation from the prior assemblies, intention, in contrast, is reflected in a sufficiently persisting state of central facilitation, producing recurrent or persistent phase sequences of cell assemblies.

Because more than one phase sequence can be operating at a time, attention and intention can be divided. For example, one phase sequence may be controlling the conscious behavior and the others may be subconscious. One must be careful not to exclude the unconscious mechanisms in this process. Incidental learning and memory can occur if the arousal from the stimulus is sufficiently strong, and the subconscious phase sequence is sufficiently well established. The person is more likely to remember the event which is afforded the conscious attention, however.

Thus, according to Hebb, set in perception would similarly be explained as a persisting phase sequence.[31] A personality is therefore defined by the preponderance of persistent, or stable, sets of a given type. When metabolic and sensory events disturb the delicate timing of these sequences, and thus expectancies are not confirmed, various types of emotional disturbance or thinking disorders are manifested in behavior. We could say that the computer brain has been confused by conflicting input.

Hebb's third major hypothetical construct is the superordinate cell assembly. This is a cell assembly based on a combination of several simple assemblies which have frequently been experienced together in consistent relationships. As sufficient degrees of consistency are reached, the common parts of the assemblies evolve into a new assembly of greater complexity than the component simple assemblies. Presumably, the more complex the cell assembly, the more diffuse the components throughout the brain. The activation of the superordinate cell assembly produces a conscious awareness of a concept. A concept is knowledge (perception) of a shared attribute, abstracted from a series of things, each of which contains that attribute. Thus, it is a label for an idea or notion that represents a category of characteristics. For example, a triangle represents a concept for closed geometric figures that include three angles and three straight sides.

Other concepts are not so easily described. For example, consider the concept of a ball. Actually, the word itself alone does not tell us whether it refers to a large assembly of persons for social dancing, or an object to be used in a game. Assuming it is the latter, a ball is usually resilient enough to bounce, and it is used in certain games and sports. It does not have to be round, or hollow or made of any particular material.

Other, even more difficult, examples would include such concepts as furniture, intelligence and freedom. Indeed, an abstract concept like fairness is very difficult to establish. For example, the child has great difficulty in perceiving any result that is adverse to him or her as fair.

As the superordinate cell assembly becomes better established through experience, it becomes more easily activated. Therefore, ultimately the particular concept can be produced by only a small fraction of the original physical stimulation in the person's environment, or by a smaller portion of the prior cell assemblies in the person's phase sequence.

Hebb's theory was later modified in terms of certain particulars.[32] The basic theory is now subsumed by the newer connectionist theories, and by the speculative extension to follow here.[33]

A key idea in Hebb's theory is that there is no clear distinction between neural traces of a stimulus and incipient neural response. That is, activity in motor areas of the cerebral cortex commingles with incoming stimulus traces to become part of the functional proximal stimulus. Moreover, such functional stimuli are structurally changed by their interaction with other proximal stimuli, and with the prevailing phase sequence. The stimuli which are held in attention by the Executive exert greater effects. In the context of meaningful daily experience, learning involves the formation of associations between this degraded stimulus representation and certain superordinate cell assemblies and an array of equivalent overt responses. Thinking, or reasoning, involves the activation of superordinate cell assemblies by the functional stimulus representations, and the activation of responses by the superordinate cell assemblies.

Different neural patterns, such as those suggested by Hebb, determine both conscious and unconscious percepts of the observer in response to the environmental stimulation. They determine the meaning of the stimulation—how it is encoded by the person (what cell assemblies are activated). In the case of perception and memory for life events, the response components include more attitudinal, affective and orienting responses than specific responses to environmental stimuli. The emotional and cognitive responses are usually more salient attributes, because they are more relevant to the motivations of the observer than the specific stimulation.

Neural patterns from various sources would be responsible for what are called meta-cognitions, an awareness that one has certain knowledge or information that cannot, however, be retrieved to consciousness at the moment. For example, you know the name of your hairdresser, but you cannot think of it at the moment. Often, then, you say, "It will come to me in a moment." The name may pop into you head a few minutes later while you are thinking about something else, indicating that another part of your mind was still trying for the retrieval cue—the necessary neural connections—to bring the name to conscious awareness (i.e., to remember it).

Thus, cell assemblies prime other cell assemblies. The mechanism works analogously to Goffman's concept of the key.[34] The key is some subtle stimulus event that is crucial in providing contextual meaning in a given situation. For example, animals can communicate cues to each other to indicate that their mock-fighting is just playing, and not real fighting. Another example would be the professional demeanor of a physician who tells the patient that a medical examination is in progress, and not sexual abuse.

If a primed cell assembly is activated, the observer may have a conscious experience of the corresponding perception or concept, depending upon relative strengths and awareness thresholds. These cell assemblies can prime other assemblies and possibly initiate a phase sequence that may or may not produce conscious experiences. At any point, an activated cell assembly can produce an overt response. The response may or may not be anticipatory. Often the overt response is not easily traceable to a specific stimulus; it is likely to be poorly defined, included within a group that involves different effectors, but all equivalent in the sense of producing basically the same act. The longer the latency of the act, the more likely the behavior will be interpreted as intentional.

As Milner proposed, learning to associate two events consists of consistent priming of one assembly by another.[35] Memory consists of the actual reactivation of an assembly. An assembly can be reactivated by similar external stimuli, by stimulation from contextual cues and by prior parts of the phase sequence. Because of a possible confluence of many such factors, the reactivation is not likely to be an exact duplicate of the original cell assembly.

Except in the most impoverished laboratory task, several distinct cell assemblies are likely to be activated simultaneously. The one that achieves conscious attention depends in part upon the relative stabilities of the assemblies. I proposed that the better-established assemblies, through greater experience with the conjunctions would ultimately gain ascendancy because of their greater stability in a kind of competition among assemblies.[36] The better-established assemblies would be activated sooner and would be less easily replaced by other assemblies. They would presumably also be most useful in the particular context. This would be analogous to scanning memory storage. A subconscious activation of an assembly would produce a meta-cognitive, tip-of-the-tongue experience—a feeling of knowing, but an inability to recall consciously.

I propose that phase sequences occur in at least three identifiable levels of organization, corresponding to three proposed executive levels of control of behavior: automatic, intentional and executive. A higher level can at any time cancel and preempt a lower level. Therefore, a higher level loosely monitors a lower level and thus gives implied consent to the behaviors controlled by the lower level by failing to disrupt the phase sequence of the lower level.

Automatic control is relatively stimulus-bound.[37] The predictability of the responses given the stimulus can reflect more than just the innate reflex mechanism because it can also include over-learned associations. When it is being monitored by the internal phase sequence, it is conscious.

The intentional phase sequence, as described by Hebb, ordinarily dominates the conscious experience.[38] By supporting the activation of the automatic phase sequence, it makes those behaviors deliberate. It involves the "housekeeping" part of the personal schema, ensuring that reasonable responses are selected toward immediate objectives. Hebb defined a voluntary or intentional act as:

> . . .one that is determined by a phase sequence or conceptual series with some duration in time, to which both sensory and central facilitation contribute constantly. These sequences are recurrent as well as anticipatory, so the voluntary act is influenced by immediate memory and set as well as by an expectancy of the future—particularly, an expectancy of the immediate consequences of the act.[39]

Thus, in Hebb's view, the difference between voluntary and involuntary behavior is between behaviors that are relatively independent of environmental simulation and those that are relatively stimulus-bound. Therefore, Hebb concluded:

> Consciousness then is to be identified theoretically with a certain degree of complexity of phase sequence in which both central and sensory facilitations merge, the central acting to reinforce now one class of sensory stimulations, now another. The cortical organization consists of a diffuse firing in a succession of assembly actions or phases that are organized first in phase cycles (conceptual activities) and then in series such as cycles that maintain a selective influence on both behavior for appreciable periods of time, but always with the possibility that the current organization may be changed or disrupted by an unusual sensory event.[40]

Although Hebb's theory of behavior is mediational, rather than Humanistic, it proposes mechanisms that can easily be fitted into a more Humanistic orientation, by a slight, but crucial, addition. In particular, his concept of semi-autonomous central process implies a relative independence of sensory control, and his concept of phase sequence entails the relevance of cognitive terms like expectancy and confirmation of expectancy.[41] The problem of retrieval cues for memory is handled by his notion that some cell assemblies are too similar to be discriminated.

The present view proposes that the highest level of control is provided by the executive phase sequence. This sequence involves the cell assemblies within the personal schema that reflect basic personal beliefs and purposes, and the associated effects. This phase sequence may support the intentional phase sequence to produce more stubborn behavior, but it may preempt it if the intentional behavior is inconsistent with the content of the executive sequence. A chronic incompatibility of the intentional and executive phase sequences is likely to be a major cause of behaviors associated with disorders of thinking.

The intentional aspect of the executive phase sequence is basically developed through learning. Therefore, activating a given phase sequence is a process of retrieval of memory. Thus, the short-term and long-term goals of a person are dependent upon which cell assemblies are reactivated (remembered) to become a part of the phase sequence. The goal of the psychotherapist, for example, is to employ learning and retrieval techniques to establish those phase sequences that produce healthy behaviors (i.e., compatible intentional and executive sequences).

The determinist stops theorizing at this point. Further theorizing must be Humanistic in nature. Therefore, the final bit of speculation in the present theory of agency concerns how the human spirit controls the personal agency. This addition of a spiritual element makes for a short section of the chapter because we do not have a good idea for how to explain it.

Thus, the present speculations do not extend to a proposed method of interaction between spirit and body. I propose only that the interaction occurs at the level of the executive phase sequence, which represents the core personality of the person. The learning that develops this part of the person is guided on the one hand by certain genetic constraints, and it is also guided by certain spiritual constraints, in a way that no one has suggested. In any case, this spiritual guidance and control means that a person cannot be reduced to some finite product of heredity and environment.

I have previously emphasized the mystery of the mechanism of the agent called the Executive.[42] We just do not know how this entity can create and control novel responses, and why such responses are often adaptive. I proposed the following speculative explanation for the mechanisms of the mysterious Executive:

> In my view of the intentional belief state, the causal factor is a spiritual agent, which operates in some mysterious way through the action of a will having two aspects or functions that are not discretely different, but distinguishable. One part comes to terms with the environmental Gestalt, or acts for the sake of those existing goals that are environmentally related. The other part carries out the dispositional agendas of the causal agent.[43]

Thus, I argued that both the reductionist and the spiritual views were equally scientific, but embodied the same weakness—ignorance of the exact mechanism of how creative changes are produced.[44] I preferred a spiritual ghost because it was more optimistic and useful in dealing with the real problems of living, and mentioned frequently in the Holy Bible.

Discussion

My proposal is an extension of the theory of Hebb.[45] Nevertheless, it finishes with an assumption that he would not approve, because he was a Cognitive Behaviorist. Hebb's theory was a new beginning for psychology. His theory is a key part of the current cognitive revolution in psychology. Hebb's theory of behavior was bold in that it proposed mechanisms that can account for a broad array of phenomena in perception, learning, memory and thinking. For example, his concept of semi-autonomous central process (S-ACP) reflects a relative independence of sensory control. His pioneer concept was a phase sequence. The phase sequence is a habitual sequence of particular activations within the S-ACP. It accounts for various cognitive phenomena.

Hebb admonished us years ago that our science would have to deal with the established reality of concepts such as attention and set. He intended his theory to apply to clinical settings as well as to laboratory research. Hebb warned that our fears of animistic thinking could cause us to become overly restrictive in the kinds of phenomena that we include in our empirical research and in our theorizing. Animistic thinking means to endow inanimate objects with the ability to feel and to think.

While opposing animistic thinking, Hebb did not agree with Skinner's opposition to theorizing. He disagreed especially with Skinner's opposition to cognitive concepts.

I have argued that the fear among some psychologists of appearing unscientific contributed to the unfortunate tendency of the profession to support divisive and divergent, Humanistic and Behavioristic, subcultures,[46] as Kimble has discussed.[47] The basic issue contributing to the division involves intentional behavior.

In general, researchers using laboratory tasks and situations in order to study learning and memory favor the Behavioristic approach, whereas those who study life-related problems prefer the Humanistic approach. Consequently, the theories and practitioners have tended to diverge. For example, I pointed out that the theoretical basis for those types of behavior therapy that are ostensibly based on familiar learning (Behavioristic) paradigms are clearly deficient in describing the actual clinical practice.[48] Specifically, they tend to ignore in theorizing the major role of the client's intentional commitment to the therapeutic process. In fact, Hebb himself pointed out the fundamental importance of the concept of voluntary behavior for psychotherapy.[49]

The present view tends to follow Hebb in destroying the conception of the various psychological processes as being discretely different, and emphasized the importance of paraprocesses, which represent some kind of transition between the different processes.[50] The major departure from Hebb is the present proposal for a spiritual entity within a person, a part of the so-called Executive, which is the final cause of a behavior.

The present term for the Executive was chosen because it is the agent that consciously attends to some stimuli and not others, and it also intentionally selects responses. Consequently, it is the agent that controls the personal will, as well as the attentional processes of the organism. Thus, the Executive is more than a passive conduit for connecting stimuli and responses. It can also create new connections through reasoning. Reasoning is an internal process of mind by which new responses are creatively and originally connected to some stimuli in an attempt to solve some existing problem of living. Although both the stimulus and the response involved in the solution are already familiar to the person, and available to him or her, the person has never experienced them connected together before. But he or she is able to connect them spontaneously when the need arises during attempts at problem solving.

The present theory of will is basically an expansion on the thought of William James.[51] James proposed what is called soft determinism. His proposed mechanism holds a potential response in a person's consciousness (the person consents to the response), thus enabling the environmentally controlled mechanism to make the final selection. In contrast, Pollio proposed the generation by the environment of potential responses from which the final selection is made by a voluntary personal choice.[52] Harcum emphasized,[53] however, the point of Bandura that the personal agent, whatever its nature, and the environment interact to produce conditions that cannot be unambiguously assigned to either one individually.[54]

The "just so" proposals of Skinner have nevertheless been serious attempts at this formidable task.[55] The reductionistic argument is that, if a behavior appears, the appropriate environmental and hereditary determinants for it must have been present. Such circularity has little, if any, advantage either theoretically or practically.

James proposed that those not wishing to suspend a decision on this metaphysical issue, in spite of the inherent ambiguity, can nevertheless proceed:

> . . .taking the risk of error on our head, we must project upon one of the alternative views the attribute of reality for us; we must so fill our mind with the idea of it that it becomes our settled creed. The present writer does this for the alternative of freedom, but since the grounds of his opinion are ethical rather than psychological, he prefers to exclude them from the present book.[56]

Therefore, the decision is between incompatible belief states, with the particular belief state determining the interpretation of how the belief state came to be. The choice of interpretation is not capricious, because there are external criteria to prevent a purely arbitrary choice of one's orientation on this issue. It should be emphasized at this point that these criteria are practical rather than scientific or philosophical. James acknowledged that the scientific and moral conceptions may actually conflict:

> But when scientific and moral postulates war thus with each other and objective proof is not to be had, the only course is voluntary choice, for skepticism itself, if systematic, is also voluntary choice. If, meanwhile, the will *be* undetermined, it would seem only fitting that the belief in its indetermination should be voluntarily chosen from amongst other possible beliefs. Freedom's first deed should be to affirm itself. We ought never to hope for any other method of getting at the truth if indeterminism be a fact.[57]

Harcum proposed that determinism and voluntarism reflect two belief states.[58] In the deterministic state of thinking, explainable factors are understood as functional relations, and the unexplained factors are considered to be residual variance, caused by unknown determinants. In the voluntarism mode, explainable factors are attributed to a responsive will that responds to environmental conditions. Unexplainable factors are attributed to freedom of a transcendental will.

The reductionistic view depends upon developmental evidence. Responses that do not appear to be determined or influenced by the current environmental situation are presumed to be affected by antecedent factors, the residual traces of earlier experience. Because such traces may last for many years—perhaps permanently—there is always a viable possibility that they could be important in all but the most stimulus-bound of responses.

The question of viable will vs. reductionism also involves the issue of purposeful behavior. The point of controversy is whether the notion of purpose for a behavior means that there is an intentional striving for the incentive, which is the conventional connotation of the term, or whether the term is a simple conventional way of saying that a given motivational state of the organism directs certain behaviors persistently until that incentive, or an equivalent one, is achieved. Because consuming the incentive reduces the motivational state that led to the success in achieving it, we can say that the behavior was purposeful, without necessarily implying that intention and volition were involved.

Therefore, the question about the type of mechanism by which apparently purposive behavior is produced has been debated by philosophers and psychologists for centuries without consensus. The determinist camp argues that the perceived or inferred purpose of an animal, even a human being, is only in the eyes of the observer.[59] Thus, the determinist argues that the behavior is in fact mindlessly produced by the interaction of personal heredity with environmental factors, past and present. Therefore, the so-called agent of change is to the Behaviorist merely a convenient label for mechanical forces that have actually been effective in securing what the organism needs. So, the alleged purpose is merely an inference by the observer, inferred from the fact that the behavior ceases when the satisfaction is achieved. Therefore, the behavior appeared to the observer to be motivated by the purpose of securing that satisfactory event.

In contrast, the Humanists, as advocates of free will, propose an agent that is in some degree independent and transcendent over the mediating mechanical forces. This agent is actually free to choose a response, albeit within some physical constraints imposed by the environment, and always subject to the will of God. The person selects behaviors for the purpose of securing some perceived object of event that will satisfy a motivation.

Both sides of this issue have been promulgated by both philosophers and psychologists. Because neither group has given up its view, clearly there is no clear proof of either position, or even proof that one must be correct and the other incorrect. Although philosophical analysis permits the possibility of both a degree of determinism and free will,[60] the opposing views are still incompatible because the strict determinist view absolutely denies the possibility of any influence by an intentional (free will) agent.

Some psychologists have attempted to resolve the issue in terms of simply proposing different perspectives.[61] This view contends that these different conceptions of the causes of behavior are simply different ways of looking at one and the same object, or function, just as different viewing angles in looking at a cylinder would produce entirely different perceptions of its shape: it could appear as a circle, a rectangle or a three-dimensional cylinder.

Harcum strongly attacked this proposed resolution of the issue, saying that such an alleged resolution is nothing other than gratuitously assigning humanistic labels to purely reductionistic interpretations of the mechanism.[62] For example, considering a response to be voluntary simply because the functional stimulus or mediating mechanism is not known does not imply a difference in the causal mechanism. Nothing is gained. Such a tactic is identical to Skinner's assertion that all humanistic terms can, and must, ultimately be explained in reductionistic terms.[63] Whereas both are using humanistic terms, paradoxically, Skinner seemed to be thinking in intentional terms—though denying it— and some of the others seem to be thinking in reductionistic terms—though denying it.

In contrast, a belief in a category of cause that is not determined by heredity and environment provides a quite different orientation for both practical explanations and the guidance of behavior. For example, only if you believed in an intentional system would it make sense to exhort a person with a phobia—an irrational fear—actually to perform the feared response as part of his or her therapy. Only if you believed in intention would you even have a rational basis to ask so-called hardened criminals or drug addicts to change. Presumably, a "hardened" criminal would be one with very strong habits of criminality. And only on the basis of a belief in intentionality would you actually believe in the validity or reality of the change, if they did change their behavior.

Rychlak agreed that we can predict behavior on the basis of human premises about the logical requirements of a situation, indicating environmental influences. But, he said, there is a real difference from the deterministic view, as follows:

> We do not deny that our willingness to assign responsibility to the individual means that at some point in the course of behavioral description we may say that the behavior is up to the person, and although we can give the odds that he will choose this way or that, what he actually 'does' is *in principle* not determined by our actuarial rule but by *his* decisions. There is no other way for a free-will psychology to operate. Either one accepts a final-cause construct as the legitimate cause of behavior in at least some situations, or he does not.[64]

Harcum argued that both methods for conceptualizing the world were valid under particular circumstances, even though they cannot be employed simultaneously.[65] The phenomenon of a disjunctive change in thinking and responding patterns of humans is real. The different ways of conceptualizing the mechanics of such change are, however, incompatible. This causal mechanism can be equally well conceived as a spiritual thing or as a neural thing.[66] Although behaviors can sometimes be predicted on the basis of the different conceptions, the ultimate causal mechanism is a mystery. As Attneave and Viney contended, the free-will conception, despite its mysterious component, still provides the basis for a viable theory of human intentionality.[67] This is no less true than for the mysterious physiological component. Plus, there is the practical advantage of the free-will conception, and it is compatible with the Christian religion.

The very nature of the human spirit means that it is not easily proved by human experience. The best empirical evidence comes from first-person accounts of persons, such as George Ritchie, who have survived a death experience.[68] For example, Ritchie was revived nine minutes after he had been pronounced dead. After revival, he reported that during the death interval, he had experienced a real environment that he had not seen before. He later recognized this real environment that he had seen before only in his state of death. As Ritchie said later, as a psychiatrist, despite the undoubted differences within the medical profession on the mind-brain problem:

> I can say, however, that I have never talked to anyone who has had a near-death experience similar to mine who wasn't as convinced as I that the brain and the mind are two different things. Like me, they believe that the brain has the same relation to the mind that a television set has to television waves. Just because one cuts off the television set doesn't mean the waves cease to exist. Just because the brain and body die doesn't mean the soul or psyche ceases to exist.[69]

Summary

This chapter describes the role of theory in psychology. In the process of testing theory, psychologists make guesses about possible causes of behavior and literally attempt to falsify these guesses. A theory is accepted as correct if the very best empirical attempts to disprove it fail, and these attempts are considered adequate tests. The different theorists are distinguished by the types of explanations they investigate. Therefore, theory guides the empirical research.

The book presents a particular proposal for a theory of the causal agent in the initiation of novel behaviors. It describes the Executive in terms of a connectionist view of brain activity after the theory proposed by Hebb, but with the crucial differences that it proposes a dualistic view, assigning an ultimate level of control of behavior to a spirit of non-material essence. Thus, the theory is compatible with religious teachings.

Notes

1. Donald O. Hebb, Alice in Wonderland or psychology among the biological sciences. In Harry F. Harlow and C. N. Woolsey (Eds.) *Biological and Biochemical Bases of Behavior* (Madison, WI: University of Wisconsin Press, 1958). 451-467.
2. Ibid, 456.
3. Benjamin B. Wolman, Concerning psychology and the philosophy of science. In Benjamin B. Wolman (Ed.) *Handbook of General Psychology* (Englewood Cliffs, NJ: Prentice-Hall, 1973.) 22-48.
4. E. Rae Harcum, *A Psychology of Freedom and Dignity* (Westport, CT: Praeger, 1994).
5. Ibid.
6. John B. Watson, Psychology as the Behaviorist views it, *Psychological Review, 20*: 158-177, 1913.
7. Sigmund Freud, *An Outline of Psychoanalysis*. Trans. J. Strachey (New York: Norton, 1949).
8. Carl R. Rogers, A theory of therapy, personality, and interpersonal relationships, as developed in the client-centered framework. In Sigmund Koch (Ed.) *Psychology: A Study of a Science*, Vol. 3 (New York: McGraw-Hill, 1959).
9. Watson, Psychology as the Behaviorist views it, 1913.
10. Donald O. Hebb, *The Organization of Behavior* (New York: John Wiley & Sons, Inc., 1949).
11. Watson, Psychology as the Behaviorist views it, 1913.
12. Freud, *An Outline of Psychoanalysis*, 1949.
13. Anthony J. Sutich, Introduction, *Journal of Humanistic Psychology, 1*: vii-ix, 1961.
14. R. Taft, Humanistic psychology: An introduction to a symposium. *Australian Journal of Psychology, 34*: 217-219, 1982.
15. Lawrence LeShan, *The Dilemma of Psychology* (New York: Dutton, 1990).
16. W. W. Harman, The transpersonal challenge to the scientific paradigm: The need for a restructuring of science, *ReVision, 11*: 13-21, 1988.
17. LeShan, *The Dilemma of Psychology*, 1990.
18. Michael Wertheimer, Introduction to psychology. In W. H. Holtzman (Ed.) *Personalized Psychology, A1* (New York: Harper and Row, 1977). 1-14, 11.
19. Wolfgang Köhler, *Gestalt Psychology* (New York: Liveright, 1947).
20. E. Rae Harcum, Parity for the theoretical ghosts and gremlins: Response to Pollio/Henley and Rychlak. *The Journal of Mind and Behavior, 12*: 151-162, 1991.
21. Hebb, *The Organization of Behavior*, 1949; B. F. Skinner, *Science of Human Behavior* (New York: MacMillan, 1953).

22. Skinner, *Science and Human Behavior*, 1953.
23. Harcum, Parity for the theoretical ghosts and gremlins, 1991.
24. Hebb, *The Organization of Behavior*, 1949.
25. Ibid.
26. Harcum, *A Psychology of Freedom and Dignity*, 1994.
27. Ulric Neisser, *Cognitive Psychology* (New York: Appleton-Century-Crofts, 1967.)
28. Harcum, *A Psychology of Freedom and Dignity*, 1994.
29. Howard R. Pollio and T. Henley, Empirical and philosophical reactions to Harcum's "Behavioral paradigm for a psychological resolution of the free-will issue." *The Journal of Mind and Behavior, 12*: 115-134, 1991.
30. Hebb, *The Organization of Behavior*, 1949.
31. Ibid.
32. P. M. Milner, The cell assembly. Mark II. *Psychological Review, 64*: 242-252, 1957; G. V. Goddard, Component properties of the memory machine: Hebb revisited. In P. W. Juscyck and R. M. Klein (Eds.) *The Nature of Thought: Essays in Honor of D. O. Hebb* (Hillsdale, NJ: Erlbaum, 1980). 231-247.
33. J. L. McClelland and D. E. Rumelhart, A distributed processing model of human learning and memory. In J. L. McClelland, D. E. Rumelhart and the PDP Research Group (Eds.) *Parallel Distributed Processing*: Exploratons in the microstructure of cognition, Vol. 2: Psychological and Biological Models (Cambridge, MA: MIT Press, 1986). 179-215.
34. E. Goffman, *Frame Analysis* (New York: Harper and Row, 1974).
35. Milner, The cell assembly, Mark II, 1957.
36. Harcum, *Serial Learning and Paralearning* (New York: Wiley-Interscience, 1975).
37. Donald O. Hebb, The American Revolution, *American Psychologist, 15*: 735-745, 1960,
38. Donald O. Hebb, *The Organization of Behavior*, 1949.
39. Ibid, 144.
40. Donald O. Hebb, *The American Revolution*, 1960.
41. Hebb, *The Organization of Behavior*, 1949, 145.
42. Harcum, Parity for the theoretical ghosts and gremlins, 1991; Harcum, *A Psychology of Freedom and Dignity*, 1994.
43. Ibid, 155.
44. Ibid.
45. Hebb, *The Organization of Behavior*, 1949.
46. E. Rae Harcum, Defensive reactance of psychologists to a metaphysical foundation for integrating different psychologies. *The Journal of Psychology, 122*: 217-235, 1988.
47. Gregory A. Kimble, Psychology's two cultures. *American Psychologist, 39*: 833-839, 1984.
48. E. Rae Harcum, Commitment to collaboration as a prerequisite for existential commonality in psychotherapy. *Psychotherapy, 26*: 200-209,

1989.
49. Hebb, *The Organization of Behavior*, 1949.
50. Harcum, *Serial Learning and Paralearning*, 1975.
51. William James, *The Principles of Psychology*, Vol. I (New York: Holt, 1890); William James, *The Principles of Psychology*, Vol. II (New York: Holt, 1890).
52. Howard R. Pollio, *Behavior and Existence* (Monterey, CA: Brooks/Cole, 1981).
53. Harcum, Parity for the theoretical ghosts and gremlins, 1991.
54. Albert Bandura, *Social Foundations of Thought and Action* (Englewood Cliffs, NJ: Prentice-Hall, 1986).
55. Skinner, *Science of Human Behavior*, 1953, Skinner, *Beyond Freedom and Dignity*, 1971.
56. James, *The Principles of Psychology*, Vol. II, 1890. 573.
57. Ibid.
58. Harcum, The relative utility of complementary disparate views on voluntarism and determinism, 1990.
59. Skinner, *Science and Human Behavior*, 1953.
60. K. Lehrer, An empirical disproof of determinism? In K. Lehrer (Ed.) *Freedom and Determinism* (New York: Random House, 1966). 175-202.
61. D. G. Myers, *Psychology* (New York: Worth, 1986); R. E. Smith, J. G. Sarason, and B. R. Sarason, *Psychology: The Frontiers of Behavior* (3rd ed.) (New York: Harper and Row, 1986).
62. Harcum, The relative utility of complementary disparate views on voluntarism and determinism, 1990.
63. Skinner, *Beyond Freedom and Dignity*, 1971.
64. Joseph F. Rychlak, *The Psychology of Rigorous Humanism* (New York: Wiley-Interscience, 1977). 491.
65. Harcum, The relative utility of complementary disparate views on voluntarism and determinism, 1990.
66. Harcum, Parity for the theoretical ghosts and gremlins, 1991.
67. Frederick Attneave, In defense of homunculi. In W. A. Rosenblith (Ed.) *Sensory Communication* (Cambridge, MA: MIT Press, 1961), 777-782; D. W. Viney, William James on free will and determinism, *The Journal of Mind and Behavior, 7*: 555-565, 1986.
68. George G. Ritchie Jr., *Return from Tomorrow* (Grand Rapids, MI: Fleming H. Revell, 1978): Ritchie, *Ordered to Return: My Life After Dying* (Charlottesville, VA: Hampton Roads Publishing Company, Inc., 1998).
69. Ritchie, Ordered to Return, 163.

Glossary

Abnormal: either greater or less than the usual or ideally normal by some criterion amount

Accountability: principle that people should be held responsible for their behaviors

Act : a description of a behavior in terms of its purpose or what it accomplishes

Actor–observer effect: the difference between the attributions of an actor and an observer concerning the causation of the actor's behavior

Affect: a feeling of pleasant or unpleasant tone or mood.

Agent: the part of a person that voluntarily selects behaviors

Anal stage: according to psychoanalytic theory, the time period of development when the child is pre-occupied with the defecation process

Analogy: showing that one thing is like another

Ancestral factors: events in the distant past which influence behavior

Anecdote: short story or anecdote about an actual instance of behavior

Animism: imputing life to an inanimate object

Antecedent variable: a special category of organismic variable which are those reflecting the effects of earlier experiences. Also called historical variables.

Applied science: research undertaken to discover the causation of a specific behavior which poses a real-life problem

Approach-avoidance conflict: conflict when a positive goal also has negative valence

Arousal: the activation or energizing of an organism

Association: bonds or connections between two things

Attention: directing consciousness toward one stimulus or cognitive event rather than others

Attitude: persistent learned mental state which predisposes a person to react to something in terms of personal evaluation

Automatic behavior: habitual responses that are so over-learned that the person requires little or no attention to them for satisfactory performance.

Awareness: response to the environment as a result of openness to parasensory experiences

Basic science: see "pure science"

Before-and-after method: experimental method in which the control condition consists of the situation before manipulation of the independent variable, and the experimental condition is the situation after the manipulation of the independent variable

Behavior: anything that an organism does

Behaviorism (cognitive): accepts the mediating role of cognitions between stimulus and response

Behaviorism (strict): theory that observable behavior is the subject matter of psychology

Belief: integrated conclusion about the nature of reality; one of the processes of cognition.

Biology: the science that deals with living organisms and life processes

Biopsychologist: person who studies the biological foundations of behavior

Biosocial psychology: attempts to account for social behaviors in terms of inherited structure

Brain wave: common term for a recording of brain activity

Butterfly effect: the result when a tiny distant causal factor causes a subsequent critical difference in behavior

Case history method: a naturalistic method of science in which the behavior of a single individual or event in natural life situations is studied intensively and recorded

Cause: an antecedent event which is invariably correlated with a subsequent event

Cell assembly: Hebb's concept of a network of neural cells in the forebrain which, when activated, produce a particular psychological experience

Central tendency: tendency for the scores in a frequency distribution to group about a central value

C.E.O. model: description of the functioning of the Executive using the analogy of a CEO in industry

Chaos: theory in physics that certain events can be predicted only within certain limits of accuracy

Choice: voluntary selection of a response from among those made available by heredity and environment; assumes freedom of will

Claustrophobia: irrational fear of closed spaces

Clinical method: studies clients with certain, possibly abnormal, experiences or conditions in order to determine effect of those conditions on their behavior

Cognition: result of a basically logical assessment of perceptual evidence to produce a view of the world; also, the process of arriving at such a belief about the world; subsumes the processes of sensation, perception, projective perception and believing

Cognitive behaviorism: accepts mediating role of cognitions between stimuli and responses

Cognitive revolution: emergence of cognitive concepts in psychology

Compact disk model: describes the production of motivations and emotions as like the playing of records on a compact disk

Comparative psychologist: person who studies and compares the behaviors of humans and non-humans

Concept: a category of things or ideas that share certain characteristics

Conflict: state within a person when two mutually exclusive desires or impulses are activated simultaneously

Confounded experiment: experiment which contains a confounding variable

Confounding variables: extraneous variables which co-vary with the independent variable, and thus may provide an alternative explanation for the change in the dependent variable

Connectionism: theory of thinking based on shifting patterns of neural activity

Conscious: awareness of one's content of mind

Consciousness: a person's awareness of aspects of his or her environment

Construct: hypothetical entity, usually within the organism, which is presumed to cause a certain effect

Control: maintaining ability to manipulate a variable, or to keep it constant, in order to make accurate inferences about the causation of behavior

Control condition: normal or reference condition in an experiment which does not experience the manipulation of the independent variable

Control group: group of subjects in an experiment who are not given the independent variable in order to provide reference or baseline results for comparison to the results of subjects who received the independent variable

Convergent thinking: bringing together two disparate lines of thought to produce the solution to a problem

Converging evidence: evidence from two or more sources that points to the same conclusion

Conviction: commitment to a strongly held holistic belief which implies action consonant with the belief

Cookbook: book that prescribes the exact ingredients and methods to produce a particular result

Coping: production of a behavior that is the solution to a problem

Correlation: empirical relationship when two variables vary together, either positively or inversely

Courage: the capacity of a person to accept and endure risks and dangers in a steadfast manner

Creativity: ability to produce novel ideas or behaviors and to perceive novel relationships

Criterion: a standard value against which other things can be judged

Cult: group of people devoted to a person, principle or system of unorthodox religious beliefs

Customer model: considers the Executive to be like a customer in a retail store

Customer theory: theory to describe the functioning of the Executive agent as making choices from among possible responses

Cut-off score: score selected to separate passing and failing performance on the test

Data: evidence used to reach conclusions

Data language: the literal description of an empirical result

Data interpretation: the conclusion of the researcher about what the data means

Decision: selecting which act to make from available alternatives

Deduction: logical process by which cognitions are developed from a confluence of perceptions

Defense mechanisms: psychological devices by which the individual's personality keeps itself from awareness of those of its impulses which it finds unacceptable to it

Delusion: false belief about reality, held in spite of sufficient evidence that it is not true

Demand characteristics: attributes of an experiment which leads the subject to reach a conclusion, true or false, about its real purpose

Dependent variable: the behavior in an experiment which the researcher is trying to explain.

Depression: general sadness, with or without adequate causation

Description: objective listing of the physical and psychological attributes of a person or thing

Determinism: an underlying assumption that our behavior, thoughts and feelings are completely caused just like events in the natural world, such that whatever happened had to have happened under the circumstances.

Deviation: difference in raw-score units between an individual measurement in a frequency distribution from the mean of the complete distribution of values or scores.

Dignity: the worth or esteem placed on a person by others

Directing: process of leading the organism to make one response in preference to another

Discovery: learning through deliberate study from personal observation, as opposed to being instructed

Disordered mental state: pathological state of thinking

Dispersion: scatter or variability of scores; variable errors which are measured by range, mean deviation and standard deviation

Distal stimulus: physical change in the environment which excites a receptor

Doctrinaire: when a psychologist's views all fall neatly and consistently into a given category of theory

Dualism: philosophical point of view that there are two fundamentally different sorts of entities in the universe—material and non-material,

Eclectic: describes psychologists who do not adhere to a single theoretical position, but shift from theory to theory as each seems useful or appropriate to them.

Education: the learning which is oriented toward the general improvement of the person to respond adjustively in many situations

EEG: see "electroencephalograph"

Effector: muscle or gland for which the action constitutes a response

Efficient cause: explanation of how an event came to happen

Ego: the part of the personality concerned with rational assessments of reality, on the basis of practical experience

Elaborated model: describes the causation of behavior in terms of stimulus, learning and multifarious internal mechanisms

Electroencephalograph (EEG): a graphic recording of so-called brain waves, which are periodic changes in electric potential at a given point in the brain

Emergent stimulus: new and different perception of a particular stimulus configuration as a result of perceptual organizational processes

Emotion: a condition of feeling, such as fear, anger, grief or joy, which combines both psychological and physical arousal

Empirical: knowledge based on sensory experience

Empiricism: belief in the value of sensory-based knowledge

Environment: the totality of the surroundings of a person

Epistemology: the philosophical study of the origin, value and limits of knowledge

E.S.P.: see "Extrasensory Perception"

Executive: term referring to the hypothetical agent in the human personality which receives and interprets stimulation and selects responses.

Experiment: method of science in which the researcher manipulates some condition for a person and then compares his or her acts to a control or reference condition to determine if they are changed by the manipulation

Experimental condition: condition produced by the manipulation of the independent variable

Experimental group: the comparison or reference group of subjects in an experiment used to establish performance on the dependent variable in the absence of an experimental manipulation.

Ex Post Facto experimental design: unplanned experiment when a variable is manipulated by a condition not controlled by the experimenter

Extenuation: notion that environmental influences can overwhelm the effects of a viable will

External validity: characteristic of an experiment which permits valid application to real-life situations

Extraneous variable: uncontrolled, and often unknown, variable which can influence behavior in an experiment

Extrasensory perception (ESP): general term for awareness of events in the environment by way of some unknown process

Extrinsic reward: an arbitrary reward that is not a natural consequence of the correct behavior

Fact: event that was observable by at least two competent observers and, therefore, provides basic empirical evidence

Faith: strong conviction about reality which is based primarily on intuitive evidence

False negative: rejected candidate who would have succeeded if they had been selected

False positive: successful candidate who later fail on the job

F.C.P.: see "Final Common Path"

Fear: unpleasant emotion produced by a perceived threat to personal welfare

Feedback: return of a response as stimulation for the next response (truly a feedforward mechanism)

Feedforward: when one response influences the next response

File-Drawer problem: problem in interpreting research results because unpublished results (often negative) are consigned to the researcher's personal files, and thus are not available to other researchers

Final cause: explanation for why an event occurred; what is its purpose?

Final common path (FCP): the concept of a limited number of motor neurons upon which many neurons in the central nervous system converge and compete for access.

First-person data: unreportable personal experience of a single observer

Fixation (psychoanalytic theory): stopping of emotional development at a particular psychosexual stage

Formal: done according to regular or established form or custom

Free Association: method of psychoanalysis requiring the client to say the first thing that comes to mind in response to a stimulus word

Free Will: idea that a person can by personal choice select the act that he or she will make when he or she could have made a different choice

Freedom of will: assumption that behavior is controlled by the joint effects of a personal will, environment and heredity

Frequency: number of times something happened, or the number of persons doing some act

Frustration: unpleasant feeling when a person is blocked from the achievement of what he or she desires

Frustration tolerance: ability to cope with problems in life despite previous experiences of failure

Functionalism: school of psychology which asked observers to describe mental operations they went through as they performed prescribed tasks. Related to Structuralism and Introspection.

Functional model: a description of the functions, or processes, that take place inside the organism

Functional stimulus: the effective or critical stimulus for producing a particular response

Gene: the physical unit of heredity

Generalization: acting the same to two different inputs; acting as if they were the same

Generativism: concept which says that human actions can be produced by factors of the environment, heredity and a viable will

Genital stage: according to psychoanalytic theory, the time period of adult sexuality

Genuine: desired quality of a humanistic therapist to manifest candor and personal integrity

Gestalt psychology: the school that maintains that the whole is different from the sum of its parts

Historical variable: see "Antecedent Variable"

Holistic: when something is considered as a whole

Holistic domain: Conceptualization of reality that involves the confluence of evidence and conclusions from the transductional and intuitive domains.

Homeostasis: Tendency of the body to maintain a balanced state of the internal environment.

Humanities: branches of learning regarded as primarily pertaining to culture

Humanity: that part of humans which only he or she has, and which makes him or her different from other things

Humanism: view of psychology that human beings are intentional with a personal will which can change their behaviors in creative ways that are not entirely conditioned by the person's heredity and environment.

Humanistic therapy: therapy based on the therapist as a facilitator to help client see how his or her behaviors are maladaptive in society, with the client ultimately responsible for the success of the therapy

Hypothesis: a possible explanation for a given act, which is not known to be true

Hypothetical construct: an inferred internal structure which affects behavior, and is described in physical terms, but its actual existence has not been proved

Id: according to psychoanalytic theory, the part of the personality that contains the libido, or unconscious pleasure-seeking impulses

Immanent truth: inherent truth; does not contain self-contradition

Incentive: an object or condition that a person perceives as capable of satisfying a desire

Independence: a personal characteristic of forming opinions and behaviors without undue influence of others

Independent variable: the manipulated variable in an experiment

Indeterminism: concept that behaviors are not completely controlled by external events

Individual differences: performance variations among individual persons

Individual psychology: the branch of psychology which studies the quality of being a person rather than a thing or an abstraction; the study of the properties that distinguish one individual person from another

Induction: generalization of response tendencies from previous experiences

Information: knowledge of reality

Inner-behavioral approach: considers that no natural data is outside science

Input: the stimulation of the person from the psychological environment

Intentional: personal awareness of aiming at a voluntary goal or purpose

Interaction: when the effects of one variable change the effects of another variable

Interactionistic dualism: philosophical belief that two essences of the universe (material and non-material) interact with one another

Interbehavioral approach: argues that no natural phenomena are outside of science, and therefore scientists can learn about human nature from examining all products of human behavior

Internal validity: design purity of an experiment which permits valid conclusions

Interpretation: process by which sensations are converted into perceptions by addition of meaning from traces of prior stimulation

Intervening variable: Expression of relationship between control conditions (stimuli) and the dependent variable (responses)

Intolerance of ambiguity: discomfort when faced with a situation that is not easily understood or controlled; desire to have everything reduced to black and white

Intrinsic dignity: unearned dignity accorded to every human being

Introspection: looking inside oneself in order to observe and report one's own actions and feelings; provides second-person data

Intuition: experiential process by which the person, through minimal cues and similarities, becomes aware, without reasoning, of information about the environment

Just-so theory: theory that contends that, whatever the objective response, the physical conditions were just right to produce that response

Key: subtle stimulus event that is crucial in providing context in a given situation

Knowledge: correct conviction about reality

Latency stage: according to the psychoanalytic theory, a time period of relative emotional calm because of submerged sexuality

Law: a principle supported by such strong evidence that it is not subject to doubt, unless new disconfirming information is obtained

Law of Effect: principle that a response followed by satisfaction (i.e., is rewarded) will tend to be repeated

Law of Least Effort: all things equal, the individual will perform the behavior that requires the least effort to achieve its goals

Law of Ultimate Practicality: principle proposed by Harcum that one is free to believe anything about the environment that is not contradicted by convincing evidence and also works for personal benefit

Learned helplessness: habit of passivity because the person believes that he or she is powerless to control events

Learned optimism: habit of confidence because the person has been successful in controlling events

Learning: process inferred from a persistent change in behavior as a result of experience

Liberal Arts: a course of study which emphasizes academic rather than technical content, and thus is characterized by openness to different ideas as opposed to rigorous thought.

Libertarianism: concept that behavior is entirely controlled by voluntary action of a will

Library model: describing memory traces as analogous to material stored in a library

Libido: a general motivation to satisfy a basic biological need for pleasure

Limbic system: parts of the midbrain and forebrain that are particularly involved in emotional and motivational responses
Logical positivism: the belief that if it cannot be measured it, it does not exist, or is nonsense
Machine: a thing of more than one part, which is built to do some work
Materialistic monism: view that only the material world is real
Mathematics: the science of the measurement, properties and relationships of quantitative forms and sets
Mature: fully developed in body and mind; able to tolerate frustration; capable of delaying or denying satisfaction of desires
Maximizing: finding the best solution to a problem
Mean: the arithematic average
Mean deviation: average of the separations between the mean and each individual score, taken without regard to sign
Measure: to quantify the amount of a thing
Measure of central tendency: either the mean, median or mode, each of which indicates the typical score in a frequency distribution
Mechanism: part of a body or machine which is responsible for an event
Median: middle point of the frequency distribution of scores on a test
Mediating process: mechanisms between stimulus and response that influence the response
Memory: ability to retain and retrieve past experiences
Memory trace: lingering effect of earlier stimulation in the nervous system
Mental: pertaining to the mind
Mental health: the condition of feeling satisfied with life and enjoying it
Mental set: see "Set"
Metacognition: awareness of knowledge that is not in attention at the moment
Metaphorical approach: a subjective method used by some scientists in which a word is used in place of another word in order to suggest an analogy or likeness between them
Metaphysical issue: an issue that cannot be solved by empirical means because it involves questions of truth about nature, of what does or does not exist, of what is real
Metaphysics: branch of philosophy that examines the nature of reality (existence) and the relationships between mind and matter
Methodological determinism: the practical assumption that all behavior is caused; this is the justification for the scientific method
Mind: a conception of the total activity in the factors that control behavior
Mind-body problem: problem of understanding the relationship between mind and body
Mode: most frequently occurring score in a frequency distribution
Model: an analogy which is used for organizing our thoughts and representing relationships to help us understand the functions of a given mechanism
Moderating variable: variable that does not directly influence behavior, but interacts with other variables to change their effects

Modernity: conception of science which recognizes a subjective element, contextual truth and practical considerations
Molar: global level of description of behavior
Molecular: fine-grained level of description of behavior
Monism: general philosophical view that mind and body are composed of one and the same essence
Mood: temporary state of mind or feelings
Motivation (secondary): the process by which certain learned desires produce certain acts
Motivation (primary): the process by which certain unlearned desires produce certain acts
Motor: related to the actual performance of an act
Mutation: spontaneous change in a habit
Natural necessity: a theory of causation which states that cause is the whole set of necessary conditions sufficient for an effect
Naturalistic method: scientific method which attempts to describe a behavior in the natural setting, without intrusion by the researcher
Need: departure from homeostatic balance
Neurohumor: Electrochemical substance which can excite neurons to fire
Normal (statistical): the response or condition that is near the middle of the normal frequency distribution; it is average and most frequent
Normal (ideal): the response or condition that is most favorable or desirable in an absolute sense
Observational method: recording behavior by direct observation
Ontology: the branch of knowledge (metaphysics) that investigates the nature of reality
Oral stage: in psychoanalytic theory, a time period when the child is preoccupied with oral gratification
Organism: the animal or person who can contribute many variables to the determination of his or her behavior
Peak experience: an extremely happy experience
Peer review: the term for the reviewing process for journal publication in psychology, which involves judgment of merit by nominal peers of the author
Perception: interpretation of a sensation by adding literal or idiosyncratic meaning to it
Person: a particular human being
Personal esteem: high regard or respect for one's self; self-esteem
Personality: the sum of the stable psychological characteristics of a person
Personality trait: dispositional factor within a person
Personality type: classification of a person according to a dominant personality trait
Personal space bubble: space about a person that he or she considers as having personal proprietorship
Phallic stage: in psychoanalytic theory, a time period when the child is pre-

occupied with exhibitionism

Phase sequence: Hebb's concept of a temporal series of cell assemblies

Philosophy: a consistent conception or system of principles about the universe, formulated with the intention to understand reality

Phobia: an irrational fear of a specific object or situation

Physiological psychology: the branch of psychology which studies the correlations of physiological processes or activities with behavior

Placebo: control procedure to keep the subjects blind to the fact that a condition in an experiment is the control condition

Placebo effect: psychological or physiological effect produced by cognition and beliefs of the person

Pleasure principle: assumption of psychoanalytic theory that the newborn is dominated by the search for pleasure, that the demands of the libido be immediately gratified

Polarize:to separate into two extreme opposites, as into radically different opinions, attributes or electrical charges.

Positivistic view of science: approach to science which deals only with facts

Post-positivistic view: liberal approach to science which accepts all types of data

PQ4R technique: active study technique involving Previewing, Questioning, Reading, Reflection, Reciting and Reviewing.

Pre-destination: religious term for an alleged foreordination by God of everything that will happen

Prejudice: opinion formed prior to the examination of evidence

Previewing: brief scanning of material to be studied in order to form a general idea of what it covers

Principle: a verbal statement of the way events of a certain class consistently and uniformly occur, thus providing a fundamental truth for guidance.

Principle of parsimony: rule to look for the simplest explanation for an event

Problem: a question raised for an answer

Process: the meaans by which things change from one state or one condition into another.

Profession: the work that a person does to earn a living

Profiling: falsely attributing certain negative personality characteristics to a member of a particular group

Proof: facts that establish truth of something to convince any reasonable person

Proximal stimulus: transduced form of a stimulus, usually represented by the small letter s

Psyche: refers to mental content

Psychiatrist: an M.D. who specialized in treating thinking disorders

Psychoanalysis (therapy): insight method of psychotherapy based on the assumption of unconscious motivation

Psychoanalytic theory: one of the three basic theories of personality based on fixation of pleasurable drives at various psychosexual stages of development

Psychology: the study of the mental and physical processes that cause animal behaviors for the purpose of understanding, predicting and controlling those behaviors

Psychosomatic: the effect of a thinking disorder on the physical body

Psychotherapy: using psychological methods to help another person solve his or her problems of living

Pure science: research undertaken to discover general principles of behavior

Questioning: asking specific questions about the material in a reading assignment

R: symbol to indicate an overt response

Random: selected such that each member of a population has an equal chance of being selected

Range: the interval in scores between the highest and lowest scores in the frequency distribution

Reactance: tendency of persons to defend themselves against he idea that their behavior can be predicted

Reading: active search for the answers to specific question posed in a study assignment

Reality principle: Freudian term for the fact that the pursuit of personal pleasure leads to personal problems if it does not take into account the exigencies of life and the desires of others

Reality testing: inducing a client to experience the consequences of his or her actions

Reasoning: connecting a stimulus and a response which were not previously associated in experience, in order to solve a problem

Reciting: active recall of the answers to the questions posed for a reading assignment

Reduced cell assembly: network of neurons produced by the common components of many networks; a lowest common denominator of network activity, whose activation corresponds to a conceptualization, cognition or a code of action

Reductionism: conception which maintains that human beings consist only of physical structures

Reflecting: thoughtful evaluation of the answers to questions in a reading assignment

Reflex: inborn, structural connection between a certain stimulus input and a response

Regression to the mean: on re-testing, a person who scored high on the first test is likely to score lower on the second test, and a person who scored low on the first test is likely to score higher on the second test, because so-called chance factors, which added to very high or very low scores on the first test, and would not be likely to occur on the second test.

Research: discovery of general laws of behavior

Response: any behavior that a person can produce

Response interference: mutual competition among different response tendencies

Response selection mechanism: some response tendencies are more likely to appear as overt responses

Response (mental) set: predisposition to respond in a certain way

Responsibility: personal characteristic of honoring one's commitments and obligations in a satisfactory manner

Responsive will: aspect of a human volitional system which responds to conditions of the environment

Responsivity: personal characteristic of awareness of conditions and circumstances in the environment, and responding in a caring manner

Reviewing: delayed recitation of the material learned in a reading assignment for the purpose of refreshing the memory

Reward: thing or event which satisfies a motivation; popular term for a reinforcement

Rubin figure: figure with an ambiguous interpretation because it can be seen as a white vase against a black background or as two black silhouettes of faces against a white background

S: symbol for an observable stimulus

S-ACP: see semi-autonomous central process

Sample: group of individuals selected to represent a larger population

Schema: inferred cognitive structure representing multiple associations among events

School: group of psychologists who follow the theoretical ideas of a prominent leader

School psychologist: person who studies and applies psychological data and methods to school-related problems

Science: a gathering of facts about nature, the search for such facts, and the way a person goes about obtaining these facts

Second-person data: report of personal (internal) experience by a single observer

Selection ratio: ratio of number of applicants to number of jobs or admissions

Selecting: process by which the organism chooses the overt response

Selectivity of perception: some stimuli are more likely to be perceived than others

Self-actualization: achieving personal aspirations for self

Self-esteem: the view or subjective regard or respect that the person has of himself or herself; personal esteem

Semi-autonomous central process: an internal mechanism for selecting responses

Sensation: The immediate existential response of the organism to a stimulation from the physical environment.

Sense organ: part of the body which receives stimulus input and passes it along the nervous system to the brain

Sensory: related to the activity of a sense organ

Set (or mental set): transient readiness to take a given view, or predisposition to make a given act

Signal: a target stimulus

Significant difference: a research effect too large to be attributed to chance

Simple functional model: description of the causation of behavior in terms of stimulus and the functions of Believing, Directing, Selecting and Learning

Social desirability bias: tendency of a research subject to make responses that will be admired by others

Social psychology: study of behavior of people in groups

Socialization: process of responding to rewards of society

Soft determinism: philosophical view that human behavior can be a joint product of environmental and inherited factors and some freedom of will

Somatopsychic: when the physical structure and state of the body exert effects on the kind of responses produced, including the content of the conscious experience in the person

S-0-R model: description of the origin of behavior in terms of the relationships between stimulus (S), organism (O) and response (R)

S-O-R cyclic model: model of stimulus, organism and response which includes the feedback (actually feedforward) from response to the new stimulus situation in a continuous cycle

Species: a distinct kind of animal or plant, in which all members of the group have the same permanent characteristics

Species-specific behavior: behavior which results from the natural characteristics of the species

Spontaneous remission: unexplained improvement in a pathology

S-R model: representing behavior in terms of correlations between stimulus and response

Standard deviation: the square root of the value obtained by summing all of the squared deviations of each score from the mean divided by the number of measurements in a frequency distribution

State: condition of consistency within criterion limits of those attributes which define it

Statistics: quantitative procedures to show the numerical relations between facts

Stimulus: object or event that influences acts by activating a sense organ

Stimulus-bound behavior: when the response is entirely predictable from knowing the stimulus

Stress: perception of an increase in unpleasant psychological arousal produced by input demands placed on a system, which strain, or threaten to strain, its ability to function because of conflicting tendencies of different coping responses

Strict behaviorism: explains the causation of behavior in terms of connections between stimuli and responses

Strong transcendence: when responses differ from what would be expected from environmental circumstances

Structuralism: the first approach to psychological theory, coming out of the research methodology of introspection

Stubborn facts: facts which are consistently obtained regardless of the theory which guided the research

Subject: person or animal whose actions are manipulated or observed in research

Sufficiency: finding a solution to a problem that will work, but may not be the best solution

Superego: the part of the mature personality structure that is concerned with issues of right and wrong, based on imitation of the same-sex parent

Superordinate cell assembly: more elaborate combination of individual cell assemblies

Survey: naturalistic research technique for determining the views of a selected population on some issue

Symbol: one thing used to represent a concept or idea

System: a thing of several components which performs a certain function

Teleological: pertaining to ends, goals and purposes

Theory: tentative explanation about how a given mechanism works to produce a class or category of behaviors

Therapeutic alliance: the trusting relationship between psychotherapist and client that provides a basis for successful therapy

Thinking: inferential process by which cognitions are integrated into convictions or conclusions

Third-person data: evidence obtained by any competent observer by observing overt behavior

Thought experiment: possible experiment for which the results would be obvious from just thinking rationally about the prevailing psychological principles in the situation

Training: the learning that is oriented toward the development of skills to accomplish a known job

Trait: an enduring characteristic of personality which disposes the person toward certain behaviors

Transaction: interaction between organisms that influences each party

Transcendental: outside the sensory system as conventionally understood

Transcendental truth: empirical truth arising from consistency with the facts

Transcendental will: aspect of human volitional system which responds independently of environmental circumstances

Transduction: process through which energy in the environment is converted into neural impulses

Transfer: carry-over of learned performance from one stimulus situation to another

Transpersonal: intuitive, non-empirical subjective evidence for a conviction

Unconscious: those views, decisions or desires of the person which are unknown to him or her

Variable: a thing which changes over time and can influence behavior

Variability: the spread or dispersion of scores about the central value in a frequency distribution

Variance: the squared value of the standard deviation, used as a measure of the variability of scores

Viable will: an alternative term for freedom of will, which asserts only some measure of independence from effects of heredity and environment.

View: a way of seeing or thinking about an object or an issue

Voluntarism: belief that all behavior is voluntary

Voluntary behavior: the behavior that is caused by the action of a viable will

Wholeness: concept of Humanistic psychology that emphasizes the healthy and good personal characteristics of individuals which make them productive and successful

References

Annett, Edward A. *Psychology for Bible Teachers.* New York: Charles Scribner & Sons, 1925.

Attneave, Frederick. In defense of homunculi. In W.A. Rosenblith (Ed.), *Sensory Communication,* 777–782. Cambridge, MA: MIT Press, 1961

Baars, Bernard J. *The Cognitive Revolution in Psychology,* New York: The Guilford Press, 1986.

Bandura, Albert. *Social Foundations of Thought and Action.* Englewood Cliffs, NJ: Prentice-Hall, 1986.

Barnhart, Clarence L. Editor-in-Chief, *The World Book Encyclopedia Dictionary, L-Z, Vol. 2.* Chicago: Doubleday & Co., Inc, 1963.

Batson, C. D., and W. Lawrence Ventis. *The Religious Experience.* New York: Oxford: University Press, 1982.

Baum, W. M. *Understanding Behaviorism.* New York: HarperCollins, 1994.

Baumeister, Roy F. Self and volition. In W. R. Miller and H. G. Delaney (Eds.), *Judeo-Christian Perspectives on Psychology: Human Nature, Motivation and Change,* 57-72. Washington DC: American Psychological Association, 2005.

Bird, O. A. The humanities. *Encyclopedia Britannica* (Macropaedia), *Vol. 20.* 731-735. Chicago: Encyclopaedia Britannica, Inc, 1985.

Boring, Edwin G. When is human behavior predetermined? *The Scientific Monthly, 84*: 189–196, 1957.

Brehm, Jack. *A theory of Psychological Reactance.* NY: Academic Press, 1966.

Browning, Don S. and Terry D. Cooper. *Religious Thought and the Modern Psychologies* (2nd ed.). Minneapolis: Fortress Press, 2004.

Buechner, F. *Wishful Thinking: A Theological ABC.* New York: Harper & Row, 1973.

Carrington, W. L. *Psychology, Religion and Human Need*: A Guide to Ministers, Doctors, Teachers, and Social Workers. Great Neck, NY: Channel Press, 1957.

Chiang, H. and Abraham H. Maslow. *The Healthy Personality: Readings,* (2nd ed.) New York: Van Nostrand, 1977.

Cook, T. D. and D. T. Campbell. *Quasi-experimentation: Design and Analysis Issues for Field Settings.* Chicago: Rand McNally, 1979.

Cronbach, Lee J. Beyond the two disciplines of scientific psychology. *American Psychologist, 30*, 116-127, 1975.

Deese, James. *Psychology as Science and Art*. New York: Harcourt, Brace & Jovanovich, 1972.

Dennett, D. C. *Brainstorms*. Montgomery, VT: Bradford Books, 1981.

English, Horace B., and Ava C. English. *A Comprehensive Dictionary of Psychological and Psychoanalytical Terms*. New York: Longmans, Green, 1958.

Eron, L. D., L. R. Huesmann, M. M. Lefkowitz and L. O. Walder. Does television violence cause aggression? *American Psychologist, 27*: 253-263, 1972.

Feinberg, J. Introduction to Part 4. Determinism and free will. In J. Feinberg (Ed.) *Reason and Responsibility*, (5th ed.) Belmont, CA: Wadsworth, 1981.

Frenkel-Brunswik, Else. Intolerance of ambiguity as an emotional and perceptual personality variable. *Journal of Personality, 18*: 108-143, 1949.

Freud, Sigmund. *An Outline of Psychoanalysis*. Trans. J. Strachey. New York: Norton, 1949.

Gelso, C. J. Two different worlds: A paradox in counseling and psychotherapy. *Journal of Counseling Psychology, 17*: 271-278, 1970.

Gleick, J. *Chaos: Making a New Science*. New York: Viking, 1987.

Gleitman, Henry, James Gross, and David Reisberg. *Psychology* (8th ed.) New York: W. W. Norton & Co, 2011.

Goddard, G. V. Component properties of the memory machine: Hebb revisited. In P. W. Juscyck and R. M. Klein (Eds.) *The Nature of Thought: Essays in Honor of D. O. Hebb*, 231-247. Hillsdale, NJ: Erlbaum, 1980.

Goffman, E. *Frame Analysis*. New York: Harper & Rowe, 1974.

Greenway, P. The methodological implications of phenomenological assumption in humanistic psychology. *Australian Journal of Psychology, 34*: 231-237, 1982.

Grunbaum, A. Causality and the science of human behavior. *American Scientist, 40*: 665-676, 1952.

Grusky, Z. The practice of psychotherapy: A search for principles in an ambiguous art. *Psychotherapy, 24*: 1-6, 1987.

Hall, Calvin S. and Gardner Lindzey. *Theories of Personality*. New York: Wiley, 1957.

Harcum, E. Rae, *Serial Learning and Paralearning*. New York: Wiley-Interscience, 1975.

——. *Psychology for Daily Living*. Chicago: Nelson-Hall, 1979.

——. A classroom demonstration of the difference between correlation and causality. *Perceptual & Motor Skills, 66*: 801-802, 1988.

——. Defensive reactance of psychologists to a metaphysical foundation for integrating different psychologies. *The Journal of Psychology, 122*: 217-235, 1988.

——. A classroom demonstration of determinism, prediction, and control of human behavior. *Psychology, 25*: 41-43, 1988.
——. The fractionary psychology we try to give away. *American Psychologist, 4:* 483-484, 1988.
——. Commitment to collaboration as a prerequisite for existential commonality in psychotherapy. *Psychotherapy, 26:* 200-209, 1989.
——. The relative utility of complementary disparate views on voluntarism and determinism. *The Journal of Psychology, 125*: 217-228, 1990.
——. Behavioral paradigm for a psychological resolution of the free-will issue. *The Journal of Mind and Behavior, 12*: 93-114, 1991.
——. The classroom test as a dependent variable in transfer of learning. *New Directions for Education Reform, 1*: 69-74, 1992.
——. Parity for the theoretical ghosts and gremlins: Response to Pollio/Henley and Rychlak. *The Journal of Mind and Behavior, 12*: 151-162, 1991.
——. *A Psychology of Freedom and Dignity*. Westport, CT: Praeger, 1994.
——. *Incidental Psychotherapy Within Christian Relationships*. Lanham, MD: Hamilton Books, 2011.
Harcum, E. Rae, Barry N. Burijon and Neill Watson. Client responsibility in the practitioners' operational definition of behavior therapy. *Journal of Human Behavior and Learning, 5*: 12-16, 1988.
——. Need for a theoretical justification of humanistic commitment components in behavior therapy. *Psychological Record, 39*: 493-500, 1989.
Harcum, E. Rae and Ellen F. Rosen. *The Gatekeepers of Psychology*. Westport, CT: Praeger, 1993.
Harcum, E. Rae, Ellen F. Rosen and Barry N. Burijon. Popular vs. Skinnerian views of the relation between human freedom and dignity. *Journal of Psychology, 123*: 257-267, 1989.
Harcum, Phoebe M. Personal communication, January 2, 2000.
Harman, W. W. The transpersonal challenge to the scientific paradigm: The need for a restructuring of science. *ReVision, 11*: 13-21, 1988.
Harré, R. *Personal Being*. Cambridge, MA: Harvard University Press, 1984.
Harré, R. and E. H. Madden. *Causal Powers*. Oxford: Basil Blackwell, 1975.
Hebb, Donald O. *The Organization of Behavior*. New York: Wiley, 1949.
——. Alice in Wonderland or psychology among the biological sciences. In Harry F. Harlow and C. N. Woolsey (Eds.) *Biological and Biochemical Bases of Behavior,* 451-467, Madison, WI: University of Wisconsin Press, 1958.
——. The American revolution. *American Psychologist, 15*: 735-745, 1960.
——. The semiautonomous process: Its nature and nurture. *American Psychologist, 18:* 16-27, 1963.
——. *A Textbook of Psychology*. (2nd ed.) Philadelphia: Saunders, 1966.
Holy Bible, New International Version. Grand Rapids: MI: Zondervan, 1984.
James, William. *The Principles of Psychology: Vol I*. New York: Holt, 1890.

——. *The Principles of Psychology: Vol II.* New York: Holt, 1890.

Jeeves, Malcolm A. *Human Nature at the Millennium*: Reflections on the Integration of Psychology and Christianity. Grand Rapids, MI: Baker Books, 1997.

Jones, E. E., and R. E. Nisbett. The actor and the observer: Divergent perceptions of the causes of behavior. In E. E. Jones, E. Kanouse, H. H. Kelley, R. E. Nisbett, S. Valins, and B. Weiner (Eds.) *Attribution: Perceiving the Causes of Behavior.* Morristown, NJ: General Learning Press, 79-94, 1972.

Kimble, Gregory. A. Psychology's two cultures. *American Psychologist, 39*: 833-839, 1984.

Koch, Sigmund. The nature and limits of psychological knowledge: Lessons of a century qua "science." *American Psychologist, 36*: 257-275, 1981.

Kohler, Wolfgang. *Gestalt Psychology.* New York: Liveright, 1947.

Korn, J. H. Psychology as a humanity. *Teaching of Psychology, 12*: 188-193, 1985.

Lefcourt, H. M. *Locus of Control: Current Trends in Theory and Research.* New York: Erlbaum, 1976.

Lehrer, K. An empirical disproof of determinism? In K. Lehrer (Ed.) *Freedom and Determinism*: 175-202, New York: Random House, 1966.

Leichman, H. Personal communication, 1975.

LeShan, Lawrence. *The Dilemma of Psychology.* New York: Dutton, 1990.

Mahoney, Michael J. Publications, politics, and scientific progress. *The Behavioral and Brain Sciences, 5*: 220-221, 1982.

Maier, Norman R. F., and T. C. Schneirla. *Principles of Animal Psychology* (enlarged edition). New York: Dover, 1964.

Manicas, P. T., and P. F. Secord. Implications for psychology of the new philosophy of science. *American Psychologist, 38*: 399-413, 1983.

Maslow, Abraham H. Humanistic science and transcendental experiences. *Journal of Humanistic Psychology, 5*: 219-227, 1965.

May, Rollo. *Psychology and the Human Dilemma.* Princeton: Van Nostrand, 1967.

McClelland, J. L., and D. E. Rumelhart. A distributed processing model of human learning and memory. In J. L. McClelland, D. E. Rumelhart and the PDP Research Group (Eds.). *Parallel Distributed Processing: Explorations in the Microstructure of Cognition. Vol. Two: Psychological and Biological Models*: 170-215. Cambridge, MA: M. I. T. Press, 1986.

McCollom, Ivan N. Psychological thrillers: Psychology books students read when given freedom of choice. *American Psychologist, 26*: 921-927, 1971.

Milgram, Stanley. Behavioral study of obedience. *Journal of Abnormal and Social Psychology, 67*: 371-378, 1963.

Miller, George A. Psychology as a means of promoting human welfare. *American Psychologist, 24*: 1063-1075, 1969.

Miller, William K. What is human nature? Reflections from Judeo-Christian perspectives. In W. K. Miller and H. D. Delaney (Eds.) *Judeo-Christian Perspectives on Psychology: Human Nature, Motivation and Change*, 11-29. Washington, DC: American Psychological Association, 2005.

——, and Harold D Delaney, Psychology as the science human nature: reflections and search directions. In William A. Miller and Harold H. Delaney (Eds.) *Judeo-Christian Perspectives on Psychology: Human Nature, Motivation and Change*, 291-308. Washington, DC: American Psychological Association, 2005.

——, and Harold D Delaney (Eds.) *Judeo-Christian Perspectives on Psychology: Human Nature, Motivation and Change*, 291-308. Washington, DC: American Psychological Association, 2005.

Milner, P. M. The cell assembly. Mark II. *Psychological Review, 64*: 242-252, 1957.

Murray, Alfred L. *Psychology for Christian Teachers*. Grand Rapids, MI: Zonderman Publishing House, 1943.

Myers, D. G., *Psychology*. New York: Worth, 1986.

Neilson, William A. (Ed.) Webster's New International Dictionary of the English Language (2nd ed.). Mayfield, MA: G. & C. Merriam Co. Publishers, 1944.

Neisser, Ulric. *Cognitive Psychology*. New York: Appleton-Century-Crofts, 1967.

Nelson, James M. *Psychology, Religion and Spirituality*. New York: Springer, 2009.

Paloutzian, Raymond F. and Crystal L. Park (Eds.) *Handbook of the Psychology of Religion and Spirituality*. New York: The Guilford Press, 2005.

Odegaard, C. E. A historical perspective on psychology dilemmas. In L. Rickman & H. Ellis (Eds.) *Preparing Psychologists for the 21st century: Proceedings of the National Conference on Graduate Education in Psychology*, 17-24, Hillsdale, NJ: Erlbaum, 1990.

O'Hara, M. Comment on Carl Rogers' "Toward a more human science of the person." *Journal of Humanistic Psychology, 25*: 25-30, 1986.

Oppenheimer, Robert. Analogy in science. *American Psychologist, 11*: 127-135, 1956.

Pollio, Howard R. *Behavior and Existence*. Monterey, CA: Brooks/Cole, 1981.

Pollio, Howard R. and T. Henley. Empirical and philosophical reactions to Harcum's "Behavioral paradigm for a psychological resolution of the free-will issue." *The Journal of Mind and Behavior, 12*: 115-134, 1991.

Ritchie, George G. (with Elizabeth Sherrill) *Return from Tomorrow*. Grand Rapids, MI: Fleming H. Revell, 1978.

——. *Ordered to Return: My Life After Dying*. Charlottesville, VA: Hampton Roads Publishing Company, Inc., 1998.

Rogers, Carl R. A theory of therapy, personality, and interpersonal relationships, as developed in the client-centered framework. In Sigmund Koch (Ed.) *Psychology: A Study of a Science, Vol. 3*. New York: McGraw-Hill, 1959.

Rogers, Carl R. and B. F. Skinner. Some issues concerning the control of human behavior: A symposium. *Science, 124*: 1057-1066, 1956.

Rosenthal, Robert. The "file drawer problem" and tolerance for null results. *Psychological Bulletin, 86*: 638-641, 1979.

Royce, J. R. Heretical thoughts on the definition of psychology. *Psychological Reports, 8*: 11-14, 1961.

——. The present situation in theoretical psychology. In J. R. Royce (Ed.) *Toward Unification in Psychology*, 11-37. Toronto: University of Toronto Press, 1970.

Rychlak, Joseph F. *The Psychology of Rigorous Humanism*. New York: Wiley-Interscience, 1977.

——. Newtonianism and the professional responsibility of psychologists: Who speaks for humanity? *Professional Psychology: Research and Practice, 15*: 82-95, 1984.

——. Some theoretical and methodological questions concerning Harcum's proposed resolution of the free will issue. *The Journal of Mind and Behavior, 12*: 135-150, 1991.

Seligman, Martin E. P. *Learned helplessness*. In J. E. Levitt, B. Rubin, & J. Brooks (Eds.) *Depression: Concepts, Controversies and Some New Facts*. Hillsdale, N. J.: Erlbaum. 1983.

——. *Learned Optimism*. New York: Pocket Books, 1990.

Sheridan, E. P. Science versus practice or science and practice. In L. Rickman & H. Ellis (Eds.) *Preparing Psychologists for the 21st century: Proceeding of the National Conference on Graduate Education in Psychology*, 223-230. Hillsdale, NJ: Erlbaum, 1990.

Shoben, E. J. Jr. Psychology: Natural science or humanistic discipline? *Journal of Humanistic Psychology, 5*: 210-218, 1965.

Skinner, B. F. *Walden Two*. New York: MacMillan, 1948.

——. *Science of Human Behavior*. New York: Macmillan, 1953.

——. *Beyond Freedom and Dignity*. New York: Knopf, 1971.

Smith, M. B. *Social Psychology and Human Values*. Chicago: Aldine, 1969.

Smith, R. E., J. G. Sarason and B. R. Sarason. *Psychology: The Frontiers of Behavior*. (3rd ed.) New York: Harper & Row, 1986.

Snow, C. P. *The Two Cultures and the Scientific Revolution*. New York: Cambridge University Press, 1959.

Sutich, Anthony J. Introduction. *Journal of Humanistic Psychology, 1*: vii-ix, 1961.

Taft, R. Humanistic psychology: An introduction to a symposium. *Australian Journal of Psychology, 34*: 217-219, 1982.

Toynbee, Arnold. Beyond freedom and dignity: An uneasy feeling of unreality. *The Center Magazine*. March/April: 58-62, 1972.

United Methodist Church. *Book of Discipline of the United Methodist Church.* Nashville, TN: Methodist Publishing House, 2004.

Van Kaam, Adrian. Humanistic psychology and culture. *Journal of Humanistic Psychology, 1*: 94-100, 1961.

Viney, D. W. William James on free will and determinism. *The Journal of Mind and Behavior, 7*: 555-565, 1986.

Watson, John B. Psychology as the Behaviorist views it. *Psychological Review, 20*: 158-177, 1913.

Weiten, Wayne. *Psychology: Themes and Variations*, (3rd ed.) Pacific Grove, CA: Brooks/Cole Publishing Company. 1995.

Wertheimer, Michael. Introduction to psychology. In W. H. Holtzman (Ed.) *Personalized Psychology.* A-1: 1-14. New York: Harper & Row, 1977.

Weston, Drew. *Psychology: Mind, Brain and Culture.* New York: John Wiley & Sons, Inc., 1996.

Wolman, Benjamin B. Concerning psychology and the philosophy of science. In Benjamin B. Wolman (Ed.) *Handbook of General Psychology.* 22-48. Englewood Cliffs, NJ: Prentice-Hall, 1973.

Yalom, Irvin D. *Existential Psychotherapy.* New York: Basic Books, 1980.

Zimmerman, D. W. A note on the completeness of the scientific method. *Psychological Record, 34*: 175-179, 1984.

Subject Index

D

P

Q

R

U

V

W

Author Index

About the Author

E. Rae Harcum, PhD., is a professional psychologist, and a long-time member of a Protestant religious denomination. He taught psychology at the college level for many years. He has authored many journal articles in psychology, and several books on psychology and on religion.

CPSIA information can be obtained at www.ICGtesting.com
Printed in the USA
BVOW021635150412

287655BV00001B/4/P

9 780761 858706